Parent Training and Developmental Disabilities

Monographs of the American Association on Mental Retardation, 13

Michael J. Begab, Series Editor

Parent Training and Developmental Disabilities

by
Bruce L. Baker
University of California, Los Angeles

with chapters by

Stephen A. Ambrose
Children's Institute International
and
Stephen R. Anderson
The May Institute

123159

Published by
American Association on Mental Retardation
1719 Kalorama Raod, NW
Washington, DC 20009

The points of view herein are those of the authors and do not necessarily represent the official policy or opinion of the American Association on Mental Retardation. Publication does not imply endorsement by the Editor, the Association, or its individual members.

No. 13, Monographs of the American Association on Mental Retardation (ISSN 0895-8009)

The studies reported in this monograph were supported by Contract 72-2016 and Grants HD-42848 and RO1 HD10962, National Institute of Child Health and Human Development; Grant No. DE G00 8435061, National Institute of Handicapped Research; and UCLA Academic Senate research awards.

Library of Congress Cataloging-in-Publication Data

Baker, Bruce L.
    Parent training and developmental disabilities.

    (Monographs of the American Association on Mental Retardation ; 13)
    Includes bibliographical references.
    1. Mentally handicapped children—Home care—United States.   2. Mentally handicapped children—Rehabilitation—United States.   3. Parents of handicapped children—United States.   4. Child rearing—United States.
I. Ambrose, Stephen, 1950—   .   II. Anderson, Stephen, 1950–   III. Title.
IV. Series.
HV894.B37   1989   649'.152   89–18493
ISBN 0-940898-22-5

Printed in the United States of America

 3

Table
of
Contents

Preface

The parents of a child who is developmentally disabled are meeting a challenge at once heroic and ordinary. The heroism, though unsought, is undisputed. Who would voluntarily change places? Yet most daily challenges for these parents and children are pretty much the same ordinary ones that occupy all families. And, like all families, those with a special child often have questions, seek guidance, or just want to make sure they are on the right track.

Parent training refers to programs that seek to help parents learn better ways to meet the ordinary challenges. The term parent training is, perhaps, ill chosen, conjuring up images of a drill sergeant barking orders to rows of parents, all folding diapers in unison. In truth, most of these programs are a blend of consultation and education. Psychologists or educators work together with parents, drawing on their respective expertise to develop ways to enhance the child's learning at home. As services to families have expanded in the past two decades, parent training has been one important component.

In this monograph I have gathered together our research on parent training for families with a child who is developmentally disabled. It was carried out over the past 18 years, at Harvard University until 1975 and thereafter at the University of California, Los Angeles. I have drawn on four major research samples and several ancillary ones—about 500 families in all. Although many of our findings have been reported previously, I have added heretofore unpublished data, conducted new analyses, invited two chapters from other programs, and addressed parent training issues that cut across the samples and the years. For perspective, I have set our studies in the context of the parent training literature, although the review of this other work does not pretend to be comprehensive.

This program of research officially began in 1971, when two events converged. At Harvard, Alan Brightman, Louis Heifetz, and I had begun to write a book for parents, to share "how-to" ideas for teaching children who are retarded. At the National Institute of Child Health and Human Development (NICHD), Dr. Michael Begab had just written a request for proposals that recognized the shortage of service providers and invited research on the effectiveness of written training materials for parents. We were fortunate to be awarded the NICHD contract, which resulted in our writing a series of teaching manuals for parents and studying the effectiveness of manuals relative to other service delivery approaches.

Subsequent grants from NICHD and, more recently, from the National Institute of Disability and Rehabilitation Research (NIDRR) allowed us to continue studies of parent training, examining the relative effectiveness of different approaches to training, predictors of outcome, alternative programs for families predicted to do poorly, and programs for special populations. A common thread throughout these studies has been the question of cost-effectiveness: How can families be given meaningful assistance in ways that minimize the cost in time to both professionals and the parents?

Two early influences introduced me to families with retarded children and set the stage for these studies. One was my efforts in the late 1960s to introduce behavioral programming—and collaboration with parents—into the Children's Unit of the Fernald State School in Waltham, Massachusetts (Baker & Ward, 1971). Three observations impressed me then and impress me to this day. First, most parents, despite their having been ignored by the institution for years, became involved in some way that was best for them. Second, many of these parents were very effective teachers of their children. Third, and most important, the parents had much to offer to one another and to us—much information, interest, and support.

The other influence was Camp Freedom, an educational residential summer program in New Hampshire that I began in 1969 and that continued for nine years (Baker, 1973). It was in this setting, living each summer with fifty retarded children, that we learned the most about children and their families. One particular lesson that energized the studies that would follow was that parents of moderately or severely retarded children must be involved for a school program to be truly worth the effort. One year we followed up on our summer campers at Christmastime, finding that those whose parents had actively participated in teaching them were showing continued gains, whereas the others were slipping back in many skills to pre-camp levels (Schwenn, 1971).

The monograph is written primarily for persons who work with parents of children who have developmental disabilities. It is organized into four units. Unit I, containing Chapter 1, introduces parent training within the context of the literature on families with a child who is handicapped. Unit II presents our program of parent training research. Chapter 2 describes the families we have studied and the Parents as Teachers training program. Chapters 3 through 7 in turn address research questions about participation in training, outcome, differential effectiveness of training approaches, predictors of outcome, and alternative programs for predicted low-gain families.

Unit III addresses research on parent training for three special populations. Chapter 8 is an invited chapter by Dr. Stephen Ambrose on adaptations of our group program for child abusive families. Dr. Ambrose, formerly a member of our research team, is presently a Psychologist at Children's Institute International in Los Angeles, an agency with multifaceted approaches to problems of abuse. Chapter 9 is on the merging of our group program with other programs for parents of children diagnosed with hyperactivity, or, as it is now termed, attention deficit hyperactive disorder. Chapter 10 is an invited chapter by Dr. Stephen Anderson on an intensive individual training program for parents of children with autism. Dr. Anderson is Director of The May Institute's Early Childhood Programs in the greater Boston area.

Unit IV contains four chapters that address broader issues in parent training. Chapter 11 examines the impact of parent training on personal and family adjustment. Chapter 12 looks at the roles of fathers, brothers, and sisters in parent training programs. Chapter 13 begins with the observation that parent training programs, despite the empirical evidence for their success, are not readily available. We report two studies of program dissemination. Finally, Chapter 14 summarizes our findings as they apply to questions that service providers might and do ask, and draws several implications for policy in service delivery. The appendices include guidelines to the Parents as Teachers curriculum and copies of our measures.

_____Acknowledgments

The "we" used throughout this monograph is far from editorial. Indeed, as I attempted to pull together about 18 years of "our" studies, a host of people who were valued collaborators and friends symbolically looked over my shoulder. As the writer always says about here: the errors are mine alone. But, for the ideas and energy and caring, I have many people to thank. First, I want to acknowledge Michael Begab, who got us started researching parent training and who, much later, got after me to write it all down here.

I owe heartfelt thanks to my former doctoral students who played a central role in "the project," at Harvard and at UCLA: Stephen Ambrose, Peggy Berlin, Alan Brightman, Richard Brightman, Duncan Clark, Louis Heifetz, Kathleen Kashima, Sandra Landen, Merilla McCurry-Scott, Rob Pasick, Mary Prieto-Bayard, Jim Shenk, Patrice Yasuda. Thanks also to my colleagues Stephen Anderson, Andrew Christensen, Donald Guthrie, Stephen Hinshaw, O. Ivar Lovaas, and Richard Wenzlaff for their contributions.

I am grateful, also, to the staff of the Regional Centers for the Developmentally Disabled in Los Angeles County, and especially to Ann Baerwald, Mildred Estes, Ron Huff, and Nancy Spiegel, for making us welcome and helping in so many ways. I also want to thank Ann Wendell (Research Press) and Melissa Behm (Brookes Publishing) for believing in (and publishing!) our parent training books.

Over the years, many wonderful research assistants and doctoral students have contributed to the parent training and research in countless ways: Lorraine Acevedo, Andrea Ackerman, Karen Bierman, Jennifer Carter, Nancy Babin Carroll, David Donovan, Ann Hazzard, Benita Blachman Heifetz, Alexander James, Claudia Kaplan, Peter Kassel, Pam Kimsey, Lisa Lieurance, Jose Lopez, Erzi Maslow, Anne Maxwell, Elizabeth Mooney, Diane Murphy, Julie Ogawa, Barbara Parks, Pat Pasick, Phyllis Prado, John Reiser, Molly Schwenn, Gary Seltzer, Marsha Seltzer, Judith Wilson, and, most recently, Moi Wong, whom I especially thank for all her help with this monograph. I wish I could acknowledge each and every undergraduate volunteer, Camp Freedom counselor, parent, and child. They played such important roles. Anyway, thanks.

And finally a warm thank you to my wife, best friend, and impartial reviewer, Jan Blacher—for everything.

Unit 1

Introduction

"Oh, Matt," I said, reaching for his hand. "How can we stand it? Other people have retarded children . . . not us." (Kaufman, 1988, p. 6).

On ancient maps, in the blank parchment beyond the known world, were inscribed the words: Here be dragons. This was a warning to the voyager that he entered the unknown region at his peril. Sandra Kaufman and Diane Crutcher describe eloquently the private dragons that await a family discovering that their child has a developmental disability and that childrearing will not follow well-travelled paths.

"What do you see as the prognosis for Nicole?" Matt asked the doctor. Why on earth was he asking that, I wondered.

Dr. McCall paused. He looked down at his papers and then at us.

"She's mentally retarded . . . she may never advance beyond the mental age of five years," he said finally. The fan continued circling. "Nothing can be done for her," he added regretfully and then mumbled something about the retarded often having short lives.

I was caught totally unaware. Retarded? Our child, retarded? This isn't happening, I thought. I dropped into a void, plummeting, plummeting.

Escape? There was no escape.

I wanted to scream at the doctor, "How can you be so calm! You've just changed the course of our lives!"

Instead I sat numbly silent. Matt and Dr. McCall continued talking. Matt got up; then I got up. He walked out of the room, and I followed him. We reached our car, and I started out alone toward the pharmacy for Nicole's prescription.

Somewhere on the walkway the tears began to come. I fled to the car. There, in Matt's arms, all the incredulity and pity for Nicole came pouring out.

"I'm so sorry," Matt kept apologizing. "I thought you suspected . . . "
(Kaufman, 1988, p. 6).

When you're going to have a baby, it's like you're planning a vacation to Italy. You are all excited. Seeing the Colisseum . . . the Michelangelo . . . the gondolas of Venice. You get a whole bunch of guidebooks. You learn a few phrases in Italian so you can order in restaurants and get around. When it comes time, you excitedly pack your bags, head for the airport, and take off—for Italy. Only when you land, the stewardess announces "Welcome to Holland."

You look at one another in disbelief and shock saying, "Holland? What are you talking about—Holland? I signed up for Italy! But they explain that there's been a change of plans and the plane has landed in Holland—and there you must stay. "But I don't know anything about Holland! I don't want to stay here!" you say. "I never wanted to come to Holland. I don't know what you do *in Holland and I don't want to learn!" But, you do stay; you go out and buy some new guidebooks. You learn some new phrases in a whole new language and you meet people you never knew existed.*

But the important thing is that you are not in a filthy, plague-infested slum full of pestilence and famine. You are simply in another place . . . a different place than you had planned. It's slower-paced than Italy; less flashy than Italy. But after you've been there a little while and you have a chance to catch your breath, you begin to discover that Holland has windmills . . . Holland has tulips . . . and Holland even has Rembrandts.

But everyone else you know is busy coming and going from Italy. They're all bragging about what a great time they had there and for the rest of your life you will say, "Yes, that's where I was going . . . that's where I was supposed to go . . . that's what I had planned." The pain of that will never, ever go away.

You have to accept that pain because the loss of that dream, the loss of that plan, is a very, very significant loss. But . . . if you spend your life mourning the fact that you didn't get to Italy, you will never be free to enjoy the very special, the very lovely things about Holland (Crutcher, 1986).

Those of us venturing into the uncharted territory of family intervention might also keep an eye out for dragons, especially the ones we unwittingly create. People who would help have often felt helpless themselves. Friends and relatives offer platitudes rather than say nothing, and professionals have advised institutional placement in one decade and decried it in the next. With helpers adrift, parents must seek their own way.

Parent training is especially perilous—and presumptuous. As professionals, we can hardly begin to appreciate what a family has experienced over the months and years before we enter their world. We could so readily overlook not just the pain but the triumphs, see the weeds and miss the tulips. We cannot truly understand what any particular family wants and needs, and we may never have even most of the answers. But only a small glimpse at the courage of these parents and their children is encouragement enough to at least try.

Chapter 1

Parents and Parent Training

Premises and Programs

Families with a child who has a developmental disability enter the 1990s with newly codified rights, more service options, and higher expectations, for their child and for themselves. Indeed, until recently, professional practices seemed to overlook the family. The child was diagnosed, treated, taught, or forgotten in special settings—clinics, hospitals, schools, institutions. The family's role was essentially to listen, watch, and wait. They were silent extras.

Now the family has been discovered and the new service delivery script offers parents not just a speaking part but a leading role! Are parents prepared for this? What roles can they occupy best and at what cost in time and effort to them? Certainly a primary role in parenting a child with retardation, as in parenting any child, is teaching. No matter how retarded the child is, society holds parents responsible for some degree of socialization. And yet no one is well prepared to become the parent (and thereby the teacher) of a child who is retarded. Teaching even the most basic skills in areas such as self-care, communication, or play comes slowly and requires a degree of motivation and ability not demanded by more typical parenting.

This monograph is about the development and evaluation of parent training programs that aim to share with families special strategies for enhancing their teaching role. Such programs are but one, albeit important, part of a comprehensive service delivery system.

FAMILIES WITH DEVELOPMENTALLY DISABLED CHILDREN

The choice of a perspective on a social problem greatly influences the nature and locus of services. No view of mental retardation has been as pervasive in this century as the conception of the retarded person as sick or permanently impaired (Wolfensberger, 1969). These beliefs justified schools in segregating or excluding retarded children as too impaired to benefit much from education, and a common recommendation to parents

5

was to institutionalize the child in one of the large state hospitals. In these settings superintendents were medical doctors, living units were called wards, staff dressed in white uniforms, and the day's main activity was inactivity. The naive visitor would have had little trouble reading the message that the people who lived here were very sick indeed.

Of course, some children do have undeniable organic impairments that will be permanent. The conceptual error, however, was to let the impairment define the person, so that it was emphasized to the exclusion of the individual's many other attributes and needs. Wolfensberger (1969) went on to note the emergence in recent years of a different perspective, that of the individual with retardation as a developing person. This view, now with two more decades to draw upon, stresses the individual's learning and adaptation, thereby encouraging settings that enhance growth. Today parents are urged to keep their child at home.

The prevailing view of the retarded child as sick was readily generalized to the family as well. Here, too, there were some truths, and here, too, they were narrowly used as exclusive guides for professional practice. First, the truths: There is little doubt that the discovery of a child's retardation is a psychological trauma for which a family is never well prepared. Helen Featherstone captures this poignantly in her recollection:

> When I was twenty-five, a friend told me that her brother had been killed in a motorcycle accident two years earlier. She said, "Nothing bad had ever happened to me before." I turned this statement over in my mind for a long time. What could she mean? Bad things happen to everyone—even to the luckiest people. Two years later I learned that my newborn son was blind; on that day I remembered her words. Now I understood them. I knew that nothing bad had ever happened to me before. (Featherstone, 1980, p. 4).

Studies have described adverse effects on parents and on brothers and sisters as well (Farber, 1959; Lobato, 1983). Many authors have tried to delineate psychological stages that parents go through, beginning with shock and a feeling of confusion and loss, followed by a period of disbelief and nonacceptance that the child might be retarded. With eventual acceptance of retardation there is guilt, and there is a relentless search for causes, for places to fix the blame. No family stone is left unturned (Schild, 1964; Solnit & Stark, 1961).

Olshansky (1962) wrote a provocative essay that argued against the concept of stages leading to adjustment, observing that "chronic sorrow" is a natural and universal reaction to a child with handicaps. There is some evidence for lasting measurable effects on mood, self-esteem, and interpersonal satisfaction; on measures of these domains, mothers and fathers of retarded children have displayed more problems than have parents of normally developing or chronically ill children (Cummings, 1976; Cummings, Bayley, & Rie, 1966; Waisbren, 1980). There is an impact on family interaction as well. Disagreements between husband and wife over childrearing, severe restriction on social life, disruption of short- and long-range family plans, disproportionate amounts of time devoted to the retarded child to the exclusion of other family members, and excessive financial burdens have been frequently noted (Gunn & Berry, 1987; McAllister, Butler, & Lei, 1973; Schild, 1971).

But that is not the whole story. Children who are retarded also bring to their parents and siblings a measure of joy, fulfillment, and compassion as any child does, and they teach very special lessons of patience and caring. These have been the focus of recent studies. Eden-Pearcy, Blacher, and Eyman (1986) found that parents' emotional reactions and certainly their sequence are much less predictable than earlier theorists believed. Turnbull and Behr (1986) pointed out the positive side of having a disabled child in the family, a view, they noted, that is obscured by research that only looks at and asks about problems. Wilson, Blacher, and Baker (1989) interviewed siblings of children with severe handicaps and found that while difficulties were acknowledged, the siblings expressed a high degree of positive involvement.

Parents as Patients

Actually, parents speaking about the impact of a handicapped child have spoken loudest about their frustration, anger, and despair with the service delivery system's unresponsiveness to their needs (Turnbull & Turnbull, 1985). Family services, where available, often meant psychotherapy for parents. Professionals, dwelling on the ill emotional effects on the family wrought from the child's birth, focused on enhancing the parents' psychological well-being. Parents often found themselves in the role of patients.

More recently, these psychiatric perspectives have been questioned. Blackard and Barsh (1982), suspecting that professionals magnify the impact on the family of a child who is handicapped, studied this directly. They compared personal responses from 43 parents of severely handcapped children with responses from 101 professionals about how they felt parents of severely handicapped children in general would respond. Professionals consistently overestimated the impact of the handicapped child on all aspects of family functioning, including the marital relationship, restriction of family activities, and effects on siblings.

Moreover, even when there are problems, the prevailing professional view has failed to see that they may stem not from the fact of the retarded child *per se*, but from daily frustrations parents faced in living with the child, from unsuccessful daily attempts to cope with behavior problems (such as temper tantrums in public or aggression against younger siblings), or from facing the multitude of skill deficiencies. The approaches that somehow worked with their other children simply fall short. In parenting normally developing children one can draw on one's own childhood experiences of being parented and on willingly offered advice from friends, relatives, and neighbors. For parents of children with retardation, however, these sources are often off the mark or silent (Wikler, 1981).

Rather than therapy, then, parents have asked for straightforward advice about what they might do to handle specific child management problems (Eberhardy, 1967) and for practical help as well (e.g., respite care). Counseling is appropriate when it can help a family over crisis points (e.g., the birth of a disabled child, decisions about schooling, adolescent concerns, planning for a future outside the family home). Of course, families of handicapped children are not immune from the psychological distresses that burden the rest of us; in these cases, therapy may also be appropriate.

New Roles and Involvements

Much has changed with the significant federal legislation of the 1970s and 1980s. Public Law 94-142, The Education for All Handicapped Children Act of 1975, guaranteed the right to a free and appropriate public education to all children with handicaps aged 5 through 21 and to many such children aged 3 to 5. Public Law 99-457, The Education of the Handicapped Act Amendments of 1986, extended services downward to include birth to 3 years of age (Gallagher, Trohanis, & Clifford, 1989). In these laws, new rights and responsibilities, especially concerning decisionmaking, have been extended to the parents of children with handicaps. Every special education program must consider ways to involve parents, and programs proliferate. Parents, long neglected, are now actively recruited to collaborate in planning and teaching.

We should ask, though, how such increased parent involvement affects the family. Proponents argue the potential spin-off benefits to the child and the family when parents become better teachers and decisionmakers. Some skeptics, however, argue that parent involvement needs rethinking (Foster, Berger, & McLean, 1981) because excessive demands may mean increased burden of care (Featherstone, 1980).

Consider this: Shrybman (1982), writing about due process in special education, listed responsibilities of parents, begining with "1. Keep written records with copies of all of their letters to and from officials and school personnel" (p. 218) and continuing through 119 items! Some school programs, enthusiastic about the benefits of parent involvement, require parents to attend a day or more each week. Turnbull and Turnbull (1982) spoke for many overwhelmed parents in pointing out that some are just not up for all of this involvement. We have noted elsewhere: "This wide swing of the pendulum from the days when parents were to be silent observers of professional practice threatens to topple parent enthusiasm in its path. Teachers who teach well and administrators who administer well are needed so that generally informed parents can make a meaningful contribution to their child's development without making this their life's focus. One hopes for balance." (Baker, 1984). We will return to the question of impact on the family in Chapter 11 and implications for policy in Chapter 14.

Parents as Teachers

Parents, whatever their involvement with the educational system, are themselves teachers. They are their growing child's first teachers. Where else will she learn about love, the toilet, sharing, green vegetables, and the word no? Parents set the foundations upon which schools and other instructors will build, and parents are the ones who will be there year after year. They will even still presume to teach her when she is an adolescent —and knows everything. We do not, then, need to give a rationale for parents assuming a teaching role: it comes with the territory.

Parents of delayed children, however, get mixed messages. Society expects them to socialize the child and their failures to do so are not unnoticed. Yet they are also faced with a dual press to abandon this teaching role. For one thing, there are personal doubts. Their child's learning is slower, teaching is less natural, and ofttimes they feel uncertain about what to do. For another, the service system long gave the message that if a child is special then professionals will take over—everything. Basic skills that other children are quite naturally taught at home—putting on a sweater, sweeping the floor, going to the toilet, riding a tricycle—become part of the school's curriculum.

The shift from a medical to developmental view of the child with retardation and the decreased use of institutional placement has brought with it a redefinition of parental roles. Parents' input into school programs became required and in some cases valued. It also came to be recognized that a home environment intentionally facilitating the child's learning would be a valuable addition to the efforts of classroom teachers. There are some skills best taught at home (e.g., toilet training) and many others where benefits are greater with a consistent school-home approach (e.g., language). Well-trained parents could carry over specific school programs and hence increase the child's learning rate and promote generalization. Finally, by more effective home management of problem behaviors and teaching of social and play skills, parents could make the home a more pleasant place and prepare the child better for other social settings.

PARENT TRAINING PROGRAMS

To meet the needs of families with developmentally disabled members, a smorgasbord of supportive services and interventions is now offered. These include information and referral services, self-help parent groups, therapy, respite care, and parent training (Intagliata & Doyle, 1984). We will be concerned with parent training, although it is not always distinct from these other services. Even this is not a single approach; there is considerable diversity in training aims and approaches, and the many variations probably differ in their effects on child and family (Baker, 1984). We will just allude to this diversity here. Orientations differ. Not surprisingly, there is no singular view of the ideal family climate for enhancing the child's development. Training orientations have been primarily behavioral or, to a lesser extent, reflective (Tavormina, 1974).

Training formats differ. Most common is an individual professional-parent approach that usually involves having the child present. Professionals counsel, instruct, and model; parents teach and receive feedback. There may be a general curriculum, but it is flexible and the number of training sessions will vary within some broad limits. Less common, primarily because of logistics, are parent training groups. In contrast to more open-ended support groups, these training programs will follow a specified curriculum to some extent. Most typically, groups will enroll from five to ten families with one or two leaders. Most group programs meet for between six and ten sessions, long enough to provide some basic instruction and help parents get one or two teaching programs underway, but not so long as to end by attrition.

Training sites and foci and methods and demands differ. Programs meet with parents in homes, clinics, schools, or even simulated homes. Some focus narrowly on carrying out a specific skill-teaching or behavior management program, while others teach general principles of behavior change that should apply in a variety of situations. Parent trainers typically use some combination of individual consultation, lectures, group discussions, videotape, live demonstrations, role playing, supervised teaching, books, and homework assignments. Finally, program requirements range from attending a single training session to teaching at home for hours each day over years.

Parent Training and Developmental Disabilities

Most parent training programs reported in the professional literature are for families with intellectually normal children who present behavior problems. These reports can only inform programs for developmental disabilities up to a point. A child who is retarded has not one isolated and obvious target problem, but a plethora of deficiencies and often no clear starting place. Although behavior problems are usually a concern, they must take a programmatic back seat to teaching new skills. Because teaching goes on for years, parent training must prepare the family to tackle new teaching after the formal program has ended. Hence, the program will of necessity be different, more concerned with assessment, understanding teaching principles, and skill building.

The parent-child interaction will be different, too. Many studies now tell us, not surprisingly, that children who are delayed differ in interactions from their nondelayed age-mates; for example, they provide less readable cues, are more avoidant of social interaction, have less positive and more negative affect, and do not take turns in interactions as well (Brooks-Gunn & Lewis, 1982; Rogers & Puchalski, 1984). Mothers of children with delays are more active and more directive, and initiate more interactions (Brooks-Gunn & Lewis, 1982; Eheart, 1982). Some programs see these maternal behaviors as less desirable, and aim to help mothers interact with the child who is delayed as they would with any child. An alternative view is that the mothers are adapting to the child's delay in ways that work and should be encouraged. When we reach a clearer understanding about the types of parent-child interaction that promote development, we will be able to set more informed goals for parent training.

In any event, when teaching children who are retarded, progress will come slowly and skills must be simplified and then simplified yet further. Presenting a task is often impeded by the child's handicap. For example, verbal control is sometimes not very effective in getting and holding a child's attention if he has autism, retardation, or a hearing impairment. Parents must learn to rely more on modeling and physical guidance, and these require a more conscious, patient, and well-planned effort.

Moreover, motivating the child to perform a task usually requires imagination and persistence. For example, authors working with children who are deaf-blind (Mira & Hoffman, 1974) or autistic (Lovaas, 1981) have noted the frequent failure of social and even food consequences to motivate performance. Finally, the use of firm contingencies and punishment, difficult with any child, is often especially problematic for parents of a child with handicaps: They are apt to indulge him or her in ways they would not treat a child who was not handicapped, with predictable consequences in unmanageable behavior.

Evaluating Parent Training

This monograph is primarily concerned with evaluating the effects of parent training. The theoretical cornerstone on which our programs were built is broadly behavioral, incorporating elements of what is now called *radical behaviorism* along with social learning theory and cognitive-behavior modification. These orientations have guided applied researchers in developing a behavior modification technology of teaching, although that term implies a degree of precision not attained and probably not attainable. Behavioral theory and the empirical findings derived from it, though, have directed our choice of where to intervene, how to intervene, and, of concern here, how to assess outcomes.

Criteria for evaluation

The criteria by which we might judge a program to be successful are quite diverse. Table 1.1 lists 11 ways a program could address the question: Does parent training work? Most of these have behavioral indicators, although a few are attitudes. It is reasonable that a program may work quite well according to some of these criteria but fall short by others. Service providers must decide what benefits are important, assess these, and then honestly advertise what the program does and does not offer. In subsequent chapters, we will look at how our program and others stack up against these criteria.

TABLE 1.1

Did the Program Work? Possible Criteria for Evaluating a Parent Training Program

---

1. SOCIAL VALIDITY: Do parents find the goals and the methods of the program worthwhile?
2. ENROLLMENT: Do parents enroll in the program?
3. COMPLETION: Do parents maintain good attendance?
4. PARTICIPATION: Do parents carry out the demands of the program?
5. CONSUMER SATISFACTION: Do parents express satisfaction with the program?
6. PROFICIENCY: Do parents learn what the program aims to teach?
7. CHILD GAINS: Do children show demonstrable gains?
8. MAINTENANCE OF CHILD GAINS: Do child gains last?
9. MAINTENANCE OF TEACHING: Do parents continue to put what they learned into practice at home months or years later?
10. FAMILY BENEFITS: Do parents' attitudes or family adjustment (e.g., stress, coping, parent-child relationship) change?
11. ADVOCACY: Do parents become better advocates for their child's education?

Trends in evaluation

We should note several trends in evaluating parent training. One has been a greater concern with long-term child changes. In 1977, Forehand and Atkeson reviewed parent training outcome studies and concluded that there had been only scant attention to the maintenance of treatment effects over time. It has become common wisdom both that long-term effects should be assessed and that maintenance should be intentionally programmed for if it is to be realized (Horner, Dunlap, & Koegel, 1988; Stokes & Baer, 1977).

Another trend has been a broadening of focus, from single variable to multivariate, from only assessing changes in specific child behaviors to also assessing changes in parents and in the family system. A related trend has been to expand parent training procedures beyond child teaching and management to other parent and family concerns. We will report the little that is known about broader effects as of this writing, but we imagine that this promises to be a major focus of study in the immediate future.

Consistent with this has been the renewed interest in consumer evaluations, or what Wolf (1978) has called social validity. Consumer self-reports were formerly eschewed as too subjective and biased. We now find, however, that some studies solicit parent judgments about the acceptability of intervention goals and procedures (Calvert & McMahon, 1987; Pickering & Morgan, 1985; Singh, Watson, & Winton, 1987) and that many programs measure parents' satisfaction with results.

Research designs and samples

Behavior therapy evaluations often employ single-subject experimental designs and present the findings with just one case or with several, as we have done in Chapters 9 and 10. The generalizability (external validity) of such reports is, of course, limited; we cannot know how typical each single case might be. This approach, however, has great heuristic value in identifying promising interventions.

Other evaluations use group designs that vary in their experimental soundness (Campbell & Stanley, 1966). Two decisions, about control groups and sample size, merit brief discussion here. With each, the essential question is: What is being evaluated? First, controls. Often in the early stages of developing an intervention, the evaluator employs a single group, perhaps a series of consecutive cases, to assess effects. A randomized control design may follow. In parent training studies, the most common design is to compare a training condition with a no-training or waiting list control and simply to ask the question: Did training work? There are disappointingly few studies with more complex designs where several types of intervention are contrasted, with or without a no-training control.

A related issue is sample size. Many studies with randomized group designs fail to detect differences because too few subjects were included. With only 5 or even 10 families in a condition, for example, outcome differences must be large and consistent to be statistically significant. The result is that many studies reporting no differences may be failing to detect clinically important effects. On the other hand, for most basic evaluation questions very large samples could also be misleading. If 100 families would be needed in a condition to demonstrate statistically significant intervention effects, these differences are likely to be clinically trivial. However, when the researcher wishes to examine predictors of within-condition variability, a somewhat larger sample size is desirable.

Parents as Teachers Research

As our program of research on parent training evolved, we considered the above evaluation issues. We evaluated not only immediate parent training outcome but also long-term effects, with 6-month or 1-year follow-ups. We studied child changes on specific targeted behaviors, but we also studied parent and family outcomes. We solicited feedback from our parent-consumers. We began with case studies, but primarily utilized randomized group designs to evaluate training approaches, with delayed training controls and/or varying intervention formats. For these studies, we assigned roughly 20 to 30 families to a condition, although untrained control groups were sometimes smaller. For our prediction studies, we aggregated for larger samples of about 50 to 100 families.

Our parent training programs have also been influenced by the evolution in parent concerns as well as the social and professional viewpoints that we have considered in this chapter. These have all changed considerably since we conducted our first parent training group more than two decades ago.

Unit II

Parents As
Teachers
Training
Program

"Looking back, you can usually find the moment of the birth of a new era, whereas, when it happened, it was one day hooked on to the tail of another." (John Steinbeck, 1986, p. 20).

The realization that we could teach retarded children better by also teaching their families sort of snuck up on us. Families, too, gradually got used to this idea. Yet with hindsight, the birth of our Parents As Teachers program was on a mild April Sunday in 1967. It went something like this.

Jon's parents turned in at the white sign with the black letters announcing WALTER E. FERNALD STATE SCHOOL and drove slowly past the cavernous red brick residence halls. The tension they had felt since the phone call was heightened in this familiar and yet always alien place. The blossoms hinting at spring in Massachusetts and the Sunday stillness belied the chaos they remembered within the building and within themselves each time they brought Jon back from his monthly weekend visit home. "He tears up the house upsets his sister frustrates us but he should have a home and this school isn't a school at all if only we knew what to do with him but . . . " The words had been said so often they just hung now in silence as Jon's parents entered the Children's Unit.

That phone call. The psychologist had said they were from Harvard and starting a program for six retarded children and Jon had been chosen. The children would live in a special unit and be taught according to behavior modification. Whatever that is. At least they would be taught. And if both parents would come to a meeting in two weeks . . . well, here they were.

We waited. Today we would meet the kids' parents. Our behavior modification project had started only days earlier, long enough, though, for us to see that there is much more to filling a child's day than the fragmented literature with its graphs and numbers implied. It would be good if the children's parents knew what we were doing and maybe carried over our programs during visits home, however infrequent. We would focus on basic skills in daily living—self-help, communication, play—and on the management of problem behaviors that interfered with learning, disrupted households, and said to onlookers, "I am different!"

We met that afternoon with Jon's parents and the others for informal talks about what we were trying to do and how they could help. Their skepticism was healthy, bred through years of bureaucratic false promises, and their questions were sound. Their involvement was soon heartening. Not every one, of course. But soon some parents were rewarding toileting successes, ignoring tantrums, or teaching puzzles one step at a time. Jon's mom quickly learned our speech imitation program and carried it through dutifully on Jon's now more frequent weekends home. She was surprised that she could do it. We were relieved.

Our initial enlistment of parents as partners was a guarded success. We admired the willingness of some to try again, their capacity to learn, their persistence; we felt good about what we were doing. It seemed a productive way to spend our time. Naturally, though, we felt many uncertainties.

One nagging question was how narrow or broad our training should be. Following the case studies, we had begun to show parents simply how to carry out one of our teaching programs. We gave some rationale, but parents' understanding it was not crucial as long as they followed through on what we were doing. We began to see that parents would be better served by training that included behavioral observation, program development, implementation, troubleshooting, recording progress. A parent with a more complete understanding of behavioral programming not only would be able to take on an expanded teaching role, but also would have skills with which to approach future programming needs without our complete help. We were on our way to realizing that the best parent training avoids fostering dependency.

So we wondered: Could parents learn broader principles and techniques of behavior modification? Would they need intensive individual training, or could they benefit from less labor-intensive groups? How else could training be made less costly in professional time? What would Jon's mother do if we stopped supervising? Would all parents do as well as Jon's? Probably not. What then?

These and similar questions drove our research. As we reflect back two decades on Jon's family and then turn to chapters describing our research, we are reminded again how much of "what it's really like" falls between the neat lines of a scientific report. For perspective, we will begin with a glimpse of three families and their concerns.

Chapter 2

Parents as Teachers Program

FAMILIES

The O'Neills rent the top floor of a triple-decker in the faded Dorchester section of Boston. Brian, their six-year-old autistic son, is a whirlwind of aimless activity. As we climb the stairs to visit, we have a fleeting image of the early 1900s, when extended families clustered together in these huge houses. Moving out often meant just moving downstairs. There weren't many services back then, but wouldn't it still have been easier, having grandparents, aunts, uncles, and cousins a floor or two away? They would have helped.

The Acostas are delighted that four-year-old Emily is in a mainstreamed preschool, although they worry that the bus ride from their suburban Los Angeles home is long. Emily enjoys feeding her rabbit and playing with her two very attentive older brothers, but her temper outbursts have become worrisome. Her dad, an engineer, and her mom, a part-time secretary, have juggled their lives a lot to meet the extraordinary challenges of a child with Down syndrome. They have tried to provide as normal a home life as possible. But they wonder: could they be teaching Emily better?

Mrs. Johnson is proud of her accomplishments. For six years she has raised her son James by herself—thanking God for his school programs and for her mother, who has watched James after school until Mrs. Johnson returns from her sales job. She has done her best to do what his teachers suggested—the potty training, playing ball, and trying to get him to talk more. He's doing pretty well, considering his retardation. But James is now ten years old, bigger, and more difficult to control when he wants his own way. Mrs. Johnson and her mother sometimes talk about it. James is almost a teenager. How much longer can they manage?

The O'Neills, Acostas, and Johnsons are not extraordinary. Their daily lives are pretty much like those of most families, except that having a child with mental retardation poses some special needs and concerns. There is more of a need for understanding and help from family and friends. There is a heightened need to keep in touch with teachers and other professionals. There are nagging doubts about how normal or how special to make the child's world. And the future hangs like a huge question mark that becomes difficult to ignore. On the demographic surface, though, our research samples of these families look representative of all families from the communities served.

Research Samples

In Chapters 3 through 6, we have compiled findings from 341 families who were trained with our Parents as Teachers curriculum and from whom extensive measures were taken. Many other families have also participated in our programs but are not included here because they were trained by other agencies, they were pilot groups in preparation for larger studies, their training had a focus or a format that significantly departed from the basic program, or their training is ongoing. Findings from some of these (e.g., other agency replications, school-based training, training in Spanish, advocacy training, training for child abusive families or families with children who are hyperactive) will be reported in Chapter 7 and in subsequent units.

The 341 families represent four large samples that we trained over 16 years, in greater Boston (1972–75) and Los Angeles County (1976–87).

1. Boston sample (n = 122). The families from greater Boston participated in the Read Project, a large-scale format comparison study conducted at Harvard University. It began in 1972, with follow-up measures taken in 1974.

2. Los Angeles sample I (n = 103). These families from Los Angeles were trained and followed up between 1977 and 1979 in studies examining parent training formats, maintenance of gains, and predictors of outcome.

3. Los Angles sample II (n = 44). These families from Los Angeles were trained and followed up between 1980 and 1981 in studies validating outcome predictors and examining intervention with predicted low-gain families.

4. Los Angeles sample III (n = 72). These families from Los Angeles were trained and followed up between 1985 and 1987 in a study comparing media-directed and live-directed training.

Characteristics

Selected demographic characteristics of these families are shown in Table 2.1. (See Appendix B for the Demographic Questionnaire and other measures.) For simplicity, we have not included standard deviations, but we should note that there was considerable variance on all of the measures for which we report central tendency. Yet the average families across these four samples were generally quite similar. The average parents were in their mid- to upper 30s and had some college education.

TABLE 2.1

Demographic Characteristics of Families

Variable	Boston	LA I	LA II	LA III
N	122	103	44	72
Mother: Age (Mean years)	39.1	36.3	33.7	35.4
Education (Mean years)	13.4	13.6	12.7	13.6
% Employed	23.3	41.7	36.4	52.8
%Employed full time	4.5	25.2	29.5	37.5
Father: Age (years)	41.7	38.2	33.8	38.1
Education (Mean years)	14.3	14.8	13.3	14.2
Family income: Median category	10,000–14,999	14,000–17,999	18,000–24,999	25,000–34,999
Marital status: % Intact	NA	83.5	79.6	77.8
Child: Age (Mean years)	7.2	6.5	5.6	5.9
Sex (% Boys)	61.9	55.0	55.8	77.8
Diagnosis: % Down syndrome	45.0	34.6	9.3	20.8
Autism	3.1	7.7	11.6	19.4
Cerebral palsy	9.4	14.4	23.3	12.5
Brain damage	16.9	NA	2.3	4.2
Mental retardation, unknown origin	14.4	25.0	30.2	22.2
Other	11.2	18.3	23.3	20.9
Level of retardation:				
% Mild or borderline	45.5	38.1	48.8	56.3
Moderate or severe	54.5	61.9	51.2	43.7
Total number of siblings (Mean)	2.3	1.5	1.3	1.5
Parent group members (%)	70.0	56.5	29.5	59.7
Used behavior modification with child (%)	4.0	30.8	13.6	23.9

Their family income was slightly above the national average and rose across the four samples, consistent with national trends over these years. The percentage of mothers employed full-time also increased from almost none in the early 1970s to more than a third in the mid 1980s.[1]

In the Los Angeles samples, about one family in five was headed by a single parent. That we did not even record this variable in the early 1970s perhaps reflects not only our oversight but also changing times. To the best we can reconstruct, virtually all of the families in the Boston sample had two parents.

The Boston sample was almost all White while the Los Angeles samples had mixed ethnicity. We did not specifically record ethnicity until

[1] In each family, the parent who would take primary responsibility for attending meetings, teaching the child at home, and completing measures was designated for data analysis as the *primary parent*. When parents planned to share attending and teaching equally, measures were taken from both, but mother was designated the primary parent for analysis. In most cases where father was designated primary parent it was either because father was raising the child by himself or mother could not read and write English and thus could not complete measures. In the Boston sample, all primary parents were mothers and in the Los Angeles samples combined only 5 were fathers, so primary parent descriptors are quite like those for mothers.

the Los Angeles III sample, where the breakdown for primary parent ethnicity was closely representative of the geographic area (White, 56%: Hispanic, 26%; Asian, 13%; Black, 5%).

In the typical family at least one parent had some experience with other parent groups, but few had specifically learned behavior modification techniques. The rise in the percentage of families who had carried out behavior modification programs at home from the Boston to Los Angeles samples reflects the increasing awareness of this approach during the 1970s.

The subject child was more often a boy and the average child's age decreased across the samples from 7.2 years to 5.9 years, reflecting the trend in parent programs, including ours, to begin at an earlier age. The most frequent diagnoses were Down syndrome and mental retardation from unknown causes, with some cases of autism and cerebral palsy with retardation in each sample.

We cannot be as certain about level of mental retardation, because we did only limited testing of the children. We had as evidence our assessments of skills and behavior problems, the Regional Center's records, and parent reports. In the Los Angeles samples, each child was present for several sessions and we could ascertain that all were retarded to some degree, most in the moderately or severely retarded range. We did exclude children who were nonambulatory, deaf, or blind. We have included parents' reports of level of retardation, although in some cases they overestimated ability, partly because of semantics. For example, many parents of children whose diagnosis was autism or cerebral palsy rather than "retardation" checked "not retarded" despite considerable delay in functioning.

Lost somewhere in all of these numbers is the reality of these families, parents who sat up at night after their child was finally settled in bed, deliberating about whether to join this program they had just talked about with us or with their counselor. Most of them were informed and concerned people who wanted to do everything possible to help their child. But often they were also tired people who had already attended many meetings and appointments on behalf of this child. They were people who had already taught much to their child but often were still haunted by feelings of not having taught enough. They were not all convinced that a parent training program could help—hadn't they already been told what to do by enough people who just didn't understand what it was like? They were people who might have wished for another, different, program, perhaps one that had come earlier, or had a different focus, or was easier to get to, or did not involve the anxiety and bother of group meetings. With it all, however, this Parents as Teachers program was what was available just now. So they decided to attend the first meeting.

GROUP PARENT TRAINING

Aims

The Parents as Teachers program was developed for families with children who had moderate or severe retardation and who ranged from about 3 to 13 years of age. Our overall aim has been to facilitate development of children with retardation by increasing their parents' ability to implement behavioral programs. The program teaches parents basic principles of behavior modification and how to apply these in a variety of learning situations with their child: increasing the child's involvement in activities; reducing problem behaviors; building basic self-help skills; and, to a lesser extent, building play, speech, and language skills.

Our ideal family after training would be able to select skills to teach, develop strategies that are systematic and manageable, implement these in a way that maximizes success, and know whether they are working. These goals require parents to be knowledgeable about behavioral principles and able to apply them in teaching interactions with their child, and to actually do so. The goals have, in turn, led us to take measures of parental knowledge of behavioral teaching principles, actual teaching skills, and implementation of programs at home. Our goals for the child were increased skills and reduced behavior problems, so we have measured these domains as well.

We expect that families like the O'Neills, Acostas, or Johnsons also derive other benefits from parent training that, although not the direct focus of the program, are perhaps even more important. They may value the social support and information from other parents in the group. They may feel more certain about how to parent their special child and better able to cope with situations that arise. They may adopt more positive attitudes toward the developmentally disabled child and his or her potential. They may even be able to apply skills learned in our program to problems experienced with their other children. Cooperation among family members and between the family and the child's other teachers may increase.

Parameters

The Parents as Teachers program typically involves a series of 8 or 9 two-hour weekly group meetings for parents only, although child care is often provided. There are also three individual assessments for parents and child: before training, at the mid-point, and after training. Training takes place in community agencies and group meetings are held in the evening to facilitate attendance by working parents. Usually there are two co-leaders who conduct training for a group of eight to ten families. In two-parent families, both are encouraged to attend. We now urge single parents to bring a friend or relative to participate in training with them.

Recruitment

In recent years, Regional Centers for the Developmentally Disabled have referred families to us. In California, a system of 21 Regional Centers registers persons with developmental disabilities and provides services to them by referral either to community agencies or to individual service providers. Our project originally recruited families from the community at large, through television coverage, newspaper articles, talks given to community groups, and directed mailings. This approach had two major disadvantages: It was very time consuming, and parents who called were distributed across a wide geographic area. The latter meant that groups had to be formed on a geographic basis, with too few families in any one area for random assignment to different conditions. Moreover, some families decided against participating because the meeting sites were still too far away.

Collaborating with Regional Centers has proven much more cost-effective. Counselors inform families of the program and compile a list of those who are interested, and the Regional Center provides meeting space. This collaboration between a university-based applied research program and community service agencies benefits both parties.

Assessment

Each family attends an individual pre-training assessment session where parents are interviewed about home teaching experiences, parent-child teaching interactions are videotaped, and parents complete a battery of measures. A detailed assessment of self-help skills is introduced in the first group session. Parents are oriented to the Self-Help Inventory, which contains 32 self-help skills in the areas of dressing, eating, grooming, toileting, and housekeeping. For each skill, from 4 to 10 component parts are arranged in a hierarchical scale, ranging from "Child cannot do any part of this skill" to "Child can perform this skill independently," with various degrees of mastery in between. Parents check the step that most accurately reflects the child's present performance. For some groups, such as the media-directed training described below, we have simplified the task by initially having parents complete a Self-Help Checklist that quickly assesses what their child can do on each skill: None, Some, or All. This is then the take-off point for selecting three skills to target for teaching, and the parents do the more complete assessment in the Self-Help Inventory just for these three skills. These measures are in Appendix B.

We acknowledge parents' own expertise from the very beginning of our training experience with them. We point out that they know their child best, and we give them a concrete and detailed assessment tool so that they can accurately report what they know (or what they find out by taking their child through the skill). We have found that even parents with limited education can complete the Self-Help Inventory. We similarly utilize the Behavior Problem Inventory (see Appendix B) and the Play Skills Inventory (Baker & Brightman, 1989) as we begin these modules of the program.

Curriculum

The group leaders guide parents through a standard curriculum. Table 2.2 shows the main topics of each meeting, and Appendix A gives a brief outline of each meeting's content. The first four sessions focus on teaching self-help skills. Parents learn basic assessment and teaching methods. They learn to set behavioral objectives, break skills down into component steps, and use reinforcement appropriately. In the fifth session, one or two families at a time attend with the developmentally disabled child. Parents demonstrate what they have been teaching at home and receive feedback from a leader and perhaps from other parents. Sessions are videotaped and sometimes the tape is replayed and discussed with parents.

The next three sessions focus on strategies for behavior problem management and toilet training, when applicable. Parents learn to identify problems to work on, to observe and record the frequency or duration of problem behaviors, to analyze the problems in terms of antecedents and consequences, to develop and carry out a behavior management or toileting program, to chart progress, and to troubleshoot when problems arise. Each family takes data on at least one problem behavior before and during the execution of a home-based program.

The final two sessions deal with applying the principles and methods that parents have learned to additional areas of teaching: play skills, speech, and language. These sessions also consider incidental teaching (working teaching into the daily routine) and future planning. Table 2.3 shows the types of skills and behavior problems that parents target at various points during the program.

TABLE 2.2

Parents as Teachers Curriculum

Prior to training	
Group	Orientation
Individual	Pre-assessment
Training sessions	
1. Group	Self-help skills: Introduction to behavior modification and targeting a self-help skill
2. Group	Self-help skills: Basic behavioral teaching strategies, including task analysis, setting the stage, modeling and guiding
3. Group	Self-help skills: Choosing and administering rewards; shaping and fading
4. Group	Self-help skills: Troubleshooting
5. Individual	Self-help skills: Session with child, to demonstrate self-help skill teaching and to receive feedback
6. Group	Behavior problems: Defining and observing behavior problems; carrying out an A-B-C (functional) analysis
7. Group	Behavior problems: Identifying consequences and locating a better consequence; planning a program
8. Group	Behavior problems: Additional techniques (e.g., token systems) and troubleshooting ongoing programs
9. Group	Generalizing the principles to play skills; incorporating teaching into the daily routine
10. Group	Generalizing the principles to speech and language, or review and future planning
Post-training	
Individual	Post-assessment
follow-up	Varied in different versions of program

Instruction

Leaders use a variety of modalities to instruct parents. They use brief mini-lectures, small group problem-solving sessions, and focused discussions to present and elaborate ideas. They use action-oriented approaches such as demonstrations with each other and role-playing with parents to illustrate teaching techniques. In preparation for each group meeting, parents read chapters from the *Steps to Independence* training guide (see below). The leaders focus discussions around what parents have learned in the manuals and supplement these with videotaped illustrations of teaching principles.

Each concept is presented in several different ways. To illustrate, one of the concepts parents learn in the second meeting is "setting the stage" for teaching—arranging the antecedents so as to maximize success. Before the meeting they should have read about this notion in the book. In the meeting, one leader will briefly describe this concept and lead a discussion

TABLE 2.3

What Parents Set Out to Teach: Targeted Skills

Brian O'Neill (Age 6)

Self-help skills:
• Making a bed
• Taking a shower

Playskills:
• Following 2-part directions
• Throwing and catching a ball

Behavior problems:
• Hitting baby sister
• Self-stimulatory behavior

Emily Acosta (Age 4)

Self-help skills:
• Eating with a fork
• Putting on a pullover

Play skills:
• Riding a tricycle
• Matching Lotto cards

Behavior problems:
• Throwing food at meals
• Crying and yelling at bedtime

James Johnson (Age 11)

Self-help skills:
• Setting the table
• Getting ready in the morning without reminders

Play skills:
• Board games requiring taking turns (checkers)
• Group play (not wandering off); After school activity

Behavior problems:
• Not following directions
• "Stealing" food between meals

---

to promote the parents' understanding of the concept. The leader will then show a 5-minute videotape of several parents setting the stage to teach (e.g., drawing a placemat to indicate where each item goes when teaching how to set the table; pinning the towel to the rack so it will not slip off when teaching how to dry hands). Finally, the leader will ask each family to note one way in which they could set the stage to increase success with the skill that they have chosen to teach their child. Presenting each idea in this manner, using several different modalities, maximizes the parents' learning.

Orientation

The orientation of this training approach has evolved much as the field of behavior therapy has evolved. The early program was rather strictly behavioral, focused on teaching techniques, formal teaching sessions, and accurate recordkeeping. Over time, the behavioral emphasis has softened somewhat. We could not ignore our own follow-up findings (see Chapter 4) that parents rarely did formal teaching or kept records once training ended. We sought ways to incorporate teaching more incidentally into the daily routine and to keep record-keeping to essentials. We also moved toward greater attention to parents' attitudes, beliefs, and thoughts, all encompassed by the term *cognitions*. The orientation today is cognitive-behavioral (Beck, 1976). The main focus is still on teaching parents behavioral techniques and supervising their application. We have, however, added a cognitive component to almost every meeting, focusing not only on what parents and their child do, but also on parents' cognitions (or *self-talk*) about those activities. We intend to teach parents to be aware of negative or interfering self-talk and to develop problem-solving strategies that can override the negative cognitions that so often impede progress.

In the first meeting, for example, we ask parents to list *reasons to teach* and *reasons not to teach*. The latter list might include statements such as "He already gets too much pressure in school," "I might do the wrong thing," or "I don't have enough time." It seems best to air such thoughts, because if unacknowledged they can effectively block progress. The group then attempts to come up with alternative, more positive, statements or ways to solve the problem posed. Hence, the parent who is worried about doing the wrong thing may be advised to say to herself: "I've already taught him many things," or "I can ask members of the group for their ideas about teaching." Similarly, the group can help the parent who complains of limited time to problem solve on this subject until a workable plan is arrived at (e.g., "I will teach on weekends and my husband will teach at night during the week"). Similar discussions take place in other meetings throughout training.

MEDIA DIRECTED PARENT TRAINING

We have had an enduring interest in developing programs that are both cost-effective and exportable. Both goals have translated for us into developing instructional materials that can be used by parents with little or no professional guidance. We began in the early 1970s to develop a series of nine self-instructional manuals covering self-help skills, toilet training, play skills, speech and language, advanced living skills, and behavior problems for parents of children with developmental disabilities. We published these beginning in 1976 as the *Steps to Independence* series. (Baker, Brightman, & Blacher, 1983; Baker, Brightman, Carroll, Heifetz, & Hinshaw, 1978a, 1978b; Baker, Brightman, Heifetz, & Murphy, 1976a, 1976b, 1976c, 1976d, 1977; Baker, Brightman & Hinshaw, 1980). Recently, we combined the manuals into *Steps to Independence: A skills training guide for parents and teachers of children with special needs* (Baker & Brightman, 1989).

Parents read sections on choosing a target skill, teaching, rewarding, and recording progress, illustrated by fictionalized mini-cases and humorous drawings. There are also detailed programs for teaching targeted skills. The chapter entitled *Behavior Problems* aims to teach an approach for understanding and modifying behavior problems rather than prescribing specific programs. Figure 2.1 shows a sample page. Throughout, we have stressed to parents that "no one knows your child as you do" and that the guidelines presented are simply that—guidelines, to be flexibly adapted to the parents' and child's particular teaching and learning styles and to their home environment.

Following parents' successes in learning from the manuals (see Chapter 5), we decided in 1984 to carry training through media a step further and produced *Steps to Independence: Self-Help*, a video program that takes a small group of families through a four-session program in self-help teaching (Kashima, Baker, & Landen, 1988). This area was chosen because it is one of the easiest in which to instruct parents. The content of each meeting is presented primarily through a 35-minute videotape; a moderator introduces each main topic, highlights important points, describes group exercises, and closes the session with a summary and homework assignment. The videotapes show an ongoing parent training group that is racially and ethnically mixed and representative of a range of child ages and disabilities. The video presentation includes mini-lectures, group discussion, and examples of parent teaching. Each videotape contains four or five interspersed instructions for the viewers to stop the tape and carry out a group exercise or discussion. The total meeting time is about 2 hours.

A facilitator is on hand to present the video program, monitor time, and stimulate group exercises and discussion. A written guide is available to orient facilitators. At present, we have only evaluated this package with professional facilitators (see Chapter 5), but we feel that it would also be successful with, for example, a parent facilitator.

CONCLUSION

This is the program, then, that the O'Neills, the Acostas, and Mrs.

CHAPTER 6

Teaching

Let's review the STEPS we've talked about so far. We've covered:

Setting out to teach
Targeting a skill to teach
Establishing the separate steps that make up the skill
Picking rewards that your child will work for
Setting the stage to maximize success

We've come a long way without even starting to teach yet! But being prepared makes all the difference in whether teaching will be fun or failure for you and your child.

In this chapter and the next one we get down to the business of:

Teaching
Observing progress and troubleshooting

We will emphasize in this chapter the two main ingredients of good teaching: instructing your child what you want him to do, and rewarding his efforts.

Tell Me, Show Me, Guide Me

Tell me something a hundred times and I still may not understand what you want me to do. Show me what you mean—demonstrate clearly and slowly—just once or twice and I'll be closer to that goal. But do it with me—put your hand on mine and guide me through it—and I'll make it!

FIGURE 2.1:   Sample page from *Steps to independence: A skills training guide for parents and teachers of children with special needs* (2nd ed.) (p.25) by B. L. Baker and A. J. Brightman, 1989. Baltimore: Brookes Publishing. Copyright 1989 by Paul H. Brookes Publishing Co. Reprinted by permission.

Johnson joined. They each came with their unique talents, needs, questions, and, no doubt, reservations. We hoped that there would be enough commonality to justify a group approach but that this approach would also be sufficiently personal and flexible. Like all service providers, we wondered: Would they complete the program? Would they benefit from it?

Chapter 3

Participation

> No one can read about a child's disability or talk to other parents without confronting the past and the future. These encounters stir up fear, uncertainty, anger, and unfathomable sorrow. If the pain is too great, parents naturally avoid it. Sadly they may cut themselves off from contacts and knowledge that would help break down the sense of isolation—settings where they could give and receive mutual understanding, where their situation might seem more ordinary. (Featherstone, 1980, p. 60).

There is probably no parent with a retarded child—indeed, any child—who has not wished for more help, better guidance, at times even just an empathic listener. In theory, parent training programs should have universal appeal. In practice, they do not. A minority of families who are offered a program will join it. For some, a professionally led program may not sit well philosophically or emotionally. For others, it may seem a good idea but the time commitment is too great or perhaps the need not great enough just now; the program may come at the wrong time in the family's developmental history. For still others, the meeting time may simply interfere with Tuesday night bowling. And even when a family joins a parent training program, they may not continue to participate.

Service providers often become discouraged when parents' response to a new training program does not mirror their own enthusiasm. Professionals in our audiences frequently comment: Our agency started a parent training program a year ago, but we could only get a small group to attend and it dwindled over time to just a few parents. Recruiting and retaining parents in a training program is the first point of program evaluation; if parents do not join and finish the program, the service providers' efforts have been in vain. Agency staff likely will be discouraged and the program may not be continued.

JOINERS AND NONJOINERS

Parents who join a training program are, then, a select group, thereby limiting the generalization of research findings. The majority of published studies are based upon small numbers of volunteer families, and investigators rarely report recruitment procedures or how many families were invited to participate. In practice, most programs are conducted by agencies where staff recruit from clients they already know, through personal contact or letters of invitation. Researchers are more apt to be recruiting from the community at large, using media and/or intermediaries (e.g., teachers, counselors) to reach parents.

Even when recruitment has involved personal invitations, a majority of families has declined to participate. In Ireland, McConkey and McEvoy (1984) invited 101 families with children who were moderately to severely retarded to join a short-term group on teaching play skills; 39 enrolled. Morris (1973) reported that of 80 families who were sent letters inviting participation in group behavioral training, 41 agreed to participate but only 14 (18%) attended the initial meeting. Hetrick (1979) mailed letters to invite parents of 369 students to participate in a group communication-skills training program; 11% came to the first meeting.

Yet programs typically offer training with one particular focus and little choice of meeting time or place. A greater proportion of parents would likely participate if they were given options. Fredericks, Baldwin, and Grove (1974) offered school-based training that was individualized in content and meeting times, and reported that about half of parents of children in special education classes participated.

We have typically offered programs on several weekday evenings and in a reasonably central facility. Our Boston families were recruited in the early 1970s through mailings, radio announcements, and newspaper articles. Prior to this very little parent training had been available in the Boston area, and there was a very large response. Of 222 families who called and met selection criteria, 165 attended orientation meetings. Several of these were deemed inappropriate and a few were not interested, but fully 160 of these agreed to participate in the program, to be assigned to training or delayed training control conditions (see Chapter 4). Our first Los Angeles sample was recruited through a combination of media (radio, newspaper, and television) and Regional Center referrals, whereas our subsequent two samples were recruited for us entirely by Regional Center counselors who described the program to parents and then submitted a list of interested parents.

We conducted two "joiner" studies to determine enrollment rates and the representativeness of families in our programs. In the first study (Baker, Clark, & Yasuda, 1981), we offered parent training to all 74 families with children in a public special school who had moderate or severe retardation and were aged 5 to 13. We sent a letter of invitation, jointly signed by us and the school principal, home with each child. Eighteen families (24%) joined the program.

In the second study, Jim Shenk (1984) offered parent training to 41 low income Spanish-speaking families who had been randomly selected from a list of 101 families referred by the Regional Center for a study of how Spanish-speaking families cope with a child who is retarded. Each family had already been visited at home twice by a Spanish-speaking interviewer from our project (Prieto-Bayard, 1987). A very high 63% of these families joined. An additional 7 families could have been offered training, but 4 had refused interviews and 3 had indicated schedule conflicts with the parent training time. If these families are included as nonjoiners, an adjusted enrollment rate of 54% is still very high for a population that has traditionally been viewed as underutilizing mental health services (Padilla, Ruiz, & Alverez, 1975). Shenk suggested that three factors contributed to the high joiner rates. First, the program was offered in Spanish. Second, the invitation to participate was personal (made in a phone call and building upon the relationship established with our project by the home visit study). Finally, the program was affiliated with and held at an agency that the families trusted.

Joiner Characteristics

The obvious next question is: How do these joiners differ from families who do not choose to join? The literature tells us little about how participating families differ from others, except that middle-class families are overrepresented in most programs (Hargis & Blechman, 1979), a phenomenon that may reflect bias by recruiters or self-selection by families. McConkey and McEvoy (1984), comparing joiners and nonjoiners, did not find a difference on socioeconomic variables. They did find, however, a difference in prior involvement: joiners previously spent more time in play activities with their children.

Studies of help-seeking have been marred by a number of methodological problems, such as relying on agency records or taking measures when the parents are entering the program or thereafter (Gourash, 1978). In both of our studies, we attempted to obtain measures independent of the decision to join parent training. In Baker, Clark, and Yasuda (1981), we obtained from the school staff each child's age, sex, diagnosis, level of retardation, a rating of extent of behavior problems, and a rating of the parents' involvement in school programs. Joiner families attended more school activities. They may also have experienced greater difficulties with their child, as children of joiners had greater retardation and had been rated by school staff as having more behavior problems that interfered with learning. Children of joiners and nonjoiners did not differ in age, sex, and diagnosis.

We also examined family demographics. We contacted the 56 nonjoiners and asked them to complete a demographic questionnaire.

Thirty of these families returned the questionnaire. They did not differ from the 26 families who failed to return the questionnaire on any variables assessed by school staff, so to this limited extent they were representative of nonjoiners. A comparison of joiners and nonjoiners on socioeconomic status indicators yielded some support for a self-selection explanation, as joiner families had higher father education and almost significantly higher socioeconomic status. They did not differ from nonjoiners in marital status (single- or two-parent families) or prior experience with parent groups and behavior modification.

In the Shenk (1984) study, there was a high participation rate in an entirely lower socioeconomic status sample, indicating the importance of other factors. Measures were taken with this sample during a prior study and before the parents were told about our parent training program and invited to participate. Four domains were assessed: (a) demographic (e.g., child and mother age and education, family acculturation); (b) reality constraints (difficulties in obtaining child care or transportation); (c) behavioral variables (e.g., child abilities and behavior problems, parent contacts with school); and (d) cognitive variables (e.g., attitudes about the child's behavior, service agencies, and expectation of benefits).

Consistent with the Baker et al. (1981) study, joiners had reported greater involvement in school activities (e.g., PTA, fund raising), although there was no difference in other types of contacts with schools (e.g., consultations about the child) or agencies. Surprisingly, the variables that significantly differentiated joiners and nonjoiners were almost exclusively cognitive in nature. Compared with nonjoiners, mothers who subsequently joined had rated a hypothetical parent training program higher relative to other services and had given higher ratings to their ability to learn how to teach new skills from such a program.

Attitudes toward the child also seemed more important than child behavior. The children did not differ in actual skills and behavior problems, as assessed by parent-completed scales. Yet mothers who joined rated for themselves and their families higher burden from the child's skill deficits, bother from behavior problems, and frustration from handling behavior problems. Thus, while Baker et al. (1981) found that the joiners' children were rated by school staff as possessing fewer skills and more behavior problems, Shenk (1984) found that it was the mothers' perception of the level of discomfort experienced by the family in response to the retarded child's behavior that was predictive of the decision to join the training program. Further studies are needed to separate out the role of actual child behavior and maternal perceptions as influencing the decision to seek help.

In any event, a clear implication of these findings is that outcome results have limited external validity. To the extent that parents who join a training program are better educated, more involved with their child, experiencing more difficulties, and perhaps in other ways different, their results may not readily generalize to other parents of children who have developmental disabilities. It would be valuable in program development to know much more about rates of joining and characteristics of joiners and nonjoiners.

DROPOUTS AND COMPLETERS

Attrition is a major concern in all mental health services, contributing to staff burnout. Parent training is no exception. Dropouts are a problem for staff morale, clinical service, and research. Staff cannot help but experience some sense of rejection and failure when families do not come back. Families who drop out are likely to be dissatisfied and may also experience some sense of failure. Program evaluators must necessarily be wary of high dropout rates, for these limit the interpretation of outcome results.

How many families who begin a training program complete it? Measurement here is straightforward. Yet most published studies do not give completion rates and those that do are not comparable. Some include as dropouts those parents assigned to training who never began (Forehand, Middlebrook, Rogers, & Steffe, 1983), others (including ours) only include parents who dropped out after starting, and still others mention no criteria. Only a few give more specific criteria, such as attending at least 50% of meetings and completing post-measures (Dubey, O'Leary, & Kaufman, 1983; Webster-Stratton, Kolpacoff, & Hollinsworth, 1988).

With these caveats, we can note that completion rates vary widely, from 100% (Hirsch & Walder, 1969) to less than 50%. Forehand et al. (1983) reviewed parent training studies in 8 behavioral journals over a 10-year period; 22 studies had usable data, with an overall completion rate of 72%. Some of the lower rates have been in programs stressing communication skills and parental attitudes, areas perhaps of less relevance to the needs of parents of children who have developmental disabilities (Hetrick, 1979; Miller, 1980).

Of the 341 families trained in our four major samples, 278 or 81.5% completed training and post-measures; 63 families—almost one family in five—were considered dropouts. A family was designated as a completer if the primary parent (see Chapter 2) attended more than half of the meetings and the pre- and post-assessments. In our Boston sample, 122 of 128 families assigned to training condition (see Chapter 5) began training and 111 (91%) finished the program, with all but one non-completer leaving the program early in training after three or fewer meetings.

However, only 100 families (82%) met the more stringent criterion of also completing the post-training assessment. In the Los Angeles samples, of 219 families who began training, 178 (81.3%) met the criteria for completion.

Why does a family drop out of training? Does it have more to do with characteristics of the program or of the family?

Dropouts and Program Characteristics

Recruitment

There are several reports that agency referred parents complete training at a lower rate than self-referred ones (Dumas, 1984; Worland, Carney, Weinbert, & Milich, 1982). We examined this relationship with the Los Angeles samples. Los Angeles I families were self-referred, recruited through the news media and targeted mailings; they had a completion rate of 91.3%. Los Angeles II and III families were staff-referred, recruited by Regional Center counselors; together, they had a completion rate of 72.4%. This difference was highly significant (χ^2 = 11.53, df = 1, p < .001). While another variable might account for this difference, referral source fits with our experience. We have often found parents referred by counselors who came to the screening session simply because they felt their counselor expected them to, and it is not surprising that some of them did not follow through as well as parents who sought out the program on their own.

Training Format

In a review of the dropout literature, we did not find that rates varied with the child's problem (e.g., conduct disorder versus developmental disability) or the type of training format (group versus individual). In our samples, completion rates did not differ much by training format employed, and some differences were confounded by the recruitment used. Individual and group training formats were remarkably similar in completion rates when referral was controlled for. For the self-referred families, completion rate was 88% for individual training (N = 16: LA I sample), 89% for group training (N = 116: Boston and LA I samples), and 88% for group training that involved individual home visits (N = 32: Boston sample).

For the self-referred families who began training through self-instructional manuals (N = 29: Boston sample), 86% met the completion criteria. In this format, however, only post-measure completion was involved because there were no meetings, so the completion rate is not really comparable to that found in other training conditions. By contrast, for a sample of self-referred families trained in a telephone consultation condition (N = 32: Boston sample), the completion rate was only 72%. This training approach was generally the least successful of those we have examined, and we will consider it further in Chapter 5.

Incentives

Many programs have remembered the law of effect in designing their intervention and have included incentives to motivate parent participation. These vary. One program made professional resources, such as extra training time and a toy-lending library, contingent upon parent participation (Donahue, 1973). Another desperate daytime program sought to reduce nonattendance by giving weekly synopses of soap operas missed during meeting time to mothers who attended (Rickel, Dudley, & Bermon, 1980). Most commonly, however, the incentive is money. In some programs a "contract deposit" is required from families and refunded according to certain performance criteria (Benassi & Benassi, 1973; Rinn, Vernon, & Wise, 1975). Hirsch and Walder (1969), for example, refunded a $50 deposit if all nine sessions were attended, with no refund at all otherwise (remarkably, all 30 mothers maintained perfect attendance).

In other programs, parents are paid for participation. Fleischman (1979) paid a $1 parenting salary for each day that parents of children who acted out carried out prescribed programs and found that this significantly increased participation for lower socioeconomic status families. Our program has successfully used a lottery in several groups for lower socioeconomic status families (Ambrose, Hazzard, & Haworth, 1980). At each meeting, parents could earn tickets for attending, coming on time, and completing homework. One ticket was drawn at the end of each meeting for a relatively inexpensive prize (e.g., houseplant, stuffed animal, canned ham, even State lottery tickets). Parents enjoyed and were motivated by the game.

Dropouts and Family Characteristics

Apart from program considerations such as referral, training format, and incentives, what individual and family characteristics relate to completion? We have found, perhaps contrary to common sense, that there is little to be learned by asking parents why they stopped attending. Rarely have parents spoken critically of the program, even when pressed to do so. Most often, they have cited changes in their work schedules causing conflict with the meeting time, prolonged sickness in the family, unavailability of babysitters, and the like. While we generally do not doubt the reality of these obstacles, we believe that they only lead to termination in families that were inclined to drop out anyway. Indeed, many families who attend regularly have similar obstacles, and we have seen countless families make extraordinary arrangements to attend despite seemingly impossible obstacles. One mother brought her 3-day-old baby with her; another mother came to training several days after having had a mastectomy; and one airline pilot negotiated his flights so as not to miss a meeting. It makes sense to look further at the characteristics of completers and noncompleters.

Demographics

In each sample, we contrasted completers and noncompleters on demographic variables. The most consistent variable related to attrition was marital status: in each sample except Boston, where we did not record this variable, single parents dropped out at a much higher rate than married ones. In the three Los Angeles samples combined, 19.2% of families were headed by a single parent. The dropout rate for these families was 40.5%, three times as high as the 13.5% for intact families ($\chi^2 = 14.4$, $df = 1$, $p < .001$).

A second variable significantly related to attrition in every sample was pre-training knowledge of behavioral teaching principles, with dropouts scoring lower than completers. This does not reflect less education or less prior experience with behavior modification or parent groups, as dropouts and completers did not differ on these variables. It may, then, indicate that dropouts were less comfortable with a behavioral approach to child problems.

It is worthwhile to note the many other variables on which dropouts were not distinguished. They did not differ on family demographic variables, including socioeconomic status, income (except in Los Angeles III), family size, primary parent age, or employment. Neither did they differ on child variables, including age, level of self-help skills, behavior problems, reported level of mental retardation, or diagnosis. In Los Angeles samples I and II, dropouts and completers were compared on their pre-training expectations about potential success, problems they might encounter, likelihood of overcoming them, commitment to teaching, and view of themselves as responsible for teaching; they did not differ on any of these variables. Contrary to our expectations, dropouts and completers did not differ on the reality dimension of how far they had to travel to the meeting site.

Psychological Characteristics

In the Los Angeles III sample, we compared dropouts (23) and completers (49) on an expanded battery of measures that also included parent depression, marital adjustment, family problems and stress, family adaptability and cohesion, and family coping strategies (see Chapter 11 for a description of these measures). We have seen that single parents were more likely to drop out. For married parents, those reporting a low or average marital adjustment had a greater dropout rate than did those reporting high adjustment. Two other psychological variables were predictive. Completers initially tended to report greater child-related stress in the family, consistent with Shenk's (1984) findings of greater perceived burden, bother, and frustration in families that joined parent training; and completers reported fewer different coping strategies available to the family for dealing with stress. This is consistent with Birkel and Reppucci's (1983) finding that a weaker social support network may be associated with a greater search for outside professional help. These results suggest that psychological variables may contribute to our understanding of dropouts, but further multivariate study with large samples is needed.

Toward Increased Participation

Our analyses of completers and noncompleters suggests several ways in which parent training programs could maximize participation rates. First, a recruitment strategy involving self-referral or at least some proactive response from families may produce higher completion rates. These may be obtained at some cost, however, for we know that initial self-referral rates will be lower than rates when agency staff directly contact families; hence, some families who could benefit from training will never begin it. Second, we are inclined to attribute the relatively high participation rates in the Parents as Teachers program to our time-limited program with program content that speaks directly to the teaching and behavior management concerns of parents who have children with developmental disabilities.

Third, there may be ways to restructure the program to increase participation of single parents and parents with low initial behavioral knowledge, our two most consistent predictors. In attempting to understand the propensity for single parents to drop out, we examined whether married parents drop out at a higher rate when the spouse does not attend. They do not. Having someone else, even at home, to share ideas and responsibilities with may help sustain interest. One wonders whether the group experience itself may be alienating for single parents, who are in the minority. Yet when clinicians have conducted parent training groups exclusively for single parents, they have still found high dropout rates (Hall & Nelson, 1981; Pinkston, 1984).

We tend toward a social support and accountability explanation. We noticed that all of the 7 dropouts in the first phase of the Los Angeles I sample ($N = 50$) attended training alone. For the second phase, ($N = 53$) we encouraged the 7 single parents to bring a friend or relative with them to training to increase their motivation to attend and to have someone to share ideas with. Five did so, and of these only one dropped out; she had brought a housekeeper, who spoke little English! It may also be helpful to schedule several individual sessions with the single parent and the group leader before the group begins, to establish rapport and commitment. These sessions could also introduce the concepts to be considered in the group meetings, as behavioral knowledge is low in dropouts.

Finally, there are some reality-based supports that make training more accessible. For lower socioeconomic status families, we have found that reminder phone calls the day before or the day of the meeting help to maintain attendence. Providing child care at the meeting site will facilitate attendance for some families. Providing make-up meetings may help to maintain parents who are marginal about continuing, although one should not be surprised when they miss the make-up sessions as well. The main value of make-up sessions is to keep the motivated parent who happens to miss a meeting from falling behind.

CONCLUSION

Completing a training program is in itself an important indicator of success. Our subsequent consideration of the Parents as Teachers program will involve other outcome measures taken from completers only. We would like to know more about the impact of training on dropouts, but to obtain further measures from these families is difficult at best, and we have not made a systematic attempt. It is important to remember, however, as we look at favorable training outcomes, that these are overestimates of the program's success. Only a small proportion of eligible families initially joined the program and, moreover, one family in five that began training did not complete it.

Chapter 4

Outcome

The most basic and often asked question about any intervention is: Does it work? Staff in every program address this inescapable question somehow, if only in informal discussions with one another. Many programs, however, take a more formal, data-based look, and no single measure or perspective on the question suffices. Indeed, here we will consider six critical outcome questions that we and others have tried to answer: Do parents like the training program? Do they learn the teaching principles that the program teaches? Can they apply these in a teaching interaction with their child? Do they actually do so at home? Do their developmentally disabled children show gains? Do parent and child gains maintain over time? We can imagine other benefits that children, parents, and families might derive from an intervention program, but we will wait until Chapter 11 to consider these. It is first important to see to what extent the answer to each of the above six questions is "yes," because these questions speak directly to what parent training programs claim to do.

CONSUMER SATISFACTION

There was a time not long ago when measures that assessed consumers' opinions about the helpfulness of mental health services were dismissed by professionals as too subjective and biased. Decades of research on psychotherapy had found clients and therapists singing its praises while more objective studies struck a sour note. The reader most likely knows of instances when parents have been highly satisfied with, and even advocated for, programs that simply do not work by more objective evaluation. Of course, the simple fact that consumers do derive satisfaction from an intervention, that they perhaps find benefits that are not tapped by more objective measures, is also important.

Moreover, consider the case where the consumer does not like a program. It will not be much utilized, despite demonstrated effectiveness. In alcohol treatment, for example, the drug antibuse that makes the patient vomit following ingestion of alcohol is a highly effective treatment, but one that is almost universally rejected by patients (Goldstein, Baker, & Jamison, 1986). In recent years the social acceptability of an intervention and the consumer's satisfaction with it have come to be seen as important parts of a multimethod assessment (Kazdin, 1977; Wolf, 1978).

Although we have always solicited feedback about our program from parents, we introduced a questionnaire measure of consumer satisfaction beginning with the Los Angeles II sample. This Program Evaluation Questionnaire was adapted in part from one used by Forehand and McMahon (1981) with parents of noncompliant children. It asks for parents' evaluation of (a) the appropriateness of the intervention for them, (b) the program generally, (c) specific components of the program, and (d) their own participation. Items are each rated on a 4- or 7-point scale (see Appendix B).

Table 4.1 shows Program Evaluation ratings obtained from 49 primary parents in the Los Angeles III sample at the end of a 9-session Parents as Teachers program. On the general evaluation, all or almost all parents found the approach appropriate, the group helpful, and the leaders helpful and competent. All would recommend the program "much" or "very much" to other parents. On evaluation of program components, however, we find more variability. Almost all parents found lectures and

TABLE 4.1

Program Evaluation: Percentage of 49 Primary Parents with High
Consumer Evaluations Following the Parents as Teachers Program

A. *General*
1. Appropriateness of approach — 100[a]
2. Helpfulness of group — 96
3. Helpfulness of leader — 100
4. Competence of leader — 96
5. Recommend program to other parents — 100
6. Overall feeling (positive) — 96

B. *Usefulness of program components*
1. Lectures by leader — 98[a]
2. Videotapes — 70
3. Group discussions — 89
4. Group exercises — 73
5. Reading manuals — 80
6. Home observations and teaching — 93

C. *Self-evaluation*
1. Attending meetings — 100[b]
2. Completing readings — 76
3. Skill teaching — 91
4. Keeping skill records — 39
5. Behavior management program — 85
6. Keeping behavior problem records — 52
7. Confidence in teaching — 81[a]

[a] Percentage of parents who reported much (6) or very much (7) on a 7-point scale.
[b] Percentage of parents who reported most (3) or all (4) on a 4-point scale.

teaching their child "much" or "very much" useful, whereas videotapes and group role-playing exercises were not rated as highly.

On the self-evaluation, most parents reported that they had done most or all of the teaching and behavior problem programming assigned, and most felt confident in these roles. Compliance with recordkeeping requests was much lower, however, even by the parents' own admission. In sum, the parents who complete training are generally well satisfied with the program; however, parent feedback on more specific questions about components of training (e.g., recordkeeping) suggests areas where the program should be examined.

KNOWLEDGE OF TEACHING PRINCIPLES

After consumer satisfaction, the outcome that is most often assessed in parent training programs is parents' knowledge of the principles that the programs have taught. Programs typically use a short-answer or multiple-choice questionnaire. One popular and general measure is the 50-item questionnaire, Knowledge of Behavioral Principles As Applied to Children (O'Dell, Tarler-Benlolo, & Flynn, 1979). Our Behavioral Vignettes Test is a 20-item multiple-choice questionnaire (Baker & Heifetz, 1976). It presents parents with brief vignettes describing situations that reflect a range of common problems encountered in formulating and implementing skill teaching and behavior management programs with a developmentally disabled child. Parents select from four alternative responses the one that they think would be most effective (see Appendix B). Here is one of the easier items, about shaping:

> You are beginning to teach Alan to name colors. During teaching sessions, especially the first one or two minutes, he looks away and often leaves his chair and walks around the room. You should:
>
> a. offer him a large reward for naming a color correctly.
>
> b. forget it for now but promise him a reward for working later.
>
> c. reward him at first for sitting quietly and looking at you.
>
> d. try to interest him by pointing at objects in the room and naming the various colors.

This measure has three advantages for us over the O'Dell et al. (1979) measure: It is shorter, it refers specifically to children who have developmental delays, and it assesses not only whether parents know behavioral principles but also how they would apply these principles in specific situations. The two measures are, however, moderately correlated; in one sample of 27 mothers where we took both measures, the correlation was $r = .67$.

The Boston sample completed two earlier versions of the Behavioral Vignettes Test (BVT), counterbalanced for pre- and post-testing. We consider these results in Chapter 5 when we compare training formats. Table 4.2 shows BVT pre- and post-mean scores and the pre-post correlation for our three Los Angeles samples and a replication of our program conducted by Tom Ball, Michael Jarvis, and their colleagues at Fairview State Hospital in California (Ball, Coyne, Jarvis, & Pease, 1984). Behavioral Vignettes Test gains were statistically significant in every sample shown as well as in studies by other investigators (Feldman, Manella, Apodaca, & Varni, 1982; Feldman, Manella, & Varni, 1983). Moreover, three studies that compared trained families with untrained control families on the BVT found that trained families showed significantly greater gains; control families gained only minimally (Baker & Heifetz, 1976; Brightman, Baker, Clark, & Ambrose, 1982; Kashima et al., 1988).

While some parents have a perfect or near-perfect score after training, most parents still show room for improvement and some parents, despite sizable gains, still score so low that they could not be said to have real understanding. Another perspective on Behavioral Vignettes Test results comes from asking: How many parents scored high enough to be considered knowledgeable? We have used 75% or more correct, or a score of at least 15 out of 20, to designate proficiency. Results from this competency perspective are shown in Figure 4.1, which shows the percent of primary parents reaching the criterion before and after training for each of the Los Angeles samples. Combined, we find 13.9% of parents reached

TABLE 4.2

Pre- and Post- Parent Training Scores for Outcome Measures

SAMPLE	N	PRE	(SD)	POST	(SD)	r	t	p
Behavioral Vignettes Test								
LA I	94	10.6	(3.8)	14.1	(3.4)	.78	14.02	<.001
LA II	33	9.5	(3.2)	14.4	(3.8)	.76	11.37	<.001
LA III	47	10.1	(4.1)	14.3	(4.0)	.76	10.20	<.001
Fairview	23	10.0	(4.0)	15.4	(3.4)	.52	7.09	<.001
Teaching Proficiency Test								
LA I	48	9.5	(4.5)	12.3	(5.3)	.42	3.65	<.001
LA II	32	7.1	(4.2)	12.8	(3.6)	.14	6.27	<.001
Fairview	17	8.9	(4.2)	13.0	(3.7)	.08	3.15	<.01
LA III	43	20.1	(7.0)	26.5	(6.1)	.38	5.75	<.001
Teaching Interview								
LA II	33	13.2	(4.8)	21.0	(7.6)	.13	5.34	<.001
LA III	46	12.2	(6.2)	21.6	(6.7)	.28	8.24	<.001

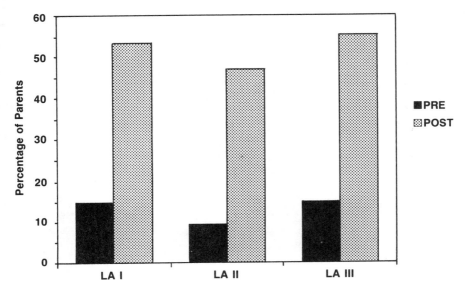

FIGURE 4.1: Behavioral Vignettes Test: Percentage of parents reaching competency criterion (75% or more correct) pre- and post-training for Los Angeles
samples. Five families did not have complete data and are not included.

the competency criterion before they began training and slightly more
than half (52.6%) attained it by the end of training. Our program, then,
boosts many parents' BVT scores to a level at which we would consider
them knowledgeable about behavioral teaching principles. Others,
however, do not reach criterion. BVT scores are correlated with parents'
educational attainment, whether we look at pre-scores, post-scores, or
gains. It may be, then, that a longer or different training program would
be necessary to bring less educated parents up to a reasonable criterion
(see Chapter 7).

TEACHING SKILL

Some programs also assess whether parents can apply what they have
learned to teaching interactions with their child. Many different
observation approaches are used, but each has some limits on its
applicability. Measures for rating behavior management in families with
conduct disordered children (Christensen, 1979; Patterson, Reid, Jones, &
Conger, 1975; Zebiob, Forehand, & Resnick, 1979) are not readily
applicable to families with developmentally disabled children, where the
emphasis is primarily on skill teaching. Several measures constructed for
parents of children who have developmental disabilities tally a score based

upon the number of behavioral techniques used while teaching (Hudson, 1982; Koegel, Russo, & Rincover, 1977; Weitz, 1981). These measures typically show significant gains from pre- to post-treatment, at least in some of the parental behaviors being coded. They do not, however, take into account whether it is appropriate to use a given technique with a particular child at a particular time.

Our Teaching Proficiency Test (TPT) was developed to score a parent's appropriate use of behavioral techniques, given the ongoing behavior of the child (Clark & Baker, 1982). This requires more judgment in scoring, so coders must be proficient in behavior modification. Each parent is video-taped in a 15-minute standardized session in the clinic teaching his or her child ability-appropriate self-help skills and play skills. Raters, blind to condition and time of administration, score the parent separately for teaching proficiency in the self-help and play tasks. They score four dimensions: organization of the teaching setting, task presentation, reinforcement, and behavior management. The self-help and play totals are summed to a Teaching Proficiency Test score. Interrater reliabilities have been high.

Table 4.2 shows TPT pre- and post-training scores for the same four samples we examined with the BVT; they are reordered because the Los Angeles III sample used a revised scoring system that resulted in higher scores (possible range: 0–56). Trained parents gained significantly in each sample shown and in another study with Spanish-speaking families (Prieto-Bayard & Baker, 1986). This measure, however, is not very stable from one testing to the next, in part because it is a "live" measure involving both the parent and the child. If the child is particularly disruptive or inattentive in one session, for example, this can depress the TPT score considerably. With considerable variability in change scores, this measure has not consistently shown greater gains for trained families than for untrained control families. Kashima et al. (1988) found that trained and control families both gained equivalent amounts after four sessions of training, while Brightman et al. (1982) found that trained families gained significantly more than controls did after nine sessions.

IMPLEMENTATION

Some parent training programs keep track of the number of teaching programs that parents carry out to some success criterion. Rose (1974a, b) found that 90% of parents modified at least one child behavior "to their own satisfaction," and O'Dell, Flynn, and Benlolo (1977), using a stricter criterion for outcome, found 68% completed one full modification project. Our Teaching Interview (see Appendix B) goes beyond this to give credit for the quality as well as quantity of teaching and to include ongoing teaching programs together with those that have been successfully completed. This structured 30-minute interview is conducted by a staff member not associated with the training. Parents are asked about teaching and behavior problem management during the previous three months (Ambrose & Baker, 1979). For teaching, they can specify up to three skills they are working on with formal teaching sessions (a regular time set aside) and three they are teaching incidentally (as the opportunity arises). For each skill they are asked a series of specific questions (e.g., how often do you teach, describe how you teach, show us any records you have kept). Raters blind to condition and administration time score audiotapes for the extent and quality of teaching and behavior problem management and these are summed into a total Teaching Interview score. Interrater reliabilities have been good.

Table 4.2 also shows pre- and post-training mean scores for the two samples where families were assessed at these points. Although we made some modifications to the scoring system between Los Angeles samples II and III, the mean scores are remarkably similar in the two samples, with trained families as a group showing significant change. Teaching Interview gains were significantly higher in trained families in two studies where they were compared with a randomly assigned, untreated control group (Prieto-Bayard & Baker, 1986; Kashima et al., 1988). We will return to this measure in our consideration of follow-through post-training.

CHILD GAINS

There are difficulties in obtaining an accurate and meaningful measure of child change. For one thing, changes in a retarded child's behavior come slowly, and for more severely impaired children gains may not be sufficiently evident to be measurable until months after training. A better time for assessment of child change might be at follow-up. By this time, however, a great many other influences will have been active, and to keep an untreated control group waiting this long does not seem clinically appropriate.

Moreover, demonstrated changes will relate to the specificity of the measures. Measures have consistently shown significant child gains when they were directly related to the content of parent training, such as tests of reading (Fry, 1977), language skills (Harris, Wolchik, & Weitz, 1981), and physical dexterity (Gross, Eudy, & Drabman, 1982), or direct observation of specific behavior problems, such as noncompliance (Dadds, Sanders, & James, 1987). When studies have used broader measures, such as developmental scales, the results have been more mixed. While some studies have found significant gains in development relative to controls (Bidder, Bryant, & Gray, 1975; Hudson, 1982), others have found that control children gained as much (Clements, Evans, Jones, Osborne, &

Upton, 1982), or, worse yet, that children of trained parents did not show significant gains (Sandler, Coren, & Thurman, 1983; Sebba, 1981). We also suspect that the amount of generalization as assessed by these broader scales would decrease with child functioning level.

We have utilized a measure of self-help skills that falls somewhere between the very specific measure and the broader one. Although the Self-Help Inventory focuses on one developmental area (self-help), it assesses 32 child self-help skills in the areas of dressing, eating, grooming, toileting, and housekeeping (see Appendix B). Initially we were concerned about whether parents' assessments would be accurate. Hence, in the Boston sample and with an earlier, 42-item version of this measure, we compared responses of parents and trained observers. For a random sample of 33 families, an observer who had not seen their scores visited the home and observed those items that were neither clearly beyond the child's ability to perform at all nor clearly already mastered. Since these middle difficulty items would be the most prone to interobserver disagreement, this was a conservative reliability check. Even then, agreement was very high (r = .89). This reliability check was repeated after training with a randomly selected subsample of 17 families, and again agreement was very high (r = .93) (Heifetz, 1974).

In this Boston sample we looked at the total self-help change scores and found that children in trained families gained significantly more than did control children. As a measure of generalization, we examined changes in programmed and unprogrammed skills separately. The average trained parent programmed 4.2 skills, representing about 10% of the skills assessed; yet changes in these programmed skills accounted for about half the total gain, indicating a specific effect of parental teaching efforts on behavioral change in their children. Changes in unprogrammed self-help skills were also statistically significant for trained families and almost significantly different from controls.

Toilet training, analyzed separately, shed light on the specificity of training effects. Training condition children whose parents programmed toileting skills during the training period improved more than three times as much in toileting skills as either control children or training condition children whose parents did not program toileting skills.

The Behavior Problem Inventory is even further from specific programming goals. Parents score the frequency, on 6-point scales, of 48 behavior problems commonly reported by parents of developmentally disabled children. These are arranged under the subcategories of acting out problems (12), mealtime problems (10), sleeping (3), fears (6), repetitive behaviors (10), withdrawal (5), and behavior when being taught (2) (see Appendix B). In the Boston sample, with an earlier version of this measure, fully half of the parents who programmed a behavior problem had targeted one that did not appear on the scale. Even with a problem on the scale, a family may be quite successful in reducing this particular problem and not have an overall scale change score.

In Los Angeles samples I and II, we found consistent increases in self-help scores and decreases in behavior problem scores. In the one comparison with an admittedly small control group ($n = 11$), children of trained families showed significantly greater improvement in behavior problems than those in control families. However, the conditions did not differ in self-help skills changes (Brightman et al., 1982). In the Los Angeles III sample, we used the entire Self-Help Inventory before training to help parents target skills to program, but we utilized a Mini-Inventory to assess change. The Mini-Inventory is an individualized subset of the next two self-help skills that the parents have targeted to teach. This allowed for an assessment of gain in targeted skills, and, not surprisingly, these gains were highly significant (Kashima et al., 1988).

It is important to realize that virtually all of the children in our samples, both experimental and control, were simultaneously in school programs; yet a very limited investment of parent teaching time—usually about 10 to 15 minutes per day—produced sizable benefits in targeted skills over and above what the school produced. Parents may have several advantages over teachers. First, parental attention and praise are especially powerful reinforcers for their children. Secondly, parents taught their child individually rather than in a group, thereby maximizing the child's attention to the task. Thirdly, parental teaching sessions typically involved repeating the skill several times, rather than running through it once and then moving on to another child. Finally, parents utilized sound behavioral principles in their teaching; they worked on a specific and appropriately targeted behavior, maintained the child's attention, and rewarded progress. A teacher who is not well trained in behavioral methods and who must divide his or her efforts among a class of students may produce much more limited change.

CASE STUDY: THE MANNS

This case study (adapted from Baker, 1986) illustrates how the outcome criteria and measures that we have considered thus far apply to one family. This family was somewhat below average on pre-training measures and about average in the gains they made.

The Manns participated in the Parents as Teachers program with seven other families in the Los Angeles II sample. Their son Jimmy has cerebral palsy and severe mental retardation; at the beginning of training, he was 7 years old. Gloria Mann was 25 years old, a housewife with a 10th grade education and the mother of two children younger than Jimmy. Dennis Mann was 28 years old, with a highschool education and full-time employment as a bus driver. They had recently purchased a small home in a new desert community east of Los Angeles, and both parents' rating of their marital harmony on the Locke Wallace Marital Adjustment Test (Locke & Wallace, 1959) was above average.

In their initial interview, the Manns acknowledged that they had no previous experience with either parent training or teaching using behavioral principles. They had tried to teach Jimmy to perform various dressing skills and to balance without his crutches; however, they did not teach on a regular basis, and felt that they had seen little recent progress. On the Behavioral Vignettes Test, Gloria scored 8 (40%) and Dennis scored only 4 (20%); these scores, both below average for this measure, indicated very little knowledge of behavioral principles. On the Teaching Proficiency Test, Gloria scored a 13 and Dennis scored 10, both above the sample mean, suggesting that despite limited formal knowledge, their natural teaching style with Jimmy was good. The Manns scored 12 on the initial Teaching Interview, indicating about an average level of home teaching for this sample.

During the 10-week program the Manns attended every meeting and evaluated the experience very highly on the Program Evaluation Questionnaire. They learned how to observe Jimmy's behavior, select appropriate skills to teach, and carry out a teaching program. For their first self-help skill, they decided to teach Jimmy to put on his pants, because he had already mastered some of this skill (he could pull his pants up from his knees after his parent had started them). At the training meetings, Gloria and Dennis reported teaching Jimmy daily, and they observed slow but steady progress.

By the end of the program, the Manns had developed some understanding of behavioral principles, as indicated by post-training BVT scores of 12 for Gloria and 11 for Dennis. There was still room for improvement, and they did not meet our proficiency criterion; however, given their limited education and low starting scores these represent meaningful gains. Gloria's TPT had risen to 16 and Dennis' to 12, indicating that both parents were teaching well.

By the last training session, they had successfully taught Jimmy to put on his pants without help. Also, they had started to teach a second dressing skill, putting on a pullover shirt. They had kept baseline data on Jimmy's hitting his younger siblings, and had carried out a behavior management program with good initial success, reducing hitting by about 60%. These programming efforts were reflected in a Teaching Inventory score of 26, higher than the sample post-training mean and indicating considerably more and better teaching during the training program than in the

comparable time before the program. Both Gloria and Dennis felt proud
of their accomplishments and were optimistic about continuing to teach in
the future.

FOLLOW-THROUGH

We have seen that with parent training a family can create a more
effective home environment for their child's learning and that their
teaching pays off in child gains. More important, however, is what
happens in the months and even years after training. Reviews of the
literature have reported that many programs did not follow up their
families after training and the follow-ups available focused almost
exclusively on child behavior (Baker, 1984; Forehand & Atkeson, 1977).
Most follow-ups have been with conduct-disordered children and have
been concerned only with maintaining the reduction in the child's
behavior problems (Strain, Steele, Ellis, & Timm, 1982). The evidence for
successful maintenance here is mixed. It seems reasonable that skill gains
of children who have developmental disabilities will be maintained if the
environment provides opportunity, encouragement, and reinforcement
for practicing them. The evidence bears this out; typically, maintenance or
further improvement are found. Learning disabled children were still
attending to task better 3 months after their parents completed training
(Diament & Colletti, 1978), autistic children showed continued language
progress 13 months after training (Harris et al., 1981), and physically
handicapped children showed continued skill gains after 3 months
(Feldman et al., 1982). In our Boston sample a 14-month follow-up found
that gains in programmed self-help skills had been maintained (Baker,
Heifetz, & Murphy, 1980).

Yet the aims of intervention with families of handicapped children are
of necessity broader than with families of nonhandicapped children who
have behavior problems. The few skill gains or behavior problem
reductions accomplished during training are but a beginning; there will
always be a great deal more to teach. Accordingly, follow-up evaluations
must examine not only whether child gains in the original target behavior
are maintained but also whether parents maintain what they have learned
and whether they apply it in new ways. There has not been much study of
the maintenance of parent teaching knowledge and skills, though in our
Boston sample parents had maintained their gains in knowledge of
teaching principles (BVT scores) at the 14-month follow-up (Baker,
Heifetz, & Murphy, 1980).

In these families we also examined formal teaching—setting aside a
period of time for planned, regular teaching sessions several times a
week—because this had been the emphasis of the manuals and training. It

was discouraging to find that only 16% of families began and followed through with formal teaching sessions for a new skill and that only 22% began a new program for behavior problem management.

Follow-up performance seemed considerably better when we examined incidental teaching: incorporating behavior modification principles into the daily routine as the occasion arose, without formal teaching sessions. Fully 76% of families reported incidental teaching that met the criteria for at least one skill. A family was credited with incidental teaching only if a specific goal could be stated and the teaching seemed beneficial and continued for at least a month, or until mastery. For example, one mother reported that she and her husband decided it was time for Julie to learn to brush her teeth. Julie's dad attached a toothbrush holder to the wall within Julie's reach, and her mother tried several toothpastes until she found one that Julie seemed to like. Each morning after Julie dressed, her mother supervised toothbrushing, using physical guidance at first, later relying on prompts. Although there were no repeated practice periods as in formal teaching and no records were kept, the mother reported that within several weeks Julie could brush her teeth unsupervised (Baker, 1983).

Overall in this follow-up, 86% of families reported some scorable teaching efforts, formal or incidental, new or continued, during the year following training. Because most families seemed to prefer to teach incidentally rather than in formal sessions, we subsequently changed the focus of the program to give greater guidance in incidental teaching and to reduce demands for formal teaching post-training.

Subsequently, Stephen Ambrose (Ambrose & Baker, 1979) conducted a 6-month follow-up of 88 families in the LA I sample with very similar results. Blind raters with high interrater reliability scored audiotapes of the Teaching Interviews on scales that summed to two scores: the extent and quality of teaching. Families who scored one standard deviation below the mean on either subscale were classified as Low follow-through (25%); others were classified as Medium (35%) or High (40%) follow-through. The High families had continued productively the programs they began during training and initiated some new teaching and/or behavior problem management following training. The Low follow-through families reported little or no continued teaching or demonstrated inadequate behavioral techniques.

In the Boston sample, we asked parents about various events that might have been obstacles to follow-through and found no relationship between this score and the follow-through score. For the LA I sample, we expanded this obstacle checklist to include 9 potential obstacles each rated on a 5-point scale. We contrasted the responses of the 22 Low follow-through families with the 66 Medium and High follow-through families. Table 4.3 shows that Low follow-through families had significantly higher

TABLE 4.3

Obstacles to Implementation Rated At 6-month Follow-up by Low
Follow-through versus Medium/High Follow-through Families

OBSTACLES	MEAN LOW	MEAN MED/HI	t
Lack of time	3.92	3.06	2.53**
Major disruptive events	3.58	2.21	3.20**
Daily interruptions	3.25	2.68	ns
Lack of patience	2.92	2.41	ns
Child's slow progress	2.67	2.38	ns
Child's lack of skills	2.33	2.47	ns
Not knowing what to do next	2.08	2.12	ns
Unable to manage behavior problems	2.00	2.38	ns
Lack of encouragement from family	1.75	1.88	ns
Total Score	24.50	21.59	1.81*

Note: Source: Ambrose and Baker, 1979. Obstacles rated on a 5-point scale (1 = not an obstacle; 5 = very much an obstacle).
* $p < .05$, one-tailed. ** $p < .01$, one-tailed.

total scores and reported that major disruptive events (e.g., death in the family, divorce) and lack of time were significantly higher obstacles than the other families. We cannot say whether these perceived obstacles merely provided a rationalization for not following through or whether these families were, in fact, more stressed and less well organized in their daily lives.

One limitation of the follow-ups we have reported is that there was no control group available for comparison. Hence, we do not know how much these families might have been teaching had they never been in a training program. Trying to maintain a control group for 12 or even 6 months is both clinically unwise and impractical, given other ways that parents can now have training needs met. In the Los Angeles II sample, we used a different strategy for addressing this issue. The Teaching Interview was reframed to ask about the previous 3-month period. It was then administered before training, at the end of the 3-month training period, and at a 3-month follow-up, so that each family's teaching could be compared with its own pre-training level.

For the first two groups ($n = 14$ families) the Teaching Interview means for these three points were 14.4, 22.1, and 17.8. Families increased significantly in the extent and sophistication of teaching during the training, but by the 3-month follow-up the level had fallen off to a point not significantly different from the pre-training level.

POST-TRAINING
INTERVENTION

In an attempt to promote maintenance of teaching, Kathleen Kashima (1983) developed and evaluated a booster intervention consisting of an in-home planning session immediately following training and biweekly follow-through phone calls for 3 months.

The planning session helped parents to set up goals and priorities, to plan specific steps for meeting them, and to anticipate obstacles using the Goal Attainment Scaling method (Kiresuk & Sherman, 1968). Parents first chose three or four skills to teach or behavior problems to reduce. Staff assisted parents in formulating goals so that they were stated clearly and were reasonable to attain (e.g., "Learn to tie shoes in three months"). For each of these target behaviors, the parents identified what they realistically expected they would do (e.g., "Teach three times a week for 10 to 15 minutes each time"). They then identified one or two levels that would not be as good as this and one or two levels that would be better. Hence, for each teaching goal the family developed performance criteria based upon their own expectations.

Following this, staff assisted parents in identifying the steps to follow in teaching, ways to reward themselves for following through, and obstacles that they might expect to encounter. Staff and parents worked together to identify alternative self-talk for interfering thoughts and to problem-solve about ways to deal with realistic obstacles.

Biweekly telephone calls lasting 10 to 15 minutes gave parents the opportunity to discuss their programming and any obstacles they may have encountered. In addition to contracting future subgoals with parents, staff offered teaching suggestions and encouragement.

This booster intervention was piloted with the next 10 families who completed cognitive behavioral training. These families were rank ordered by predicted follow-through score based upon criteria that we will consider in Chapter 6. One member of each successive pair was randomly assigned to the booster follow-through for 3 months ($n = 5$) and the other to a no-intervention follow-through ($n = 5$). The Teaching Interview scores from before training, after training, and at a 3-month follow-up were compared for booster and no-booster group families (Kashima, 1983). The results are shown in Figure 4.2. Using a multivariate analysis of variance for repeated measures, the group-by-time interaction was significant ($F(2,7) = 7.30, p < .025$). The no-booster group showed a drop in teaching at follow-up similar to reports of other authors and to our own earlier cognitive-behavioral groups. The booster groups, though, had maintained a high level of teaching.

Scores on the Goal Attainment Scale for the booster intervention group indicated that four of the five families attained or did better than their expected efforts at teaching. The one family in the booster program that did not benefit from the additional programming was, according to the predictive criteria in Chapter 6, the family that was predicted to do the least follow-through. The booster program may prove to be most useful

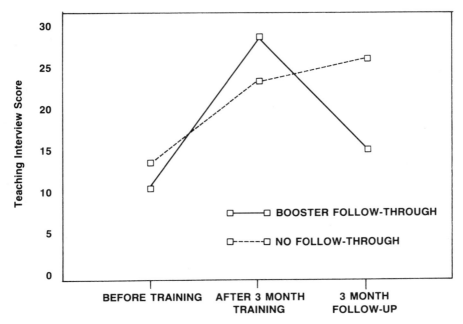

FIGURE 4.2: Teaching Interview scores, pre-training, post-training, and follow-up, for families who received the booster follow-through intervention versus those with no follow-through intervention. Scores reflect the extent and quality of teaching at home during the preceding 3 months.

for parents who have the capacity and inclination to teach but need some further guidance and accountability. However, we do not yet know whether this increased level of teaching would persist after the follow-through consultation ends.

CASE STUDY CONTINUED: THE MANNS AT 3-MONTH FOLLOW-UP

Two weeks after training, two project staff visited the Manns at home for a follow-up goal planning session. The Manns set the following four goals, stated in terms of behavioral outcomes: Jimmy puts on a pullover shirt by himself; Jimmy washes his face; Jimmy does not hit his brother or sister; and Jimmy balances without crutches. They discussed teaching plans for each goal area and the obstacles to teaching that might arise. Gloria mentioned that at times she felt overwhelmed by her responsibilities. After some problem-solving, Gloria and Dennis agreed to divide the responsibilities more; in particular, when one was teaching Jimmy, the other would keep the other two children occupied. In addition, they made a plan to reward themselves for their teaching efforts every other week by going out to dinner by themselves.

In the biweekly phone conversations, primarily with Gloria, we discussed progress and problems. At one point, Jimmy was ill for two weeks and no teaching took place. Three months following training the Manns were interviewed again by a staff member who had not been involved in their training. Their total Teaching Interview score had increased to 36 (from 12 before training and 26 after training). Dennis had taken primary responsibility for teaching Jimmy to put on the pullover shirt, and now stated that he could almost do every step by himself. Also, the Manns reported that Jimmy was able to balance without his crutches for 1 1/2 minutes and had progressed in face washing. Hitting still occurred occasionally, although much less than before the program. Both parents expressed more optimism about Jimmy's learning ability and their own ability to work together as a couple to teach him.

CONCLUSION

Thus far, we have looked at the question of whether group parent training works from six perspectives: parents' satisfaction with the program, knowledge gained, skills acquired, implementation at home, follow-through, and child gains. From our outcome data and from reports of other investigators, it seems fair to say that, by these six standards, group parent training generally seems to work. A next logical question, then, is: Does it work better than some other approach?

Chapter 5

_____Formats

Seeing the plethora of parent training formats, or models, a clinician might wonder which is best. This chapter will report four controlled studies where we examined different approaches to parent training. The first study assessed training outcomes from self-instructional manuals and increasing levels of professional involvement. The second study contrasted outcomes from the two most commonly used parent training approaches, individual and group training. The third study evaluated the effectiveness of groups that are primarily media directed, in the search for an exportable training package. The fourth study addressed the more methodological question of whether the consistently good outcomes found with parent training are simply nonspecific effects of being in a program or are really linked to specific components of training. Taken together, these studies have something to say about how a service delivery agency might structure an array of parent services.

A consistent theme through our studies of training models has been a search for more cost-effective approaches. In light of chronic shortages of child mental health services, it seems wise to develop and study alternatives to long-term, individualized, clinic interventions with families. One alternative activity for professionals is to package what we know into manuals and books, so that parents can inform themselves about teaching needs and methods without any professional involvement. It seems reasonable that if some people are following written instructions to rebuild Volkswagen engines, enjoy better sex, or plant bonsai, then it should be possible to write useful instructions about how to teach children. The popularity of the how-to idea is witnessed in bookstores by entire sections devoted to books on child care and even self-help. Until recently, however, there were very few instructional books aimed at parents of children with developmental disabilities. Most of the books that are available even today have not been systematically evaluated (Bernal & North, 1978; Rosen, 1987). Also, although written materials now seem to be part of almost all parent training programs, professionals are still reluctant to rely too heavily on them.

We recognize that all professionals will not become authors, that agencies will indeed stay in business, and that most parents will want professional guidance at some point. Another cost-effective alternative is to develop group approaches. If five, ten, or more families can come together to learn how to help their children without an enormous loss in effectiveness when compared with individual consultation, then there is obvious cost savings. Moreover, parents may derive special benefits from hearing about the experiences of other parents: The modeling, support, suggestions, and feedback have special meaning when received from another parent. And, in sharing ideas with parents, the chance to be not only a receiver but also a provider of expertise is an added appeal. There will always be times, of course, when individual help from a professional will be desired and will be best, but groups have a relatively untapped place in service delivery.

STUDY 1: MANUALS ONLY
VERSUS PROFESSIONAL
TRAINING

Our first and largest study of training formats responded to a Request for Proposal authored by Dr. Michael Begab and issued by the National Institute of Child Health and Human Development in 1972. Begab observed, in issuing this RFP, that many thousands of families with children who have developmental disabilities live in areas where there is only limited access to professionals trained in mental retardation and behavior modification. Thus the primary question of interest was how effectively parents of mentally retarded children could learn behavioral teaching strategies and teach their child when their only training was from self-instructional materials. Our study design also addressed the extent of added benefits from other training conditions representing various degrees and types of supplementary professional help (Baker & Heifetz, 1976; Baker, Heifetz & Murphy, 1980; Heifetz, 1977).

The study involved 160 families with a retarded child aged 3 to 14 years old. This was the Boston sample described in Chapter 2. Most of the children were classified as organically retarded, with functioning levels ranging from dull-normal to severely retarded; none met the criteria for cultural-familial retardation (Grossman, 1983). These families were randomly assigned to one of five experimental conditions, with increasing professional contact, described here with estimated per family implementation cost in 1972 dollars.

1. *Control:* ($n = 32$) Delayed Training. No parent training for 4 months.

2. *Manuals Only:* ($n = 32$, $38). All contacts were by mail, including provision of teaching manuals (see below), child assessment measure, and teaching log books.

3. *Phone:* ($n = 32$, $77). Manuals plus phone consultation. Use of manuals was supplemented by biweekly scheduled phone calls of 20 to 30 minutes' duration. Trainers consulted on current teaching programs and helped formulate plans.

4. *Group:* ($n = 32$, $118). Manuals plus group training. A nine-session group program following the Parents as Teachers curriculum, with eight families and two trainers (one male and one female) in each group.

5. *Group-Visits:* ($n = 32$, $211). Manuals plus group training and home visits. The same program as the Group condition, with six biweekly home consultation visits.

Trainers were experienced with behavior modification as well as with retarded children and their families. Each trainer either co-led a Group condition group and made calls to four Phone condition families or led a Group-Visit condition group and made home visits to four families.

The percentage of families assigned to training conditions who began and completed training as well as post-measures was not significantly different across conditions (Manuals Only = 78%; Phone = 72%; Group = 75%; Group-Visits = 88%). Teaching logs favored the greater contact conditions; the combined percentage of days logged was significantly higher in the two group conditions (59%) where logs were handed in, than in Manuals Only and Phone conditions (45%), where they were mailed.

Knowledge acquired and child gains presented a very favorable picture of training by Manuals Only. Figure 5.1 shows gains on the Behavioral Vignettes Test for mothers and fathers by condition. Mothers' scores in each condition gained significantly, and three training conditions (Phone excepted) gained significantly relative to Control mothers. An F test for differences among the four training conditions fell short of statistical significance ($F(3,89) = 2.41$, $p = .07$). The most substantial gain was in the Manuals Only condition and the least in the Phone condition. Father knowledge increased with the amount of potential trainer contact, but only Group-Visits fathers significantly outgained Control fathers.

Child self-help and behavior problem gains were assessed on earlier versions of the Self-Help Inventory and Behavior Problem Inventory (Chapter 4), with 42 self-help skills broken down into component steps and 32 behavior problems. Figure 5.2 shows the mean gain in self-help skills for children in each condition; although each training condition differed significantly from controls, the differences among the training conditions did not approach statistical significance. When unprogrammed self-help skills were examined separately as a measure of generalization, each training condition showed significant gain; however, Manuals Only

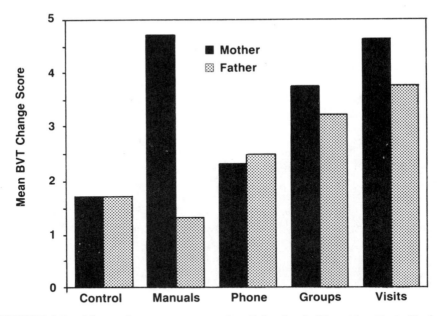

FIGURE 5.1: **Mean change score on the Behavioral Vignettes Test (I) for mothers and fathers by training condition.**

was the only condition to differ significantly from Controls. With toilet training, where the number of families in each condition was small, Manuals Only was the only condition to show statistically significant gains.

The success of the Manuals Only training format was contrary to our expectations, which were clearly revealed even in the research design itself. We expected that the benefits derived from professional contact conditions would probably be progressively greater than benefits emerging from Manuals Only. The research question had asked about cost effectiveness: Would the added benefits of professional support be worth the added price? Yet if one training condition could be said to be superior for self-help training, it would be Manuals Only. We noted at that time:

> It seems understandable, with hindsight, that a mother who is highly motivated to teach her child might read a manual more carefully when it is her only source of information and might teach more consistently without trainers and other parents available to be 'understanding' of lapses. The high motivation of the volunteer sample and the strictures of the research context should not, however, be underestimated. It is possible in other (non-research) samples that a smaller proportion of parents would make the commitment to initiate and carry out programs

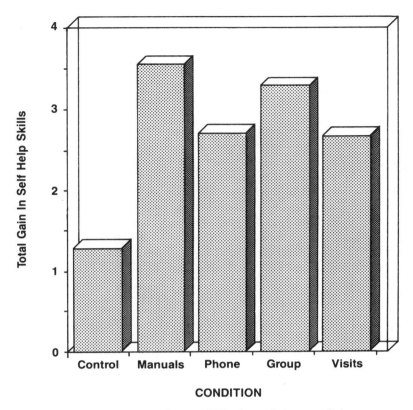

FIGURE 5.2:   Total gain in self-help skills, by training condition.

without professional prodding, but the present results suggest that those who do make such a commitment will be quite successful. (Baker & Heifetz, 1976, p. 365)

Conclusions

Although we could have been encouraged about the potential of instructional manuals for training, there were several reasons to be cautious about concluding that training parents could best proceed through manuals alone. First, in managing behavior problems, the Group conditions showed some superiority. This is an area where instructional manuals cannot be as specific and where parents might also need the added encouragement of group members and leaders. Although all families were given the manual *Behavior Problems* (Baker et al., 1976b), families in the Group conditions were significantly more likely to carry out a program than were the Manuals Only and Phone families (79% versus 29%). Also, of families that did carry out a program, records were kept more consistently by families in the group conditions. The Behavior Problem Inventory did not prove to be a good index of change in specific, targeted problems, in part because about half of the problems targeted did not appear on it. Nonetheless, only condition Group-Visits was superior to Control families, and this condition was significantly superior to the other three training conditions combined.

Second, at the end of training, Manuals Only families reported less confidence in teaching skills and managing behavior problems than did either Control families or those in all the other training groups combined. As we have noted elsewhere, "Whereas they were at least as knowledgeable and effective in teaching as parents receiving professional consultation, they did not experience their effectiveness as much, perhaps in part because they were teaching without feedback from others. Not only was there no expert available to affirm their successful efforts, but also there was no one to forgive their occasional lapses" (Baker, 1980, p. 207).

Follow-up

We wondered if parents would maintain what they had learned and if children would maintain their gains over time. We particularly wondered if parents trained through manuals only would continue to teach their children once the demands of the training program were over. Perhaps at some later time, the training conditions would be found to have produced different outcomes. One year after training, we followed up the 100 families who had completed training and post-measures, first with a letter and then with a phone call. We were able to conduct Teaching Interviews with 95 families and to readminister the original outcome measures. We reported the overall extent of follow-through teaching in Chapter 4; here we will examine the differences among the original training conditions.

Unfortunately, we were not able to maintain the original Control group over this follow-through period, because we had promised them delayed training and had provided this. Thus, overall levels of parent and child performance are difficult to interpret.

At follow-up, mothers' BVT scores decreased only slightly and nonsignificantly from post-training levels and did not differ across training conditions. Figure 5.3 shows the Performance Inventory programmed self-help skill scores for children. Here too, gains were maintained. There was no continued improvement in these skills, however, in part because at post-test many skills were approaching ceiling level. The unpro-

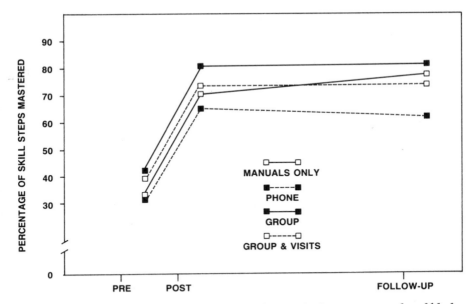

FIGURE 5.3: Performance Inventory (early version) programmed self-help skills at pre- and post-training and one-year follow-up, by training condition.

grammed self-help skills provided a pool from which parents could select new skills to teach. With these, there was continued gain for all training conditions except the Phone condition, which declined some. Gains were at a much slower rate than during training, however, and were difficult to interpret without a continuing Control group to indicate changes that might have occurred from maturation, schooling, or other factors independent of parent training.

Table 5.1 indicates the mean follow-up Teaching Interview scores by prior training condition. Individual Teaching Interview scores ranged widely, from −6 to +37, with Manuals Only families scoring lowest as a group; however, the condition means did not differ significantly by an analysis of variance. We examined family variations in follow-through behaviors and reduced these to five fairly discrete patterns varying in the type, extent, and sophistication of programming. Table 5.1 also shows the distribution of these patterns, which did not differ across conditions. When parents were asked in the follow-up interview about what training condition they might have preferred, however, parents in every condition ranked Manuals Only last, with preferences increasing with professional contact.

Based on these findings and considerations, we subsequently revised the Parents as Teachers curriculum to rely heavily on manuals

TABLE 5.1

Follow-through Score and Patterns of Follow-through: Percentage of
Families in Each Pattern by Condition and Total

	M[a]	P	G	GV	T
N	23	23	22	27	95
Teaching Interview Mean Follow-up Score	8.1	14.6	13.6	13.2	12.6
Pattern/Description, with percentage of families					
Pattern 1: Very useful teaching Continued programs begun during training; moderate amount of new teaching (formal and/or incidental); technique acceptable-to-good.	13	17	32	33	24
Pattern 2: Useful teaching Moderate amount of new teaching (mainly incidental, not formal) with technique acceptable-to-good; programs begun during training either discontinued before reaching criterion or not continued at all.	17	30	18	15	20
Pattern 3: Minimal teaching Less teaching activity than Patterns 1 and 2; all new teaching and most of the continued teaching incidental; technique acceptable.	17	26	18	7	17
Pattern 4: Poor teaching Some identifiable teaching (new or continued, formal or incidental) but with poor technique, suggesting little real utility.	30	22	14	33	25
Pattern 5: No teaching No teaching sufficiently evident to be scored.	22	4	18	11	14

[a] M = Manuals Only; P = Phone; G = Group; GV = Group-Visits; T = Total families. From "Behavioral Training for Parents of Mentally Retarded Children: One-Year Follow-up" by B. L. Baker, L. J. Heifetz, and D. M. Murphy, 1980, *American Journal of Mental Deficiency, 85,* p. 36.

for transmission of information about principles of teaching and to utilize group meetings for reviewing concepts, providing feedback on teaching, and furnishing individual guidance in the area of behavior problems. Because several studies demonstrated the superiority over didactic lectures of role-playing and/or viewing video models in training parents to execute behavioral programs (Nay, 1975; O'Dell, Mahoney, Horton, & Turner, 1979; Watson & Bassinger, 1974), we subsequently produced a series of illustrative videotapes and incorporated them into the curriculum (see below).

We should not leave the Boston study without underscoring the success of training by manuals alone and its implications for families who live in rural areas or who otherwise do not have access to an array of services. Begab (personal communication, January 1989), in reexamining our findings, suggested that for such families manuals might be followed up by regular visits from a social worker or public health nurse whose primary role would be to sustain the parents' energies and motivation to teach.

STUDY 2: INDIVIDUAL VERSUS GROUP PARENT TRAINING

Most studies that have contrasted models of training have compared clinic-based individual training to group training. Individual consultation with parents dominated early reports of parent training and is still the most common practice in clinical settings, but group training holds a promise of greater cost-effectiveness for agencies and social support benefits for parents. Two studies have reported better outcomes with individual than with group training (Eyberg & Matarazzo, 1980; Mira, 1970), but these had methodological problems that make them inconclusive. However, comparisons with parents whose children were developmentally delayed (Kogan & Tyler, 1978), mentally retarded (Salzinger, Feldman, & Portnoy, 1970), emotionally disturbed (Thomas, 1977), and nonhandicapped with behavior problems (Christensen, Johnson, Phillips, & Glasgow, 1980; Kovitz, 1976) found no difference between individual and group training on measures such as programs completed, parent perception of child problems, parent behavior in play sessions with the child, or observational data from audio recordings made in the home.

There is, then, no striking superiority of one method over the other. Small samples in the above studies may have prevented format differences from emerging as statistically significant. Also, these studies did not report follow-up comparisons, so we do not know whether the approaches had differential effects in the long run.

Our study of alternative training formats involved a sub-set of the families in the LA I sample (Brightman, et al., 1982). We randomly assigned 66 families with moderately to severely retarded children ages 3 to 13 to group parent training ($n = 37$), individual parent training ($n = 16$), or delayed training control ($n = 13$). The eight parent trainers were experienced in developing behavior modification programs for developmentally delayed children and had worked previously with families of such children; five trainers conducted both group and individual trainings.

The training curriculum was kept as similar as possible across group and individual formats. In both, parents attended a large group orientation meeting followed by nine training sessions, 2 hours each in the group format and 1 hour each in the individual. The first six sessions were weekly, the last three biweekly. The curriculum utilized the *Steps to*

Independence manuals and was consistent with the Parents as Teachers program as outlined in Chapter 2.

The process of training differed markedly in the two formats. Parents in the five groups attended meetings without their children at one of four community-based centers; each group had seven or eight families and two trainers. Training included brief didactic presentations as well as media, role-playing, discussions, and small group problem-solving. Parents in the individual format brought their children with them to one of two centers to meet with a trainer who observed their teaching and provided suggestions, modeling, and videotaped feedback.

The rate of program completion was 87% and was essentially equivalent for the two training formats; 14 of 16 individual training families and 32 of 37 group training families completed the program and post-measures. We had hypothesized that group training would be superior in increasing knowledge of principles but that individual training would be superior in increasing actual performance in a teaching session, because the group format contained more information and the individual format more teaching experience and feedback. The formats showed significant but nearly identical gains on the measures of knowledge (BVT) and teaching (an earlier version of the TPT). The latter measure included self-help skills (a major focus of training) and play skills (only dealt with briefly in training and hence a measure of generalization). Group and individual training, however, showed nearly identical gains. Similarly, child gains in self-help and behavior problems did not differ between the two training conditions. Moreover, a 6-month follow-up conducted with 41 of the 46 families who completed training revealed no differences between families trained in group and individual formats in the extent of continued teaching or in the quality of that teaching.

Group and individual training produced indistinguishable results. It may be important that the strong reliance upon written and visual media in both training formats and the use of a standardized training curriculum served to reduce the variability between formats. In clinical practice, a potential advantage of individual training is that it affords greater flexibility. Here, however, in attempting to keep curriculum content consistent across format, trainers tended not to address clinical issues that went beyond program content and thereby did not fully exploit the potential flexibility of the individual format. On the other hand, group training provides peer support and the opportunity to exchange information about experiences and services and may have produced other benefits that our measures did not assess.

In any event, our findings were consistent with other studies and strengthened the argument that there is no clear superiority of individual or group training across families. Because group training required half the number of professional contact hours per family as did individual training, we considered it the more cost-efficient approach. These findings argue that service providers should consider adoption of group training where possible.

STUDY 3: MEDIA-DIRECTED
TRAINING

The two studies just described found that self-instructional manuals and training in groups were cost-effective approaches to family intervention. A next logical step was to combine these into a format that had the advantages of both. We have described the media-directed program in Chapter 2. We reasoned that if parents met in groups but could be trained primarily through standardized media, then the approach would be both cost-effective and more readily exportable to other agencies and organizations. We first conducted several pilot groups to see if parents were receptive to the approach and could benefit from it. On the basis of very encouraging results, Kathleen Kashima, Sandra Landen, and I revised the program and then conducted a format comparison study (Kashima et al., 1988).

Sixty-one of the families in the Los Angeles III sample participated in an evaluation of the media-based program. They were recruited from three Regional Centers and within each agency they were assigned at random (with several unavoidable exceptions) to one of three conditions: media-based training ($n = 22$), live-led training ($n = 19$), or delayed training ($n = 20$). Subsequently, the three delayed training groups were randomly assigned to training format, with two media and one live. Parents participated in a four session behaviorally oriented training program on self-help skill teaching, followed by four weeks for teaching and then an individual assessment and consultation session. Content of the two training conditions was the same—the first four sessions of the Parents as Teachers curriculum—but the media-directed format we have described was contrasted with live training groups receiving instruction from an experienced parent trainer.

The three groups in the media-based condition were facilitated by individuals who had experience working with families of children who have developmental disabilities but had not conducted parent training groups. They were a research associate with a BA in psychology, an MA level agency counselor, and a PhD clinical psychologist. The three groups in the live-led condition were led by staff of our program who had each led numerous parent training groups utilizing the Parents as Teachers curriculum: an advanced graduate student in psychology and two PhD clinical psychologists. During each meeting a nonparticipating observer scored the progress of the meeting to validate that the content of the program in the two training conditions was the same and that the manner of presentation differed as planned.

To search out any possible differences between the training conditions, we used a wide variety of measures. We assessed parents' participation and compliance with training demands, consumer satisfaction, parents' gains in behavioral knowledge and teaching skill, family program implementation, and child gains in self-help skills.

Participation Measures

We first examined whether families' participation in or evaluation of the training program differed by condition. For these analyses, we also included data taken during and after training for the three delayed training groups, so in all there were four live and five media groups. Criteria for completion were that the primary parent attend at least 3 of 4 training sessions and both assessments.

Completion rates were essentially equivalent for the two training conditions: 91% for live-led and 85% for media-based training. Completion of daily teaching logs was higher during training for families in the live condition; during the four weeks subsequent to training, however, teaching log completion was low in both conditions.

Consumer Satisfaction

The parents' satisfaction scores are shown by training condition in Table 5.2. Parents in both conditions gave comparably high evaluations of the appropriateness of the approach, the helpfulness of the meetings and the leader, and whether they would recommend the program to others. We were concerned that the media-based format might adversely affect the group experience for families, so we included relevant items (e.g., feeling free to express oneself; feeling supported by group members). Evaluations of the group experience were generally positive, especially given that the program is instructional and short. Despite our misgivings, parents in the media-based format did not evaluate the group experience any differently from parents in the live format. On self-evaluation items, where parents rated the extent of their own involvement and benefits, again the two training formats did not differ.

Outcome Measures

The three experimental conditions changed differentially over time on knowledge acquired (Behavioral Vignettes Test, $F(2,44) = 6.45$, $p < .01$)

TABLE 5.2

Consumer Evaluation of Live Versus Video-directed Parent Training
(All Participants)

	LIVE $n = 27$	VIDEO $n = 32$
A. General[a]		
Appropriateness of approach	96	91
Helpfulness of group	93	94
Helpfulness of leader	96	91
Competence of leader	93	100
Recommend program to other parents	100	97
Overall feeling (positive)	93	78
B. Usefulness of program components[a]		
Lectures by leader	100	86
Videotapes	69	79
Group discussions	80	76
Group exercises	44	50
Reading manuals	68	62
Home observations and teaching	80	79
C. Evaluation of group experience[b]		
Free to express ideas/feelings	85	75
Communication open and frank	85	81
Supported by group members	46	50
Look forward to future meetings	69	62
D. Self-evaluation[c]		
Attending meetings	100	100
Completing readings	80	83
Teaching	77	73
Keeping records	31	27
Understanding material	100	100
Participation	80	77
Confidence in teaching[a]	56	50

Note. From "Media-Based Versus Professionally Led Training for Parents of Mentally Retarded Children" by K. J. Kashima, B. L. Baker, and S. J. Landen, 1988, *American Journal on Mental Retardation, 93*, p. 214.
[a] Percentage of parents in each condition who reported much (6) or very much (7) on a 7-point scale. [b] Percentage of parents in each condition who reported much (3) or very much (4) on a 4-point scale. [c] Percentage of parents in each condition who reported most (3) or all (4) on a 4-point scale.

and implementation of programs at home (Teaching Interview, $F(2,44) = 3.63$, $p < .05$). On both measures, media-based and live families increased significantly and differed significantly from the control families, who did not change. On the knowledge measure, live-trained families improved significantly more than did media-trained families, whereas on the implementation measure the training conditions did not differ. Trained families also improved significantly on the measure of teaching skill in a simulated situation (TPT), but control families also showed a significant gain; gains across conditions did not differ. Gains on the specific self-help skills that parents taught during training were significant for both live and media-based training, but here, too, the training conditions did not differ.

We concluded from this study that a brief media-based training program, even when implemented by service providers with no prior experience in conducting parent groups, can be a useful and cost-effective intervention. Parents participated in the program and evaluated it highly. They benefitted on a number of dimensions, although they did not gain as much programming knowledge as live-led groups where the leaders had extensive behavioral background. To test the robustness of this approach to training, however, it is necessary to investigate other training content (e.g., social skills, advocacy) and long-term benefits. We also wanted to know the extent to which service providers will utilize media-based programs; we will return to this question in Chapter 13.

STUDY 4: PROGRAM-SPECIFIC OUTCOMES

In the three format studies we have considered, two consistent findings stand out. The good news is that trained families consistently surpassed no-training control families on parent and child outcome measures. The more puzzling news is that different training conditions did not produce different outcomes. A finding of no differences is consistent with the results of other studies that have contrasted several types of behavioral group training (Adesso & Lipson, 1981; Firestone, Kelly & Fike, 1980; O'Dell et al., 1977; O'Dell, Krug, Patterson, & Faustman, 1980).

One explanation for the similar impact of training conditions is that despite apparent differences among the models, they have much overlap in the goals they set and the means they use to achieve them. To be sure, there is considerable within-condition variance, so if training models do not account for outcome variance it may be fruitful to examine individual family differences. We will do this in Chapter 6. Before moving on, however, there is an alternative explanation to consider. Perhaps simply being in a training program is enough to produce benefits on whatever measure is administered. Researchers investigating psychotherapy and drug effectiveness have written extensively on the nonspecific factors and placebo effects in accounting for favorable outcomes. Perhaps the demonstrated gains resulted from nonspecific aspects of participating in a group: observing one's child's behavior and one's own behavior more carefully, responding to encouragement from the trainer, and the like.

We addressed this question first with a study looking at the specificity of program outcome in two different components of a parent training program designed to increase parents' proactive participation in their retarded child's education (Baker & Brightman, 1984). One component was the Parents as Teachers program, with the goal of increasing parents' knowledge of teaching principles and their actual teaching skills. The other component was the *Parents as Advocates* program, a group parent training curriculum developed by Richard Brightman (1984) that aimed to increase parents' knowledge of their legal rights to services and also to enhance their actual advocacy skills, especially in the legally mandated Individualized Educational Program (IEP) meetings with the school.

We assigned 15 families (drawn from Los Angeles sample II) to either a 7-week Parents as Teachers group ($n = 8$) or a 7-week Parents as Advocates group ($n = 7$). All parents were assessed before and after training on two teaching measures (Behavioral Vignettes Test, to measure knowledge of principles, and Teaching Proficiency Test, to measure teaching skill) and on two advocacy measures (Advocacy Information Questionnaire, to measure knowledge of rights under the Education for All Handicapped Children Act, and Parent Talk, to measure advocacy skills in simulated situations). The Advocacy Information Questionnaire (AIQ) is a 20-item multiple choice questionnaire assessing knowledge of parental rights under the law. In Parent Talk, a teacher, school administrator, and psychologist each appeared four times on a video monitor making 15-second statements about services to the viewer's child (e.g., "I realize that you want your child to have speech therapy three times a week, but you must realize that our resources are limited and we have many children to serve"). The parent had 30 seconds between scenes to respond verbally, and this was audiotaped. In a previous study participants in the Parents as Advocates program had improved significantly on the AIQ and on Parent Talk codes reflecting the parents' expressing their rights under the law, stating a behaviorally specific desired outcome, and responding in a manner that was "quite likely to influence and impress." (Brightman, 1984, p. 456).

We reasoned that the content of these two programs was sufficiently dissimilar that training outcomes should be program-specific; parents in each training program should improve on the measures related to their program but not the other. The demonstrated gains were program-specific on three of the four indices of outcome. Gains on measures assessing advocacy-related knowledge and skills were sizable for parents in the Parents As Advocates program and significantly greater than for parents in the Parents as Teachers program, who showed some, but much less, change on these measures. Similarly, gain in knowledge of behavioral principles was considerable for parents in the Parents as Teachers program and significantly greater than for parents in the Parents as Advocates program, who changed little on this measure. Gains in teaching skill, though greater for parents in the Parents as Teachers condition, did not reach significance for parents in either condition. In general, parents' gains were program-specific; parents did *not* change across the board as a result of being in a parent training program. Rather their gains reflected the unique content of each program.

MEDIA-BASED TRAINING
STUDY REVISITED

Kashima et al. (1988) also addressed the specificity question in the media-based training study. Each of the four outcome measures had two parts, one that evaluated gains specific to the training area of self-help skills, and the other that evaluated change in a nonspecific training area. The Behavioral Vignettes Test and Teaching Interview each also had items concerned with behavior problem management, and the Teaching Proficiency Test also included play skills; these were areas not addressed in this shortened training program. The Mini-Performance Inventory included a nontargeted self-help skill and also included toilet training, a nontargeted skill area. If changes were specific to the training content, we would expect to find greater changes for each measure on the items related to self-help skill teaching than on the other items. This is a more subtle test of the specificity question than the previous study, which contrasted quite different curricula and measures. Here, we might reasonably expect some generalization from the specific to the nonspecific part of the same measure.

On all but one measure, however, trained families showed significantly greater gains on curriculum-specific items than on unrelated items. Teaching Proficiency Test changes were higher for the curriculum-specific subtask, but, consistent with the previous study, not significantly so. Behavioral Vignettes Test per item gains were more than 10 times higher for curriculum-specific items and Teaching Interview gains were exclusively accounted for by curriculum-specific teaching: +2.8 for self-help skill teaching and 0.0 for behavior problem management. On the Performance Inventory, the average improvement was 5 times greater for the targeted skill than for either the untargeted skill or the untargeted area of toilet training. Parent and child gains were, then, specific to the content of the training program.

CONCLUSION

What can we conclude, then, about training formats? Our studies of manuals only versus professional training, individual versus group training, and live-led versus media-directed training all point to the conclusion that when different formats are employed to present similar content, outcomes do not vary significantly. Less costly training formats (such as training by manuals, or groups, or by media) can be employed without notable loss in effectiveness. Moreover, positive outcomes seem to be the result of the training program content, rather than nonspecific effects of being in an intervention program. A next logical question, and the one we turn to in Chapter 6, is: Who benefits most, and least, from the Parents as Teachers program?

Chapter 6

Predictors

Although behavioral parent training by quite different formats produced comparable results, all families did not benefit equally. Aggregated gains masked individual failures, cases where improvement was slight or nonexistent. These two consistent findings, of small variability between formats and large variability within them, suggested that variance in outcomes may be related more to characteristics of the participants than of the program. We therefore began to pay less attention to differences among interventions and more to differences among families.

We examined outcome in light of a new question: Which families are least—or most—successful in parent training? The simple version of this question hypothesizes that some families will do well and some will do poorly regardless of format. The more complex version suggests that some families would do best in one training format, other families in another format. Because of our small sample sizes, however, we have not been able adequately to address family by program interactions. Therefore, we concentrated on prediction of outcome in our largest format, group training.

PREDICTION STUDIES

Duncan Clark and I began our study of predictors with the 49 families in the two group training conditions of the Boston sample (Clark, Baker, & Heifetz, 1982), and we subsequently did similar analyses with the Los Angeles I sample (Clark & Baker, 1983) and the Los Angeles II sample (Baker & Clark, 1987). We hoped to identify variables that differentiated families who did poorly in our program from the remaining families. We reasoned that knowing about predictors of outcome would help service providers determine whether referral to parent training might be appropriate for a given family. Moreover, if we could predict potential low gain families in a standard parent training program, this knowledge might help program and policy makers develop alternative and potentially more effective interventions for such families.

Although we have considered a number of outcome indicators, it seemed to us most important to identify predictors of two types of outcomes: proficiency in behavioral teaching at the end of the training program and implementation of teaching strategies during a follow-up period. We assessed post-training proficiency in the Boston sample by the parent's knowledge of teaching principles (scored on the Behavioral Vignettes Test). For the Los Angeles samples we broadened the criteria to include proficiency in a clinic teaching session (Teaching Proficiency Test) and the trainer's evaluation of the parent's proficiency. For each of the three outcome measures, a proficiency cut-off point was set at the lowest point at which the outcome could be considered a success. Parents who did not reach the cut-off on at least two measures were categorized as low proficiency. The percentages of families classified as low proficiency in the Boston, LA I, and LA II samples were 34%, 34%, and 40%, respectively.

Follow-up status was assessed by the Teaching Interview, described in Chapter 4. As we noted there, in the Boston sample, follow-up was conducted 1 year post-training and covered teaching done throughout that period. In the Los Angeles I and II samples, follow-up was conducted 6 months post-training and covered teaching done during the previous 3 months only. Interviews were scored on two subscales: amount and quality of teaching. Families were classified as low follow-through if they scored one standard deviation below the sample mean on either subscale, because this would suggest that useful teaching was not taking place. The percentages of families classified as low follow-through in the Boston, LA I, and LA II samples were 34%, 24%, and 28%, respectively.

We should note before moving on that not all low-proficiency or low follow-through families would place themselves where our numbers put them; some regarded themselves as very successful. For example, knowing better ways to teach or handle behavior problems when they arise may give a family much comfort, even if at present they do not choose to carry out the teaching programs. We, like others who have studied prediction of outcome, have defined success from our own, not the families', perspective. We do think that most families joining our program would agree from the onset that our criteria—knowing more about teaching and doing more teaching—are desirable outcomes. Nonetheless, an alternative approach to consider for future research would be to have each family, in advance of or early in the program, develop their own criteria for success, and then to use these individualized criteria as outcome indices. This would be similar to the goal attainment scaling that we used with one small sample during follow-up (see Chapter 4).

Predictor Variables Studied

From our perspective, then, some families were categorized as low proficiency and/or low implementation. There are a great many possible explanations for why a family does not achieve proficiency by the end of training or does not carry what they have learned in training over into the home. Parent trainers and the parents themselves typically advance idiosyncratic reasons. However, we find few studies that have systematically examined the relationship between parent, child, or family characteristics and intervention outcome, especially in programs for parents of handicapped children. Those that are available have focused on a narrow band of variables, primarily socioeconomic. An adequate approach to this question would involve measuring a wide range of variables, utilizing a large sample, and employing multiple regression analysis to determine the unique contribution of each variable. Only a few studies have attempted to do this (Blechman et al., 1981; Sadler, Seydon, Howe, & Kaminsky, 1976).

Case Example

We introduce a consideration of possible predictors with the following case illustration:

We categorized Peg as "low proficient" after training. She had been very enthusiastic about teaching and had only missed two meetings. She evaluated the program highly and felt that it had been beneficial. Her Behavioral Vignettes Test score had improved from 20% correct to 50% correct, but was still short of our 75% proficiency criterion. Similarly, Peg's teaching with Angela, her 9-year-old severely retarded daughter, was somewhat more skilled than before the program, but short of the Teaching Proficiency Test criterion score. The group leader evaluated her participation highly, but noted much room for improvement in teaching.

Peg was 31 years old, a housewife with two younger, normally developing children. She had married Jack, a machinist, shortly after they both graduated from high school, and she had worked as a waitress until Angela was born. Then everything seemed to change. Peg remembers the early years of being home alone with Angela as a nightmare; she had come to doubt her ability to be an adequate mother and had experienced periods of depression. In an odd way life had become easier four years later when Jason was born. He grew up "by the book" and Peg's self-esteem seemed to grow along with him. And, also, Angela was home less, having begun a series of school programs.

Although Peg had found sporadic counseling from the Regional Center useful, she had not joined a parent group or training program ("I didn't know much about them and I was always so busy."). She cared well for Angela, but did not try to systematically teach her very much, feeling that teaching was the school's responsibility. When she entered our program, it was with some reservations. She expected to encounter problems in teaching and wasn't confident that she could overcome them. For one thing, she didn't feel Jack would be much help. She expressed average satisfaction with her marriage and said that Jack was a good father, especially to the younger children, with whom he enjoyed playing. Angela had been "too much for Jack," though, and his involvement with her was more limited. He did not attend any group meetings.

Could Peg's lower post-training proficiency have been predicted, and perhaps prevented? Where would we look for possible predictors: to Angela's slow learning? to Peg's limited education? to Peg and Jack's relationship? to Peg's previous childrearing experiences? to her attitudes and expectations?

Predictors

We have been interested in the following five types of variables that might be related to success in parent training:

1. *Child characteristics:* As considered in Chapter 1, a child's retardation strongly influences parents' mood and behavior. Extending this perspective, the degree of the child's disability might be expected to relate to the family's capacity to act positively on the child's behalf. A child who learns more quickly, for example, might be expected to reward a parent's efforts, leading to more enthusiastic and extensive teaching. There is some parent training evidence that child developmental gains are less in more severely retarded children (Barna, Gray, Clements, & Gardner, 1980; Brassell, 1977) but we do not know whether that is attributable to the child's more limited ability to learn or to reduced parental teaching efforts. It is important to assess parental follow-through directly as a function of child ability.

Moreover, few studies have related outcome to other child characteristics, such as sex, age, diagnosis, or the age at which the child was diagnosed. Our samples were a good testing ground for the relationship between child characteristics and family outcome, for although all of the children in our samples were mentally retarded, they were otherwise quite heterogeneous (see Chapter 2).

2. *Parent demographic characteristics:* Socioeconomic status (SES) has received the most attention as a correlate of parent training outcome. Two definitional problems have been pointed out (Baker, 1984). First, indices of SES have varied. Some studies, including ours, have followed Hollingshead (1957) in combining father's education and occupation; others used mother's education or reading level; still others used income. Second, cut-off points have varied. In some studies, including ours, low SES has

meant that families are low relative to others in the sample, while in others it has meant scoring below an absolute cut-off on one dimension (e.g., receiving welfare payments).

In Chapter 3, we noted that lower SES families have been less likely to join parent training but that studies have been contradictory as to whether lower SES families, having joined, are less likely to complete training. There is more agreement that lower SES families, by various definitions, are less likely to fulfill programming objectives, such as carrying out programs (Rinn, Vernon, & Wise, 1975; Rose, 1974a) or producing child change (Brassell, 1977; Dumas, 1984; Patterson, 1974; Sadler et al., 1976; Webster-Stratton, 1985b). Here, too, our samples are ideal to study this relationship further, for they are quite diverse on the socioeconomic variables of education, occupation, and income.

A second demographic variable of particular interest is marital status. We have seen in Chapter 3 that single parent status is the most consistent predictor of noncompletion, and that single parents, as well as those in unhappy marriages, have been noted anecdotally to be poorer bets for parent training (Bernal, Williams, Miller, & Reoger, 1972).

3. *Parents' related experience and skills:* As behavioral programs and parent involvement have become more pervasive in special education, it is more likely that parents will enter our program having already had some related experiences. An obvious prediction is that such experiences accumulate and that parents will score higher, at least on post-training proficiency, if they have had some previous experience with parent groups and/or behavioral teaching and if they already demonstrate some proficiency in behavioral methods when they enter our program. Yet there has been little study of parents' prior experiences and skills as predictors of outcome.

4. *Parent attitudes and expectations:* There has been very little study of parent attitudes as predictors of program outcome. Strom developed the "Parents as a Teacher Inventory," and reported that in his parent training parents who perceived themselves as more comfortable in the role of teacher were more likely to be considered successful, although data were not presented (Strom, Ress, Slaughter, & Wurster, 1980). We have been interested in parental expectations and have assessed these by a self-report Expectancy Questionnaire that we factor analyzed with the Los Angeles I families. The four factors that emerged were expected success in the program, expected problems in teaching, commitment to teaching, and responsibility for teaching.

5. *Progress during training:* We have also been interested in the predictive power of parents' participation in training as it unfolds. Therefore, we have related attendance at training sessions to post-training proficiency, and post-training proficiency to follow-through.

Prediction of Proficiency

We compared families categorized as high versus low proficiency post-training on the variables that we have described. Table 6.1 indicates with Xs the measures that we took with each sample and indicates with asterisks where significant differences were obtained by independent *t*-tests.

We noted in Chapter 3 that child characteristics may influence which families join a parent training program in the first place. We consistently found, however, that child characteristics did not relate to their parents'

TABLE 6.1

Prediction Measures: Post-training Proficiency

	BOSTON	LA I	LA II
Child characteristics			
Sex	X	X	X
Age	X	X	X
Age at diagnosis	X	X	X
Self-help skills	X	X	X
Self-help quotient (skills/age)	X	X	X
Behavior problems	X	X	X
Demographic variables			
Socioeconomic status	X*	X**	X*
Family income	X*	X*	X(*)
Primary parent's education	X**	X***	X***
Marital status	—	X	X
Primary parent's age	X	X*	X
Primary parent employed	X	X	X
Mileage from meeting place	—	X	X
Older siblings	X	X	X
Younger siblings	X	X	X
Prior related experience/skills			
Knowledge of behavioral principles	X**	X***	X**
Teaching proficiency	—	X	X
Previous teaching at home	—	X*	X
Membership in past groups	X**	X	X*
Behavior modification exposure	X**	X**	X
Parents' expectations			
Success in program	—	X	X
Problems in teaching	—	X***	X
Commitment to teaching	—	X	X
Responsibility for teaching	—	X	X
During training			
Primary parent's attendance	X	X	X
Both parents' attendance	X	—	—
Teaching sessions logged	X	—	—

Note. In Boston, proficiency = post-BVT; in LA, proficiency = combination of post-BVT, TPT, and Trainer's evaluation.

(*) $p < .05$, one-tailed. * $p < .05$, two-tailed. ** $p < .01$, two-tailed. *** $p < .001$, two-tailed.

teaching proficiency after training. For these relationships, we must turn to measures of the parents and the family.

One dimension consistently predictive of post-training proficiency was the family's *socioeconomic status*. A strong and consistent finding was that the primary parents in low-proficiency families had fewer years of education. Low-proficiency families also had lower income and scored lower on an SES index (Hollingshead, 1958) that weighed father's education and occupation. Our data may help us to understand previous findings of less successful programming by lower SES families. They are less likely to have become proficient in teaching methods, and may therefore be less inclined to implement teaching at home, or may be less successful when they do. We will consider SES further in Chapter 7.

A second dimension that predicted post-training proficiency was *prior related experience and skills*. We found pre-training Behavioral Vignettes Test scores to be strongly predictive; this is not surprising, as BVT score was a component of our proficiency indices. Primary parents categorized as low-proficiency post-training began training with lower knowledge of behavioral teaching principles. Despite the fact that parents gained in knowledge of behavioral principles during training, their pre-training scores were highly related to their scores at the end of the program (see Table 4.2). Also, parents in the low proficiency group were less likely to have participated in other parent groups or to have had first-hand exposure to behavior modification programming.

One factor of the parents Expectations measure, *problems in teaching*, was related to proficiency. This measure asked questions about six expected obstacles: not being able to change the child's behavior; generally having problems teaching; lack of time; lack of encouragement and help from the family; slow progress; and lack of patience. Each of these items was followed by a question asking the extent to which the parent felt he or she could overcome the problem. The total problems score was a combination of expected obstacles and expectation of overcoming them; in the larger LA I sample, it differentiated low- and high-proficiency families.

Predictor Equations

Although several variables were related to outcome, we knew that some of these were intercorrelated and we wondered how much unique variance each was accounting for. We also wanted to combine the variables to maximize predictive power. We addressed these questions by generating prediction equations using forward step-wise discriminant analyses (Brown, 1977; Kleinbaum & Kupper, 1978). Families were dichotomously classified by this prediction equation, and the actual outcome was compared with the predicted outcome.

Given the small sample size and the large number of predictor variables, we wanted to limit those considered for the prediction equation. A common statistical problem in predictor research is "overfitting"—an equation derived from one sample by entering a large number of variables seems to explain considerable variance but performs poorly on cross-validation (Forsythe, May, & Engelman, 1971). For our predictor studies, only variables that were significantly related to the outcome variable ($p <$ .05, two-tailed) were used in the discriminant analysis. This relatively conservative approach reduces the likelihood of idiosyncratic results in a small sample. Moreover, we did not include pre-training scores on the Behavioral Vignettes Test, because this variable is one part of the proficiency criteria. The LA I formulae were cross-validated with the LA II sample and also by a within-sample leaving-one-out analysis, a variant on the split sample technique. All possible splits of one subject in one group and the remainder in the other are used. An equation is derived for this latter group of N minus 1 subjects, and the left-out subject is classified using this equation. By repeating this procedure for all subjects, one obtains an unbiased error estimate (Lachenbruch, 1975).

The prediction formula generated from the large Los Angeles I sample incorporated four variables. Low proficiency families had lower family income, less primary parent education, greater expectation of obstacles to teaching, and less previous behavior modification experience (Clark & Baker, 1983). The formula correctly classified 25 of 32 (78%) low-proficiency families and 47 out of 62 (76%) high-proficiency parents, for a total rate of 77% correct; this was significantly different from chance. Many mispredicted families received predicted scores near our rather arbitrarily determined proficiency cut-off scores, as shown in Figure 6.1. When we eliminated the middle values that had virtually no predictive utility (between 0 and -1.00), and added the families from the LA II sample, this same equation made 82% correct predictions (Baker & Clark, 1987).

What does this tell us? Our program is in many respects like a course. The parents who do not learn enough of what the course teaches will have had less formal education, perhaps reflecting less learning ability but certainly reflecting less familiarity with a learning situation. Moreover, the content of training is more foreign to them and their expectation of difficulties high. We were curious whether the relationship with parental education held only for group training, which resembled school, or whether it would hold in an individual one-on-one training format as well. We looked separately at the correlation between education and proficiency for the 16 families in LA I who were individually trained (Chapter 5, Study 2) and found that here too education strongly predicted proficiency. It seems likely that the often-found relationship between SES and parent

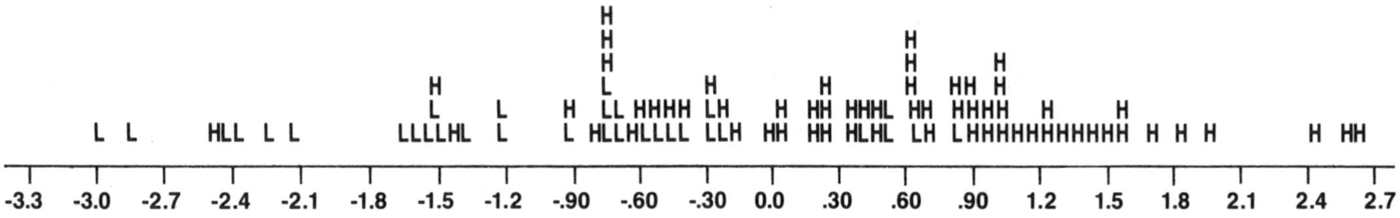

FIGURE 6.1: Histogram of canonical variable for proficiency prediction: (.24 × income) + (.21 × primary parent's education) + (.13 × expectation of problems) + (.22 × previous behavior modification experience) − 10.8. H = actual high proficiency. L = actual low proficiency.

training outcome is in large part attributable to the fact that parents with less education do not feel as comfortable in training that follows a fixed curriculum and do not learn as much of what is taught as do more educated parents. We will consider possible alternative approaches in Chapter 7.

Prediction of Follow-through

When we compared families categorized as high versus low follow-through, we used the same measures as in the proficiency prediction, but we also included measures of the parents' participation in training and scores on post-training outcome measures for both parent and child. Table 6.2 shows the measures taken with each sample (X) and significant results.

Here too, child characteristics did not relate to outcome. With the other pre-training indices, some relationships did emerge in the largest sample. However, these did not hold up in the smaller samples, perhaps because stronger relationships would have been necessary to reach statistical significance. The most consistent relationships were with process and outcome variables. Low follow-through families had done less teaching during the program itself and had emerged from the program with a lower level of proficiency on the outcome measures.

Prediction Equations

Again, we selected the variables that significantly differentiated high and low follow-through groups in the Los Angeles I sample and ran a discriminant analysis. The resulting prediction formula included three variables: lower follow-up families had lower post-training proficiency, were more likely headed by single parents, and had done less pretraining teaching of the child (Clark & Baker, 1983). The formula correctly classified 14 of 20 (70%) low-implementation families and 49 of 63 (78%) high-implementation families, for a total of 76% correct. The result was significantly different from chance. In the Los Angeles II validation sample, components of post-training proficiency replicated as predictors, although the total score fell just short of significance. Marital status was an indicator in the same direction but only 3 single parents remained in the sample. In this sample, teaching before training was not related to follow-through, but teaching during training was. As in predicting post-training proficiency, most mispredicted families at follow-up had prediction scores near our cut-off point, as shown in Figure 6.2. When we combined the LA I and LA II samples and excluded this middle group, the same formula correctly predicted 90% of families (Baker & Clark, 1987).

TABLE 6.2

Prediction Measures: Follow-through Teaching

	BOSTON	LA I	LA II
Child characteristics			
Sex	X	X	X
Age	X	X	X
Age at diagnosis	X	X	X
Self-help skills	X	X	X
Self-help quotient (skills/age)	X	X	X
Behavior problems	X	X	X
Demographic variables			
Socioeconomic status	X	X**	X
Family income	X	X	X
Primary parent's education	X	X*	X
Marital status	—	X**	X
Primary parent's age	X*	X	X
Primary parent employed	X	X	X
Mileage from meeting place	—	X	X
Older siblings	X	X	X
Younger siblings	X	X	X
Prior related experience/skills			
Knowledge of behavioral principles	X**	X*	X
Teaching proficiency	—	X	X
Previous teaching at home	—	X*	X
Membership in past groups	X	X	X
Behavior modification exposure	X	X*	X
Parents' expectations			
Success in program	—	X	X
Problems in teaching	—	X**	X
Commitment to teaching	—	X	X
Responsibility for teaching	—	X	X
During training			
Primary parent's attendance	X	X	X
Both parents' attendance	X	—	—
Teaching during training[a]	X*	—	X*
Post-training			
Trainer's follow-through prediction	X**	—	—
Proficiency	—	X**	X
Knowledge of behavioral principles	X**	X**	X*
Teaching proficiency	—	X*	X(*)
Child self-help change	X	—	—
Child behavior problem change	X	—	—

[a] Boston, teaching = number of sessions logged; LA II, teaching = Teaching Interview.
(*) $p < .05$, one-tailed. * $p < .05$, two-tailed. ** $p < .01$, two-tailed. *** $p < .001$, two-tailed.

In the Los Angeles III sample, we broadened the scope of predictors to include family factors, such as the marital relationship, family stress, adaptability, cohesion, and satisfaction. We will consider the predictive value of these family dimensions in Chapter 11, where we describe the measures.

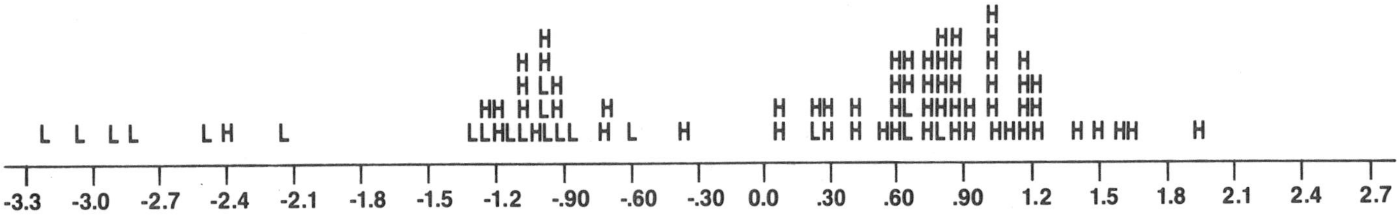

FIGURE 6.2: Histogram of canonical variable for follow-through prediction: $(1.74 \times \text{proficiency}) + (1.60 \times \text{marital status}) + (.15 \times \text{previous teaching at home}) - 4.6$. H = actual high-implementation. L = actual low-implementation.

CONCLUSION

To conclude here, then, parents who were involved in teaching before and/or during training and who left training well equipped with teaching knowledge and skills were most likely to be doing useful teaching six months after training ended. It may be most fruitful, then, to change the training program to ensure that more parents are actively teaching and learning. In Chapter 7 we examine some efforts in that direction.

Chapter 7

_____Alternatives

We found that the best predictor of follow-through was proficiency, and the best predictor of proficiency was parent education or, more broadly, socioeconomic status (SES). It seemed especially important, then, to develop alternative interventions that would boost proficiency for lower SES families. Our standard group curriculum may be too quickly paced and too didactic for these families. There is some evidence that lower SES teacher-aides learned better from more action-oriented approaches than from didactic ones, whereas middle SES aides learned equally well from both (Schneiman, 1972). Accordingly, we experimented with three variations on the Parents as Teachers program for lower SES families. Each had the developmentally disabled children present, so that parents could learn from observing and teaching (Baker, et al., 1984).

ENHANCING PROFICIENCY IN
NONPROFICIENT PARENTS

Richard Brightman and Stephen Ambrose were instrumental in organizing the first program (Brightman, Ambrose, & Baker, 1980). Participants were parents in the Los Angeles I sample who had completed the Parents as Teachers program but who had not met criteria for proficiency. We established a 3-week summer day camp for their children and included a parent training component. Of 28 low-proficiency families recontacted and invited to participate, 9 joined the program, 5 were not interested, and 14 were interested but could not participate because of schedule conflicts (e.g., vacations, ongoing school programs). We chose 9 comparison families from this latter group, closely matched with participants on post-training measures. While this was less desirable than random assignment, it was the only method available to us given the small number of possible participants. The comparison group was asked to come to one testing session that coincided with post-camp measures for the mini-camp parents, and 7 did so. Hence, we were able to study how much our camp parents gained and contrast them to similar families who had not participated.

The mini-camp program was based upon a model for designing individualized child programs that we had developed at a residential

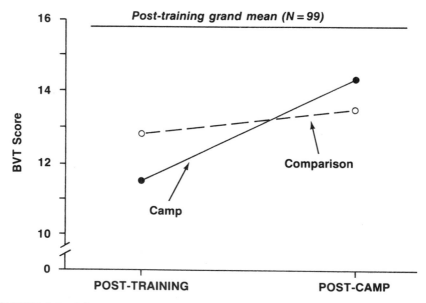

FIGURE 7.1: Mean number of Behavioral Vignettes Test items correct for mini-camp and comparison group parents following standardized training and following the mini-camp program.

camp for children with mental retardation (Baker, 1973). From information provided by parents and teachers, five or six target goals were established for each child in areas of self-help, pre-academics, perceptual motor skills, play, language, and behavior problem management. The activity schedule was then designed to maximize attention to each child's target goals. Parents attended for at least one full day each week, for a program that involved them actively.

There were four primary components to the parent training. First, each parent was assigned an *individual consultant* to help formulate programs, monitor progress, and generally offer suggestions and support. Second, parents did *active teaching* in the mini-camp program, beginning with observation of camp staff and then becoming involved as co-teachers for their child and other children. Third, each training day parents received *videotaped feedback* of a teaching session with their child. They evaluated their own performance by viewing the tape and completing a scoring sheet for rating the extent to which they utilized behavior modification techniques (e.g., Did you break the skill down into small enough steps? Did you remember to reward your child for sitting, looking and waiting?). The trainer and the parent then reviewed this guide and portions of the tape to highlight parent strengths and focus on areas needing improvement. Fourth, the two or three parents present each day met together with a trainer for *group feedback*; they reviewed each other's videotaped sessions and offered consultation to one another.

Camp families showed considerable gain following this brief but intensive program. Figure 7.1 shows the significant Behavioral Vignettes Test gains for camp parents, which significantly surpassed gains for comparison parents. The group post-score still fell a little short of our proficiency criterion. Figure 7.2 shows teaching session performance, which was only obtained at the post-session for comparison families. Here, too, camp parents gained significantly in teaching proficiency and their children gained significantly in attention to task. Only the parent measure significantly surpassed controls, however.

There was some carryover from the special program into better teaching at home. Teaching Interviews were conducted at home 1 month later. Camp and comparison families did not differ in amount of teaching. However, camp parents scored significantly higher in quality of teaching and behavior problem management.

Parents evaluated the program by a Q-sort procedure whereby they sorted 15 attributes of the mini-camp into three equal categories: most, somewhat, and least beneficial. Similarly, they assessed the value of seven components of the parent training program. Table 7.1 shows the perceived program benefits, rank ordered. We see that parents most valued improvement in their teaching and in their child's skills. We should note that the Mini-Camp program for children was highly effective. One 6-year-old child with Down syndrome increased her signing

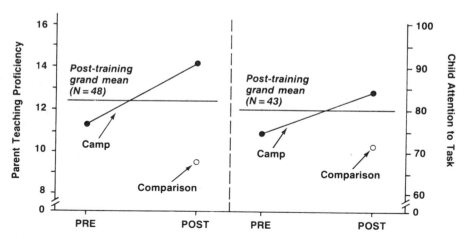

FIGURE 7.2: Mean camp and comparison group scores for Parent Teaching Proficiency (left) and Child Attention to Task (right).

TABLE 7.1

Parent Evaluation of Mini-Camp Program by Q-sorts into Most (2), Somewhat (1), and Least (0) Beneficial

RANK	ITEM	MEAN RATING
	Program Benefits	
1.0	Provided new ideas of skills to teach and how to teach them	1.78
2.0	Improved my child's skills	1.67
3.0	Improved my teaching skills	1.56
4.0	Improved my ability to handle behavior problems	1.44
5.0	Increased my confidence in my teaching	1.33
7.5	Increased my child's willingness to learn	1.22
7.5	Increased my expectations of my child's abilities	1.22
7.5	Increased my motivation to teach	1.22
7.5	Increased my motivation and ability to work for a good school experience for my child	1.22
10.0	Helped my child learn to play and work with other children	0.89
11.0	Decreased my child's behavior problems	0.67
13.0	Provided a fun time for my child	0.22
13.0	Familiarized me with a range of developmentally disabled children	0.22
13.0	Provided me with support from other parents	0.22
15.0	Provided me with some time for myself while my child was at camp	0.11
	Program Components	
1.0	Watching staff members *individually* teach and handle behavior problems with my child	1.56
2.0	Watching and discussing videotape of myself teaching my child one-on-one	1.44
3.0	Watching and discussing videotapes of other parents' teaching	1.22
4.0	Receiving trainer's suggestions about home programming	0.89
5.5	Watching staff members teach and handle behavior problems in *classes*	0.78
5.5	Teaching a class and receiving suggestions from trainer	0.78
7.0	Watching staff members *incidentally* teach and handle behavior problems during free play and lunch	0.33

vocabulary by 60 words in 3 weeks; another child learned 20 signs and pronounced her name for the first time; while several others decreased the rate of their problem behaviors by 70%. Parent performance was quite likely enhanced by a training program that took place in the context of such notable changes in child behavior. Table 7.1 also shows perceived value of the program components. Parents rated observing staff teaching their child as the most valuable component of the training program, while the two next most valued components involved the videotape feedback procedures.

This brief program was effective at raising the proficiency of parents who had completed group training but were still classified as nonproficient. In a second mini-camp program we took this training model a step further, applying it to families who were predicted in advance to demonstrate low teaching proficiency.

PARENTS PREDICTED TO
DEMONSTRATE LOW
TEACHING PROFICIENCY

Merilla McCurry Scott and Patrice Yasuda assumed primary responsibility for organizing this summer program, which was held in the school building of a church in South Central Los Angeles (Baker & McCurry, 1984). Transportation was provided and children attended for 5.5 hours per day, Wednesday through Saturday, for one or two 3-week sessions. Criteria for family selection, in addition to having a moderately to severely retarded child aged 2 to 13, were low family income and mother's education of no more than 12 years. Clark and Baker's (1983) prediction formula that we considered in Chapter 6 was used to compute prediction scores for all referrals, and the 20 families who were predicted to achieve low proficiency in group training (along with three other families) were enrolled. This was very much a low SES sample. All but one family had an annual income under $10,999, and 40% were on welfare. Only 20% of mothers were employed, and education ranged from 2 to 12 years, with a mean of 9.3 years.

Participants were all ethnic minorities, 11 Hispanic and 9 Black. Although it had not been our intent in selection to have an exclusively minority sample, these families were representative of families living in the part of Los Angeles where the program was located. All of the Hispanic families spoke Spanish predominantly or exclusively, and all training for these families was conducted in Spanish.

Parent training was quite similar to the earlier mini-camp program, emphasizing individual consultation, active teaching, videotaped feedback, and group feedback. Parents attended one pre-camp session and a half-day session each week during camp (except that a few parents whose children were only enrolled in the second 3 weeks had their final 3 meetings post-camp). For illustration, a typical day looked like this:

9:00 Meet with trainer in a small group, to report on teaching at home

9:30 Brief lecture on one aspect of behavioral teaching (e.g., rewards)

9:45 Observe in classrooms and record some aspect of teacher's behavior (e.g., each time rewards are used)

10:00 Reassemble, compare notes, and view videotapes on teaching methods

10:30 Participate as co-teachers in activities. Also, conduct a brief videotaped teaching session with own child and receive feedback

11:45 Discuss morning teaching experiences

12:00 Help to supervise children's lunch period and eat own lunch

12:45 Meet for additional information on teaching, presented in role
        plays, demonstrations, and/or videotape. Discuss homework
 1:30 End training session

Eighty-five percent of families completed training and their evaluations of the program taken at a 6-month follow-up were very positive.
Here, too, parents found the experience of watching a teacher individually
teach and handle behavior problems with their child particularly valuable.
As with the previous mini-camp, participants showed significant
improvement on all outcome measures, including the two primary
components in our definition of teaching proficiency: knowledge of
behavioral teaching principles (BVT) and ability in a simulated teaching
session (TPT). Post-training levels were still below those previously found
in the sample that was used to generate predictors. The post-level BVT of
9.5 was considerably lower than the 14.1 average in the predictor sample,
and the post-level TPT of 10.7 did not reach the predictor sample mean of
12.3. Mini-camp families began training with low scores on these
measures and actually showed considerable gains; perhaps a longer
program would have raised them closer to the proficiency cut-off.
Moreover, some vocabulary and the multiple-choice format of the BVT
was unfamiliar and difficult for many parents in this low education
sample, and the Spanish translation was less than perfect. A different
approach to measurement might have given more credit for knowledge
acquired. It is interesting to note that, consistent with the predictions, the
three parents who participated in the mini-camp but were excluded from
data analysis because they were not predicted to be low gain scored above
the predictor sample mean on both measures ($\overline{X}$ = 15.7 on the BVT and
13.3 on the TPT).

The Teaching Interview score increased post-training, but by the
6-month follow-up the average scale scores for both amount and quality of
teaching had returned to pre-training levels. We cannot say from the
present evidence whether these families did not desire to teach further,
lacked the skill to apply what they had learned to new target behaviors, or
were disrupted by other life stressors that interfered. We further
compared high and low follow-through families, and found differences on
several pre-training variables. Consistent with previous findings, low
follow-through families in this program had lower education ($\overline{X}$ = 6.1
versus $\overline{X}$ = 10.7 years) and lower post-training BVT scores ($\overline{X}$ = 6.7
versus $\overline{X}$ = 12.1). It seems that for those families with the lowest
education, the program did not "take" as well, at least by the index of
home teaching.

A third program was developed specifically for Spanish-speaking
families. The curriculum and measures were in Spanish and adapted to be

understood by parents with greatly limited education. This program speaks further to concerns about how to raise proficiency and whether such training effects last.

SPANISH-SPEAKING FAMILIES

There had previously been little extension of behavioral parent training to Spanish-speaking families, despite an enormous need for such services. Our Spanish parent training program was developed primarily by Mary Prieto-Bayard, Cathy Acevedo, and Phyllis Prado on the UCLA staff and Ron Huff at the South Central Los Angeles Regional Center (Prieto-Bayard, Huff, & Baker, 1981). In a controlled evaluation, monolingual Spanish-speaking families with mentally retarded children participated in an adaptation of the Parents as Teachers group curriculum (Prieto-Bayard & Baker, 1986).

The 10-week program followed the curriculum described in Chapter 2, with several modifications. One UCLA and two Regional Center staff members jointly conducted groups in Spanish. We translated manuals into Spanish, simplified the standard curriculum by eliminating less central concepts, and focused training exclusively on self-help teaching and behavior problem management. To facilitate access, we gave each family $2 for each meeting they attended to defray transportation costs, and we provided child care by UCLA students trained in behavioral teaching methods. Several students were Hispanic and bilingual, which facilitated communication with the families. Staff modeled appropriate teaching and supervised parents' teaching. We provided incentives for participation, including a package of child-appropriate educational toys and a certificate upon completion of training.

The 20 families were lower SES. Most (75%) had immigrated from Mexico within the previous 10 years, and most (75%) had intact marriages. Families generally reported low income and education; 80% had annual incomes below $11,000 and the mean level of education for mothers, usually undertaken in Mexico, was 5 years. We randomly assigned these families to training ($n = 9$) or delayed training control ($n = 11$) conditions (one training family had to delay beginning). Nine of the eleven delayed training families subsequently participated in training.

We wanted our measures to accurately assess these families' knowledge and abilities. They were administered by three female staff members, all of whom were Hispanic and reasonably fluent in Spanish. (Spanish versions of measures are available from the author.) The Teaching Proficiency Test (TPT) and Teaching Interview (TI) do not differ markedly from the English version. An abbreviated Child Behavior Checklist (CBC) assessing self-help skills and behavior problems was administered verbally. The main change was in assessing parents' knowledge of behavior modification principles, for which we developed the Verbal Behavioral Vignettes Test (VBVT). In this verbally administered adaptation of the written BVT, 12 items are read to the parent, who gives an open-ended verbal response of how best to deal with the problem. Coders, blind to condition and time of testing, score these audiotaped responses for effective use of behavioral principles according to a scoring manual. Interrater reliability of the total score for a randomly selected subset of tapes in this sample was quite high ($r = .91$)

Of 18 families who began training, 14 (78%) completed the program. Figure 7.3 shows the scores on outcome measures for training condition families, for the delayed training families during their waiting period, and for these same families during training. In comparisons of the initial training condition versus delayed training control, trained parents gained significantly more on the knowledge of principles (VBVT), child behavior problems (CBC-behavior problems) and home teaching (TI); differences on the TPT (teaching skill) and child self help skills (CBC-self help) did not reach significance. When initial training and delayed training conditions were combined, families improved significantly ($p < .025$) on all measures. At follow-up 6 months later, families scored significantly higher on the Teaching Interview than pre-training levels but had fallen off some from post-training levels.

We noticed two variables, one demographic and one programmatic, that related to outcome. We have seen that education, and all that it conveys, is a powerful predictor of outcome. Even within this reasonably heterogeneous sample of low-education parents, mother's education correlated strongly with our measures of proficiency: for VBVT, $r = .50$, and for TPT, $r = .62$. It also seems that delayed training families benefited more from training than did families in the initial training condition, although this difference reached significance only for the Teaching Interview where they were doing more teaching at home. Training for these groups differed in only one way: the delayed training made more use of participant modeling. In the initial training group, modeling and supervised teaching occurred about every other week. In the delayed training, this occurred weekly and was a major focus of training. The design, however, does not allow us to draw conclusions about whether delayed training families' greater teaching resulted from the participant modeling experience or from some other factor.

In a later program for Spanish-speaking families, we conducted three groups for 24 of the families recruited in Shenk's (1984) study of joiners (see Chapter 3). This program was shorter (7 sessions), included participant modeling in every session, used one-page concept handouts rather than the longer manuals, and had parallel sibling training groups

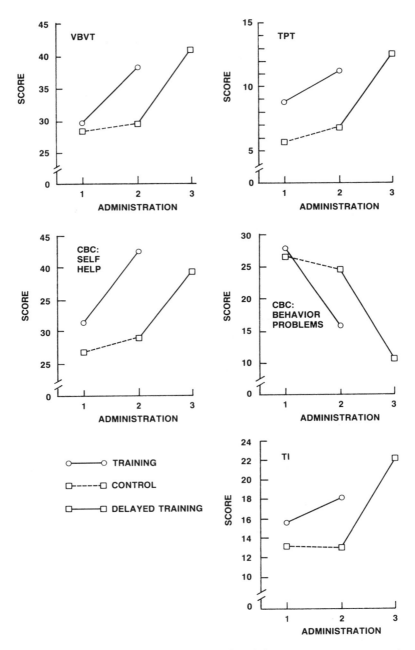

FIGURE 7.3: Training and control/delayed training group scores on outcome measures across three administrations. VBVT = Verbal Behavioral Vignettes Test; TPT = Teaching Proficiency Test; CBC = Child Behavior Checklist; TI = Teaching Interview. Source: Príeto-Bayard and Baker, 1986, p. 140.

that involved children in 12 families (see Chapter 12). In this revised program, all but one family met completion criteria.

CONSIDERATIONS FOR
MAXIMIZING PROGRAM
OUTCOMES

Access to Services

Of 71 families who began the programs described in this chapter, 63 (89%) met completion criteria. This may seem surprising, since the majority of these families were poor, had lower than average education, and were ethnic or racial minorities. There is evidence that families of lower socioeconomic status have been underrepresented in parent training programs (Hargis & Blechman, 1979) and have been less likely to complete programs (McMahon, Forehand, Griest, & Wells, 1981; Sadler et al., 1976). Moreover, Hispanic families have been traditionally viewed as underutilizing mental health services (Acosta, 1979; Padilla, Ruiz, & Alvarez, 1975) and one might expect underutilization to be even greater in monolingual Spanish-speaking families. Yet in Chapter 3 we noted a very high enrollment of lower SES Spanish-speaking families in our parent training program (Shenk, 1984), and in this chapter, we found a high program completion rate. Why?

It is likely that one factor contributing to increased enrollment and completion was increased access. Reports of service utilization have been confounded by issues of access. Most obviously, programs must be offered in a family's primary language and they must be publicized in ways that reach families. Moreover, they must be at an accessible facility that has gained the parents' trust. Much so-called underutilization has been the natural result of having so few linguistically and culturally appropriate programs as well as inadequate outreach. We attribute the high enrollment and completion of Shenk's families, for example, to the Regional Center's programs (where many bilingual staff had already addressed clients' needs and gained their trust) and to our outreach (where staff had conducted prior in-home interviews and the invitation to participate was made personally). We might not have had even a single case to report if, for example, our program had been located at UCLA and publicized by mail.

Moreover, program completion is facilitated by lowering other barriers to access. These include resource barriers, such as difficulties in getting transportation to the program or arranging child care. They also include motivational barriers, such as feeling uncomfortable in a program that is a lot like school, and the difficulty of mobilizing to attend when a day is filled with other demands and problems. In the alternative programs described above, we addressed the resource barriers as much as we could by meeting at a familiar community facility, and/or providing or reimbursing transportation, and/or providing child care.

We also addressed motivational barriers. Parents were personally invited to participate by us and/or their Regional Center counselor. We placed a reminder call to each parent the day of each meeting to encourage attendance. We invited parents to bring anyone they wanted to with them to the meeting. We tried to keep the content at an understandable and useful level and to use active approaches that involved participant modeling. We included incentives for participation. We served coffee and cookies. It is impossible to weigh how any of these ingredients contributed to a rather successful overall completion rate. The most important component actually may have been the group itself. Although a group format makes it impossible to reschedule appointments to meet individual needs, this may not be all bad. The fixed group schedule may encourage parents to make a special effort to keep up. Finally, most families seemed to value sharing experiences with other families in the group.

Parent Training and School Programs

Beyond just completing the program, most parents showed meaningful gains in knowledge and practice of behavioral teaching. Combining videotaped feedback, participant modeling, and co-consulting among parents with more traditional didactic approaches seemed particularly useful. The model of group training followed by more active and individualized involvement that was utilized in the two mini-camp programs could be incorporated into most special education school programs. Sandler and Coren (1981) reported a similar approach, beginning with four group sessions using the *Steps to Independence* manuals. They next conducted four individualized sessions, where the trainer modeled teaching and gave parents feedback as they taught their child. At this point, parents began a series of short planning meetings with the teacher every 3 weeks or so to target teaching goals and to compare notes on progress. This seems an ideal combination of roles. The behavioral specialist does initial group and individual training, activities that do not fit easily into the classroom teacher's role. Then, when parents are more proficient in behavioral programming, teachers can follow through with parents in a cost-effective way.

Home Implementation

Despite the successes of these alternative programs, we found less than optimal follow-through implementation. Typically, the amount and quality of teaching increased during training but dropped by follow-up, in some cases to pre-training levels. Why don't lessons learned in the clinic transfer smoothly into daily life at home? One consideration is proficiency. Although these families gained, many had still not met proficiency criteria. Because post-training proficiency has been our best predictor of subsequent implementation, we must still search for ways to boost proficiency further. One suggestion comes from a program of individual training for mothers with noncompliant children (Rogers, Forehand, Griest, Wells, & McMahon, 1981), in which outcomes were independent of SES. Training was individualized and competency based, requiring parents to master each step before moving on. Different families moved at different rates. Unfortunately, the authors did not report whether the number of sessions differed by SES, but in any event, this self-paced, criterion-based type of program may be a viable alternative or addition to group training.

Another consideration is that parent training makes demands on a family to change its patterns of interaction, and these demands may be resisted for a host of reasons untapped by a program that focuses on skill teaching. Dadds, Schwartz, and Sanders (1987), for example, found that in families with distressed marriages, behavioral parent training produced changes only if accompanied by a program that focused on parental communication. As we learn more about family factors related to long-term outcome, we will have a better idea of ways to modify and supplement training.

Finally, we know very little about cultural factors that influence how well a program such as ours "takes" in lower SES families with children who have developmental disabilities, and especially in racial and ethnic minority families. The results in this chapter suggest that program content need not be highly culture-specific for families to complete and be satisfied with a program; however, cultural factors may most influence actual behavior change at home. We are beginning to see parent training programs specifically designed to be culturally appropriate, such as the Effective Black Parenting Program (Alvy, 1987; Alvy et al., 1988), and the Multicultural Training-of-Trainers Project (Chan, 1986a, 1986b), that bring culturally and linguistically appropriate services to Black, Asian, and Latino parents. These programs are typically much broader in their coverage than ours, with more emphasis on acquiring information and less emphasis on specific in-home teaching.

Although a discussion of cultural factors is beyond our scope here, one illustration may indicate the complexity of the issues. Wahler (1980) was also concerned about parental follow-through at home. He suggested that social support rather than SES per se may be the main factor influencing outcome. He defined insularity as the extent, quality, and value of social support networks for mothers, and found that low gain mothers were more insular—their few contacts outside the immediate family were primarily with relatives and helping agencies—and they evaluated many contacts negatively. High gain mothers had more contacts with friends and more positive contacts. Wahler (1980) explained how insular mothers may be more locked into behavior patterns with their families and less receptive to outside influence. Prieto-Bayard (1987), however, noted that Wahler's families were low SES Black and White U.S. citizens, with a history of (possibly negative) agency contacts. She posited that for first generation Spanish-speaking mothers there would not be a negative history with agencies (Buriel, 1975) and the extended family would provide more support and have less fixed behavior patterns than in more established families. Consistent with this, she found that in a low SES Spanish-speaking sample, insularity as measured by Wahler was not predictive of maternal coping with a disabled child. Rather, positive coping was related to the total number of interactions mother had and the positive valence she ascribed to them, regardless of source.

All this is by way of saying that identifying culturally relevant factors is quite complex. We need considerably more research that examines such variables in specific ethnic or racial groups. Moreover, we ultimately need to know which among the many cultural differences that might be identified must be addressed to actually make a difference in program outcome.

Unit III

Parent Training for Special Populations

The three chapters in this unit present alternative parent training approaches for problems that would not be sufficiently met by group training that stands alone, such as our Parents as Teachers program.

The problems of child abuse, hyperactivity, and autism all huddle, at least at times, under the umbrella of developmental disabilities. In Chapter 8, Steve Ambrose faces the problem of intervening with families where there is child abuse. This problem has more than tangential relevance to developmental disabilities. Many abusive parents are themselves mildly mentally retarded. Moreover, abused children or those at risk for abuse are a high-risk group for developmental disabilities; and the reverse is also true—that is, children with handicaps are at high risk for abuse (Embry, 1980). When Dr. Ambrose worked with our group at UCLA, he modified the Parents as Teachers group program for low SES parents who had abused a child.

Dr. Ambrose has continued to work with abusive families at Children's Institute International in Los Angeles, and he reports here some encouraging benefits of family intervention. However, he realistically weighs these benefits against the incredible needs and bleak resources of these families, and he underscores the need for embedding parent training in more comprehensive services.

In Chapter 9, I consider families with a child diagnosed as "hyperactive," or, in more recent terms, Attention Deficit Hyperactive Disorder (ADHD) (American Psychiatric Association, 1987). Hyperactive children find their way into most special education textbooks, and in some cases fall under developmental disabilities legislation. Although these children typically score within the range of normal intelligence, their unfocused attention, impulsivity, distractability, and erratic performance usually lead to delays in academic and social arenas, and there is therefore considerable diagnostic overlap with learning disabilities. There is also much overlap with conduct disorders, and the behavior management challenges posed by these children are considerable, requiring more help for their parents than a brief group program can provide.

Intervention for these families is illustrated primarily with data from a parent training program six doctoral students and I conducted at the University of California, Irvine, as part of a comprehensive summer program for school-aged hyperactive children directed by Dr. Jim Swanson. We combined aspects of the Parents as Teachers program with components of other programs that were directed primarily toward children with behavior problems, and we combined group and individual training.

In Chapter 10, Stephen Anderson writes about programs for families of children with autism. This developmental disability has been well represented in our UCLA study families. We have found that the parents of children with autism showed benefits from training equivalent to those of parents whose children had other diagnoses. Yet the child target behavior changes do not generalize well to other behaviors or other situations. Moreover, these changes represent a small proportion of the enormous overall educational task. We have come to realize that parents of children with autism must receive much more intensive and individualized training and carry out much more complex teaching if there are to be meaningful gains. The characteristic behaviors associated with autism (e.g., aloofness from people, insistence on routine, self-stimulatory and even self-injurious behaviors, and limited or aberrant language) require a structured world at school and at home, with technically good teaching to get and maintain the child's attention.

I have followed first hand the intensive home-based programs that Dr. Ivar Lovaas developed experimentally in Los Angeles and that Dr. Anderson and the May Institute staff then adapted to a clinical program in Massachusetts. I invited Dr. Anderson's contribution to illustrate an extension of, or alternative to, group training that seems better suited for this population.

Chapter 8

_____Child Abuse

Stephen A. Ambrose
Children's Institute International

In the child abuse field, a focus on parenting skills seems to be replacing the more traditional psychiatric focus on intrapsychic disturbance within the individual parent. Parent training programs for parents who have been identified as abusive or neglectful by social service agencies and the courts have proliferated over the past ten years. Abusive and neglectful parents have now been offered training in their homes (Nomellini & Katz, 1983), in clinics (Wolfe et al., 1982), in groups (Brunk, Henggeler, & Whelan, 1987; Egan, 1983), and individually (Wolfe et al., 1982) using theoretically diverse curricula ranging from Parent Effectiveness Training (PET), to Systematic Training in Effective Parenting (STEP), to behavior modification. Of the various parenting models that have been proposed, we would argue that behavior modification is the most readily comprehensible to the majority of abusive and neglectful parents. Published reports of behaviorally oriented programs have generally indicated favorable outcomes, although the majority of these published evaluations have lacked methodological rigor.

While behavioral parent training seems to offer promise with this very challenging population, it is clear that abusive and neglectful families often present many predictors of poor outcome (e.g., low socioeconomic status, limited education, single parenthood, lack of motivation to learn, and anger/defensiveness about intervention in their lives). In this chapter, we will describe the Active Parenting Project, a behavioral parent training program developed jointly by the UCLA Project for Developmental Disabilities and Children's Institute International (CII), specifically for abusive and neglectful parents (Ambrose, 1983; Ambrose, Hazzard, & Haworth, 1980). We will describe the assumptions and mechanics of the curriculum, present outcome data, and highlight some of the clinical and research issues that we have struggled with in our efforts to develop a program that can overcome parents' limitations and resistances and enhance their child care skills significantly enough that their children can remain safely in their homes.

THE ACTIVE PARENTING
CURRICULUM

The Active Parenting Curriculum is guided by several key assumptions regarding the parental deficits underlying abusive and neglectful behavior. One of these assumptions is that the majority of parents who abuse and/or neglect their children do so at least partially because they lack more appropriate parenting skills. The inconsistent, ineffective, and overly punitive child management techniques of these parents have long been convincingly documented in the child abuse literature (e.g., Elmer, 1967; Young, 1964). While we recognize that a small proportion of parents willfully abuse and/or neglect out of malice, we assume that the vast majority aspire to be good parents and will try out new methods if convinced it is in their child's best interest.

Another key assumption is that many abusive/neglectful parents lack self-control, especially, although not exclusively, in managing anger impulses. Furthermore, many of their families live almost continually under conditions of high stress that further tax their self-control mechanisms. We also assume that most abusive/neglectful parents lack the skill and/or motivation to stimulate and teach their children appropriately. This is reflected in the developmental delays invariably found in samples of abused and neglected youngsters.

In view of these assumptions, we developed a curriculum designed to:
1. Teach parents effective, nonviolent child management skills;
2. Teach parents anger control strategies and methods of coping with stress;
3. Teach parents teaching skills and encourage them to be more proactive vis-a-vis their child's development.

The curriculum is comprised of 12 weekly 2-hour group meetings. The first eight meetings focus on teaching parents nonviolent behavioral methods. These include contingent positive reinforcement to encourage prosocial child behavior; restructuring of situational antecedents to reduce the likelihood of problem behavior; and the use of ignoring, time-out, hands-on physical guidance, and privilege loss to manage problem behavior that does occur.

As in the Parents as Teachers program (Appendix A), parents are taught an A-B-C (Antecedent-Behavior-Consequences) problem-solving model to help them understand the reasons for their child's behavior. Using this model, each family in the group designs individualized programs for modifying specific child behavior problems in the home.

The final four meetings focus primarily on cognitive strategies for managing anger. Parents are taught to identify unrealistic, anger-producing cognitions and to replace them with more realistic and constructive coping thoughts. Structured discussions also cover the rights of both parents and children. Emphasis is placed on problem-solving and on interacting assertively with children and adults as opposed to responding either passively or aggressively on impulse. The curriculum also includes at least one home visit and one individual session at the clinic in which staff can model techniques, give support, and encourage generalization of skills learned. The curriculum is action oriented, involving demonstrations, role-plays, and supervised practice in teaching children.

Finally, to promote parent cooperation, a lottery system is included in the curriculum. Parents can earn lottery tickets for arriving on time, doing homework assignments, performing role-plays in the group, and for any other accomplishments deemed noteworthy. At the conclusion of each session, a drawing is held and winning parents receive prizes donated by businesses in the community.

EVALUATION

A comprehensive evaluation of the Active Parenting Program was conducted over a 2-year period between 1981 and 1983 (Ambrose, 1983) with 42 families, most under court order. During the first pilot phase of the evaluation, 10 families received the Active Parenting Program. During the second phase, 32 families were randomly assigned to either the Active Parenting Program or to a control condition in which they received 12 weeks of group training in areas of parenting unrelated to behavior management, such as child development, nutrition, and health care. A battery of objective and self-report measures was administered to all parents pre- and post-training. A subsample of 15 families participated in follow-up interviews six to 14 months after training.

Measures

During the course of this evaluation we became quite disillusioned about the meaningfulness of the self-report measures we employed. Parents were, of course, encouraged to be honest and assured that their responses would have no bearing on later reports to the court. Clearly, many still felt suspicious and defensive. Indeed, there were several parents who, despite much evidence to the contrary, rated themselves as excellent on all of the parenting dimensions assessed on one of the self-report measures. Given the unreliability of parents' self-reports, for the purposes of this discussion we will focus on two more objective measures developed specifically for this evaluation, the Verbal Vignettes Test (VVT) and the Parent Proficiency Test (PPT).

The VVT consists of a series of 12 vignettes, each depicting situations that parents commonly encounter with their children. Interviewers read each vignette aloud and parents are asked to suggest specific ways of responding to the child in the vignette. Ten of the vignettes involve typical child behavior problems; two describe incidents of positive child behaviors. Parent responses are tape recorded and later scored according to the behavioral sophistication of the suggestions offered.

The PPT was adapted from the Teaching Proficiency Test described in Chapter 4. This in vivo measure of parent skill in teaching and managing child behavior has proven to be quite reliable. In a clinic play room, parents spend 5 minutes teaching their child an age-appropriate play skill (e.g., doing a puzzle); 5 minutes engaged in free play; and 5 minutes having the child put toys away. Videotapes are later scored with global ratings of parents' proficiency at teaching and managing child behavior problems along three dimensions: structuring of antecedents; contingent reinforcement of positive child behavior; and appropriate consequating of behavior problems.

Dropouts

A program's dropout rate is a critical indicator of both its effectiveness and its perceived relevance to the population served. Particularly with abusive and neglectful parents, a group notorious for evading intervention efforts, the challenge of developing a program sufficiently rewarding and sufficiently attuned to parents' perceptions of their own needs to ensure 12 weeks of regular attendance is formidable. Indeed, Wolfe, Aragona, Kaufman, and Sandler (1980), in perhaps the only published report providing dropout rates from a behavioral training program specifically for abusive parents, acknowledged, over a 3-year period, a 32% dropout rate among court-ordered parents and an 87% dropout rate among parents for whom parent training was recommended by a child protective agency.

Of 42 parents who began our program, we found 8 dropouts (19%). Consistent with findings in families with a child who is retarded, single parents were much more likely to drop out. Of the 22 two-parent families only 1 (5%) dropped out, whereas of 20 single-parent families, 7 (35%) dropped out. We also examined court jurisdiction for a subsample where we had this information and, consistent with Wolfe et al. (1980), this was also related to program completion. Of 26 court-ordered families, only 15% dropped out, whereas of the 8 families not under court supervision, 50% dropped out. Because these two predictors—single-parent status and court supervision—were related, a larger sample would be needed to determine their relative contributions.

Parent Knowledge and Behavior

The primary goal of the Active Parenting Curriculum is to teach parents behavioral alternatives to physical punishment. Virtually all of the abusive/neglectful parents we see have relied on some method of inflicting physical pain to control child behavior and many have clearly gone beyond socially acceptable limits in the severity of the physical punishments they administer. The Active Parenting Curriculum attempts to restructure parents' attitudes toward physical punishment by teaching effective behavioral alternatives, emphasizing the rights and feelings of children, pointing out the long-term ineffectiveness of excessive physical punishment, building upon whatever guilt parents experienced after punishment episodes, and reinforcing prosocial changes in attitude. Heated discussions commonly take place in the groups, with many parents, probably the majority, arguing vehemently that it is their right as parents to punish their children as they see fit and that, if they refrain completely from spanking, hitting, or whipping, their children will be spoiled and out of control.

The data from our program evaluation indicate that parents who received the Active Parenting Curriculum did indeed show positive changes in these kinds of attitudes and in their knowledge of behavioral alternatives to physical punishment. At the conclusion of the program, the VVT revealed that the trained parents had improved dramatically relative to control parents in their ability to verbally generate effective, nonviolent behavioral strategies for dealing with child misbehavior. Whether these gains truly indicate a clinically significant restructuring of parental belief systems or merely a superficial compliance with accurately perceived situational demands remains an important and difficult question. Of course, learning the material presented in the groups well enough to comply could be considered a significant first step in itself. More germane, though, in assessing the long range efficacy of this program in reducing abusive parenting practices is whether the parents can incorporate the attitudes and behaviors espoused by the Active Parenting Curriculum into their ongoing interactions with their children.

Our data addressing this question are more equivocal. The PPT showed inconsistent results. To date, we have administered the PPT pre- and post-training to three groups of parents receiving the Active Parenting Curriculum. The parents in the first group showed dramatic improvement. The parents in the other two groups, however, did not show clear gains relative to control parents. The explanation for these differing outcomes is not immediately clear.

For the purpose of the evaluation, every effort was made to administer the Active Parenting Curriculum in the same way for each group.

However, the clinical impressions of the group leaders suggested some differences in the ways the different groups reacted to the material. The two groups that showed less gain on the PPT generally seemed more hostile and resistant than did the more successful group. Whether this stemmed from differences in the composition of the groups or in the presentation of the material, these kinds of process issues undoubtedly play a role in what parents learn.

In any case, the PPT still does not assess how well parents are faring at home during their day-to-day interactions with their children and during potential crisis situations. It may be that some parents who do well with their children under the structured conditions of the PPT still cannot maintain adequate control when stressed at home. Conversely, the likelihood of some parents resorting to physical punishment may have diminished substantially as a result of their participation in the program, but this inhibition of impulsive, violent responding may not be reflected in their PPT scores. Extended, systematic home observation of parent behavior prior to, during, and following training would clearly be the best way to address these questions but, of course, this poses tremendous logistical difficulties.

Another way to evaluate the impact of the program is to look at re-abuse rates. Of the families who received the Active Parenting Curriculum during this evaluation, we became aware of two families in which there were incidents of re-abuse that came to the attention of the authorities with 6 months of the conclusion of the program. Furthermore, follow-up interviews with a subsample of 15 families 6 to 18 months after the program were generally encouraging, with all parents indicating that the group had been helpful and most being able to articulate specific behavioral methods they continued to use.

CASE EXAMPLES

To highlight and bring to life the complexity of issues involved in work with these families, three case examples are presented. These specific cases were chosen because they exemplify a diversity of presenting problems as well as a range of outcomes. The names employed are, of course, fictitious, but the stories of these children and their families are unfortunately quite real.

Case #1

Sammy and his parents were referred to the Children's Institute when Sammy was about 20 months old. On first impression, Sammy was not a particularly appealing child. His baleful eyes, wrinkled skin, and slightly misshapen head made his face look like that of a tired old man. Much of the time Sammy seemed quite disgruntled and only vaguely interested in his surroundings. When adults made even simple demands on him, he was likely to respond with a loud, miserable wail. Sometimes, too, he would cry for no discernible reason at all and would be inconsolable, much to the consternation of his 19-year-old mother, Patricia.

Shortly after Sammy's first birthday, Patricia had brought him to the hospital. He was filthy, emaciated, and close to death. The diagnosis given at the time was Failure to Thrive syndrome. Patricia very defensively maintained that he just would not eat, no matter what she tried. Despite her denial of wrongdoing, the hospital reported the case to the Department of Children's Services (DCS), which was shortly thereafter given jurisdiction over Sammy by the juvenile court. Sammy responded well in the hospital and was soon discharged to a foster home, where he stayed for approximately 6 months before being returned to his parents on a trial basis, still under DCS supervision.

As Patricia's story unfolded, it became evident that she was of low-normal intelligence and that during the months preceding Sammy's hospitalization she had been under considerable stress. Her mother, who was still a very influential figure in her life, was far from enamored with Patricia's 20-year-old, common-law husband, Manuel, an undocumented worker from Mexico employed at the time as a busboy. The angry critical feelings were mutual. Patricia found herself caught in the middle and decided to cut off relations with her mother.

In the midst of all this turmoil, and without her mother's support, she soon felt overwhelmed by the responsibility of parenthood and simply did not have the internal or external resources necessary to take care of Sammy. His feeding, bathing, and sleeping schedules became more and more haphazard. Managing her own life was difficult enough. She knew little about housekeeping, budgeting money, or feeding a hungry and demanding child. Whenever she lost patience with Sammy's demands, which was at least two or three times a day, she spanked him. These spankings had begun during Sammy's first few months. Physical punishment had been a constant throughout Patricia's own development, and she perceived spanking as an important part of the parental role. She did not even think to conceal it from the authorities when asked about her disciplinary practices.

Shortly after Sammy was returned home, the family moved into a single apartment in a neglected, run-down building profusely decorated with gang graffiti. They lived on the second floor, overlooking an untended swimming pool filled with murky, brown water. Most alarming was the absence of a railing to protect children from falling off the second floor and into the pool. The landlord had been unresponsive the one time they had complained. Sammy was only returned home on the condition that his mother and father participate in a treatment program to help them become more competent parents. Patricia and Manuel were resentful, hostile, suspicious, and frightened, but maintained that they did want Sammy home. They agreed to participate.

Particularly noteworthy in reviewing this family's progress in training is Patricia's performance on the pre-VVT. In response to virtually every behavior problem depicted in the vignettes, she recommended physical punishment. In fact, she scored lower on this measure than any other parent in the sample. A typical response was, "I don't know what the mother should do—hit him, I guess." Her pre-PPT was a little better, but still fell considerably shy of her group's pre-training mean.

In the group meetings during the early stages of the program, both parents maintained their sullen, distrustful posture. The turning point seemed to be their first home visit. The two staff members who made this visit brought along some fruit and an inexpensive toy for Sammy. Unlike some parents who feared visits to their homes by authority figures, Patricia seemed grateful for both the visit and the gifts and cooperatively role-played a time-out procedure to use with Sammy when he bit the children next door. Manuel, too, became much more involved in the program following this visit. While both Patricia and Manuel remained quiet and tense in the group, they became noticeably more attentive and cooperative.

Patricia's performance on both the VVT and PPT measures improved markedly, with post-training scores slightly above the mean for all parents who received the Active Parenting Curriculum. Staff reported that Sammy's hygiene had improved significantly, that his affect was more animated and positive, and that his behavior had become more cooperative and affiliative. Patricia, too, reported that his behavior had improved at home and she spoke proudly about his physical and intellectual growth. She was especially excited about his rapidly expanding vocabulary. Follow-up data, unfortunately, are not available on this family because they did not maintain contact with CII, and they moved during the 14-month follow-up period.

Case #2

William was 10 years old and James was 8 when their family was referred to CII by DCS. They lived with their mother Eunice and her common-law husband Jackson. The boys' biological father had abandoned the family 5 years previously. Apparently, he had been very abusive to both mother and children. Jackson, the boys' stepfather, was a street musician who spoke in colorful street vernacular. Eunice worked as a nurse's aide in a convalescent home.

The small single apartment in which they all lived was located in a seedy neighborhood populated primarily by street people and transients. Eunice did not want the boys roaming about the neighborhood when she was at work, especially because James had already been caught shoplifting. The boys, however, hated to be confined to their small, often very hot apartment and snuck out whenever possible. What most enraged Eunice, though, was when they lied to her to avoid punishment. Sneaking out, lying about it, and being punished had become a chronic pattern. She began to believe they were just "bad kids" whom she simply could not control. She felt helpless and depressed.

The incident that brought the family to the attention of the courts occurred after Jackson discovered that some of the change he had earned playing his saxophone on the street was missing from his hiding place. He was livid. It was the last straw. Despite the boys' denial of guilt, he took off his belt and thrashed them both until neighbors heard the boys' cries and summoned the police. The juvenile court decided that the boys could stay with Eunice if Jackson moved out until he successfully completed a treatment program. Jackson pretended to move out and agreed to participate.

Eunice accompanied Jackson to the first few meetings and brought the boys with her. However, soon only Jackson came, although resistant to being legally coerced into treatment. In the group meetings, at least initially, he was often disruptive and argumentative. Except for a few brief occasions, he maintained his street-wise facade throughout the program. He was late to virtually every meeting. He passively-aggressively avoided arranging a time for a home visit from staff, no doubt concerned that we would find out he was still living with his family and report him. And finally, he failed to show for his post-assessments three times despite repeated pledges of cooperation.

As it turned out, the home visit was one of the few times either parent was willing to discuss their difficulties openly. Eunice and Jackson were both able to share their concerns about the boys' unmanageable behavior and their inability to provide better supervision, especially in the afternoons after school. Eunice revealed her profound sense of hopelessness regarding their chances of meaningfully improving their living conditions. Jackson followed the author outside as the visit concluded and privately confided that he was concerned about Eunice's depression.

As a result of the home visit, arrangements were made for the boys to attend a nearby Boys' Club after school. Jackson expressed gratitude but seemed to retreat after the visit to his previous noncommittal stance. Eunice still would not come to group, despite much encouragement to do so. And Jackson was not seen again after receiving his diploma in the last group meeting. Not surprisingly, at the follow-up assessments this family could not be located.

Case #3

During a crying binge when he was 10 months old, Anthony was thrown up against a wall by his teenage father. He suffered a severe subdural hematoma and was placed in foster care. As is often the case, both of his parents had similar histories of abuse and both had spent most of their childhoods in foster care.

For 3 months after the incident neither parent would admit any knowledge of how Anthony's injuries had occurred. Finally, after considerable urging by her therapist, Anthony's mother Nancy, also a teenager, implicated Anthony's father in spite of her fear of losing him. This fear turned out to be justified, as he did in fact soon depart for parts unknown. She remained in individual therapy, though, and Anthony was finally returned to her under DCS supervision.

Soon after Anthony's return, Nancy went to work in a factory. The job was exhausting. Adding to the stress of single parenthood was Anthony's increasingly difficult behavior. His tantrums had become so severe that both Nancy and the staff at his daycare center avoided placing demands on him; Anthony had learned to control the adults in his world. Complicating the picture was Anthony's speech aphasia, most likely attributable to the head injury suffered at the hands of his father.

Anthony was still under DCS jurisdiction when he reached his third birthday. It was around that time that Nancy decided to join the parent education group to get help in handling his behavior. She was furious with him. Compounding her sense of helplessness was her guilt about his injury and its long-range ramifications. Struggling with these strong and confusing emotions and Anthony's provocative day-to-day behavior, she worried about losing control.

Approximately one year prior to beginning this program, Nancy completed a briefer, less structured parent education class also conducted by the author. She apparently learned the material well. On her pre-VVT she scored higher than any other parent in the sample, pre- or post-. Virtually all of her responses reflected considerable behavioral sophistication. To illustrate, the following is Nancy's response to Item 2 of the VVT which asks for suggestions regarding handling bedtime tantrums:

That's a problem I hope to bring up in the group because I have the exact same problem. There's a lot involved. With a normal kid I'd tell the mother to just ignore it and to read a book with him before he goes to bed. And make his playtime slowly slow down to where you read a book and then it's time for bed. You know, make it a bedtime habit—like reading a book means it's time to go to bed right after. You could also give him milk and cookies—that might gear him down. Kids usually are running around all the time, playing all hyped-up and then you give them one minute to go to sleep. If I were them, I wouldn't do it either. If he starts crying after the story you gotta ignore it. I might also offer him a reward for going to bed on time and give it to him in the morning.

Note that she recommended appropriately restructuring the antecedents ("read a book with him"), rewarding alternative behaviors ("give him a reward in the morning") and appropriate consequating of the tantrum behavior ("ignore it"). On the PPT, as well, her performance suggested considerable competence in teaching and in managing problem behavior. In the group, perhaps because of her ability to articulate issues clearly, she quickly emerged as a leader and seemed to have a constructive influence on a number of the other parents. What she seemed to need most for herself from the group was support and encouragement to use in her relationship with Anthony the knowledge and skills she already possessed. At the follow-up interview 14 months after she completed training, she described clearly and convincingly her continued use of behavioral techniques and was very positive in relating her retrospective views on the helpfulness of the program.

Discussion

These three case examples are fairly representative of the performance of families in the Active Parenting Program. Some parents made only superficial, token efforts at learning the material and incorporating behavioral methods into their interactions with their children. They came only because they were ordered to by the court and, in some cases, even the court order did not prevent them from dropping out. Other parents entered into the program with a high level of resistance but became engaged in the process of the group over the course of the program. Some of these parents clearly needed more than the 12 weeks of the program to derive clinically significant, lasting benefits. Finally, some parents participated actively and appropriately throughout the program and seemed to learn and constructively employ the ideas presented after the group concluded. These case examples also illustrated some important clinical issues, which we will consider next.

CLINICAL ISSUES

Reducing Resistance

Abusive and neglectful parents are often characterized as angry, defensive, sensitive to criticism, and generally resistant to treatment efforts, especially those which more directly seek behavior change (Martin, 1980). And unfortunately, as Jahn and Lichstein (1980) pointed out regarding the behavior therapy and psychotherapy literatures generally, ". . . research into techniques for the management and resolution of resistance has been woefully lacking" (p. 305). In the behavioral child abuse field there are but a few anecdotal reports of successful strategies for contending with some of the more frustrating manifestations of parent resistance: sporadic attendance at treatment sessions, noncompletion of homework assignments, continued belief in and use of physical punishment, and disruptive behavior in group meetings. Obviously, these kinds of behaviors must be dealt with effectively for a behavioral treatment approach to be viable.

The approach to parent resistance in conducting the Active Parenting groups involved systematically rewarding cooperative behavior via a lottery system; predicting resistance and eliciting from parents the forms it might take, a paradoxical strategy designed to preempt resistant behavior; attempting to form empathic and supportive relationships with each individual parent; and explicitly informing parents of the behaviors expected in order for them to complete the program and receive a favorable letter to the court. While all of these approaches seem potentially useful, resistance to forced treatment can be very strong, and unquestionably some proportion of the parents made it through the program primarily by "playing the game," with only intermittent intentions of changing behavior or improving family relationships.

To increase our chances of meaningfully reaching families we now offer individual counseling to parents participating in the group who evidence signs of resistance early on. We provide bus passes to those who might otherwise be legitimately unable to attend. We have also become very attentive to cultural issues, and we utilize treatment staff reflecting the ethnic diversity of the families we serve. To the maximum extent possible without sacrificing systematic training in parenting skills, we try to be flexible in giving parents a voice in what gets covered in the weekly group meetings. While we do not collude in parents' efforts to externalize responsibility for their difficulties and focus group discussion on "blaming the system," we are willing to set aside our agenda for any given meeting and discuss whatever pressing concern a parent might raise. Finally, it has been our experience that it is critical to work with protective services workers closely and cooperatively toward mutually determined goals. Lack of effective coordination opens the door for manipulative "splitting" by parents and heightened resistance.

Generalization to the Home Environment

The VVT data indicate that parents can learn to verbally generate behaviorally appropriate alternatives to physical punishment. Whether they can also behaviorally generate these alternatives in their spontaneous interactions at home with their children without the support and surveillance of program staff is much less clear.

Despite the feelings of being checked up on that home visits engender in some parents, there does not seem to be an adequate alternative method of assessing parent-child home interaction and of implementing home behavior change programs. Indeed, it is likely that many of the parents in the Active Parenting program would have profited from more than the one or two consultations that they received and that their wariness about being checked up on and reported would have gradually diminished as time proved these apprehensions unwarranted.

Assuming that additional visits would further promote in-home implementation of behavioral techniques, a remaining question is whether trained paraprofessional parent aides can serve this purpose or whether much more expensive professional therapists are needed. In this regard, it is interesting to note that the Berkeley Planning Associates' (1977) evaluation of child abuse programs found that programs employing parent aides had higher success rates than those which did not. It seems reasonable to assume that paraprofessionals will be more effective if well trained in behavioral techniques, sufficiently skilled and supervised to handle the multitude of problem behaviors parents present, and sufficiently dedicated to immerse themselves in the often minimally rewarding lives of multiproblem families.

Improving Maintenance of Gains

Encouraging, if open to question, are parents' reports in the follow-up interviews of their continued use of behavioral techniques. As we have noted, though, not all parents have fared as well after training as we might have hoped; in fact, there were at least two incidents of re-abuse. These particular incidents may or may not have been preventable, but in retrospect it is clear to us that for many parents a 12-week program is simply not long enough. It is also clear that most multiproblem families will need systematic monitoring and follow-up services for a year or longer after group participation.

We now strongly encourage parents who seem to make only marginal improvement in their first 12-week group to participate in a second, or even a third cycle. Sometimes we seek a court order to require parents to participate again. We also now offer ongoing daycare to some families to provide respite to the parents, monitoring of the child's well-being, and crisis intervention as needed. Another possibility is to have paraprofessional parent aides maintain involvement with families after formal treatment has concluded. In the context of a long-term helping relationship with the parent, the aide can both monitor parent-child interactions and, when necessary, remind parents of the behavior management strategies learned in the program.

Providing Additional Services

As we have noted, the families who participated in this project faced a multitude of problems in addition to difficulties in managing their children's behavior. The vast majority were struggling just to subsist. Many were extremely isolated and had virtually no support system outside the CII. Many were unemployed and unskilled. A significant proportion functioned in the dull normal to borderline range in intelligence. Virtually all had major difficulties in relating to spouses, parents, and other significant others. Alcohol and drug problems were common and on several occasions parents even came to the group under the influence.

Indeed, almost every group session brought to light some new crisis. For example, a family would report that they had been evicted and were living in their car. Or a father would inform the group that his wife was in jail on drug charges. Or a single mother with two children would report being pregnant again with no source of support other than welfare. Or a wife would break into tears during a meeting and after much coaxing finally admit that she had been beaten up by her husband again. Or a child would be brought to group unbathed for days with both diarrhea and a blistering diaper rash.

To be truly relevant to multiproblem families, a parent training program clearly must be flexible enough to address these kinds of crisis situations as they emerge. Moreover, a weekly group will simply not be enough for many families; individual, marital, and family therapy may also be needed. Costs can be kept down if these additional services are viewed as an adjunct to the less expensive group treatment and offered only for as long as necessary. Trained parent aides can also inexpensively fulfill some of the functions of a therapist.

It is important, too, that a program provide parents with concrete assistance in finding apartments, jobs, day care, health care, and other community resources. In addition, the child abuse agency should serve as much as possible as a drop-in crisis center. The more open the doors of the agency are, the more likely the socially isolated parent is to develop a sense of community and to use other parents and staff as a support system.

When a family receives multiple services, coordinated case management is essential to prevent confusion on all sides and manipulative splitting by families. This coordination becomes particularly problematic when the family is being seen at more than one agency. In our experience, the children's services workers are often so overloaded with cases that they are unable to provide the necessary case coordination, in which case it is incumbent upon the treatment team to fill the void and to schedule regular case conferences with all concerned.

Applicability of Approach

It has been our experience with the families who participated in the study described here and with families we have seen subsequently that a proportion of parents will derive little discernible benefit from the Active Parenting Curriculum. Clearly, it would be helpful to be able to identify in advance those parents least likely to benefit. Unfortunately, in the child abuse field there remains a dearth of hard data addressing these kinds of questions. We do know from the current study that single and non-court-ordered parents are more likely to drop out. However, it certainly does not seem appropriate to disallow them participation, because some of these parents do indeed succeed. What is necessary instead is to find ways to modify the approach to maximize their chances of successful program participation.

There are other factors, though, based on our clinical experience, that do contraindicate the Active Parenting Program for a given parent. Foremost among these factors is ongoing chemical dependency. Until the chemically dependent parent achieves a period of sobriety, he or she is likely to disrupt the group and benefit little. We now require concomitant treatment for chemical dependency and, when appropriate, drug testing as a condition of acceptance into the Active Parenting Program. Similarly, an Active Parenting group would be inappropriate for the parent with a severe psychiatric disorder until the condition is controlled. Parents with significant intellectual limitations will likely also need a modified approach that emphasizes hands-on demonstrations with children rather than discussion of abstract concepts. Finally, parents who are extremely resistant or who have long histories of antisocial behavior may have to be screened out to prevent their negatively influencing other parents.

CONCLUSION

As the child abuse literature amply documents, abusive and neglectful parents have typically had years of training in abusive parenting practices from their own parents. Further compounding their parenting difficulties is the host of current socioeconomic and systemic stressors with which most court-identified parents must grapple. Difficult yet profound decisions must be made about which parents can be helped sufficiently to allow their children to remain in their care and about how best to help these multiproblem families given limited resources.

No simple solutions or panaceas are offered here. The Active Parenting Program that we have described in this chapter is, however, an attempt to address directly the abusive/neglectful interactional patterns between parent and child through teaching parents nonviolent disciplinary methods, self-control strategies, and effective child-teaching skills. While the challenges presented by this population are formidable, even untreatable at times, our experience suggests that a behavioral parent training approach combined with other support services and a careful, sensitive response to parental resistance can for some families significantly impact the cycle of abuse and neglect.

Chapter 9

Hyperactivity

In the past two decades, there has been a flurry of professional activity around the hyperactive child. Generally speaking, this child, usually a boy, has normal intelligence but an assortment of annoying behavioral characteristics that interfere with academic and social activities—most notably hyperactivity, impulsivity, inattention, distractability, and erratic performance (American Psychiatric Association, 1987). This behavior disorder is typically first diagnosed in the elementary school years, although it often appears much earlier; it tends to continue in different forms into adolescence and even into adulthood (Weiss & Hechtman, 1986).

From several perspectives this is a problem of considerable magnitude. In the school-aged population, hyperactive children account for the greatest number of referrals to child guidance agencies (Ross & Ross, 1982) and it is estimated that half a million children begin each school day by taking psychostimulant medication for hyperactivity (O'Leary, 1980). The enormous interest in this problem among researchers is underscored by Whelan's (1989) statistic that in a representative 3-year period (1977–1979) there were 7,000 published studies on hyperactivity!

Despite all of this clinical and scientific interest, we are far from a clear diagnostic picture. The American Psychiatric Association's most recent *Diagnostic and Statistical Manual* (DSM III-R; 1987) calls this behavior disorder *Attention Deficit Hyperactivity Disorder* (ADHD). The term "attention deficit disorder" was coined because studies showed that an inability to regulate attention and behavior to the demands of the situation is a primary deficit. Although the previous version of DSM III (American Psychiatric Association, 1980) held that attention deficit disorder can be present with or without hyperactivity, the APA decided upon the single ADHD diagnosis. Some researchers believe that a more prognostically useful diagnosis would distinguish whether or not aggression is present (Hinshaw, 1987). In any event, we can expect future refinements in how this childhood problem is defined.

Many experts subscribe to medication as the treatment of choice (Gittelman-Klein, 1987). There is, indeed, impressive evidence for the effectiveness of psychostimulant drugs in reducing attention-related problems, but there are drawbacks. Some children do not benefit, and many parents are wary of medication. Moreover, although studies have not found physical side-effects to be very problematic, we need to learn more about the psychological effects of the child's long-term reliance for good behavior on pills (Whalen & Henker, 1980). Other researchers are finding some success with classroom management strategies and cognitive behavioral procedures for teaching the child to self-regulate his or her own behavior (Hinshaw & Erhardt, in press).

FAMILIES AND ADHD

Regardless of other approaches used, there is a clear need to involve the family in what will usually be a multimodal treatment plan for the child with ADHD. There is some evidence for higher rates of family disturbance, marital discord and divorce, and parental psychiatric illness in the families of hyperactive children (Cohen & Minde, 1983; Emery, 1982; Schleifer et al., 1975). Parents of hyperactive children, in comparison with control parents, report lower levels of self esteem, more maternal stress, and self-perceptions as less competent with respect to their skill and knowledge in being good parents (Mash & Johnston, 1983). Indeed, interactions between mothers and their hyperactive children are characterized by more maternal negative and coercive behavior and more child demanding and noncompliant behavior than are found in control mother-child interactions (Campbell, 1973; Cunningham & Barkley, 1979). These findings are, of course, correlational, so we cannot say whether parenting qualities play a causative role in childhood hyperactivity or are a reaction to living with a difficult child. Parent training, in either case, should help to ameliorate the problems.

The next logical question, however, is what should intervention focus on. Are there key child behaviors that might be pivotal, in the sense that normalizing them would have a positive ripple effect on the child's other behaviors? Similarly, are there key parental behaviors to modify? Although these questions will require a good deal of further study, we based our parent training program on some tentative assumptions. For hyperactive children, *noncompliance* is usually a concern and is likely to spark annoyance and rejection from parents and teachers. We decided to make this a primary focus of intervention. Secondarily, we were concerned with children's *self-control* abilities, especially those surrounding problem-solving and anger management. Although there is evidence that some cognitive-behavioral techniques produce short-term benefits (Hinshaw, Henker, & Whelan, 1984), there is little generalization (Abikoff, 1987). We reasoned that training children and their parents in these methods would promote carryover into the child's subsequent social interactions at home.

With parents, we desired to break the *negative pattern of behavior and attitudes* we have noted above. This would in part involve providing information about hyperactivity to parents and giving them opportunities to share experiences with one another, to normalize the problem and to reduce blaming both themselves and their child. This would also mean having parents experience themselves with their child in non-conflictful interactions. It would gradually involve teaching more positive ways of relating, including ways to present demands and to consequate behavior. We reasoned that if parents learned behavior management strategies that improved their child's behavior even somewhat, they themselves would have an enhanced sense of competence in child rearing and more positive attitudes toward the child.

EVALUATION OF A
PARENT-TRAINING PROGRAM

A team from UCLA implemented parent training within a 6-week multimodal program for hyperactive children at the University of California, Irvine. The program had medication, academic, social skill, and cognitive components. It was obvious from the start that with so many aspects to the overall program it would be virtually impossible to isolate the effects on the children of the parent training program per se, so we decided to focus our evaluation on the parents. We recognized that, because we could not hold some parents out as no-training controls, we would be limited in our interpretations, but we saw this as an ideal opportunity to explore the promise of a group training program.

Families

The parent training program enrolled 33 families, with 31 boys and 2 girls aged 6 to 13 years. Seventy-six percent of families were intact. Mothers averaged 38 years of age with 14 years of schooling, although only 22% were college graduates. Thirty percent of mothers were employed full-time. Families came from Orange and Los Angeles counties to attend the program, with a mean roundtrip distance of 31 miles. It was the Irvine program policy to require participation in parent training by at least one parent.

Curriculum

The format combined six group and six individual sessions. Each Tuesday, parents attended a 2-hour group session that was repeated three times (8 AM, 4 PM, 7 PM) so that parents could attend at the time that was most convenient. Later each week, each child's parent(s) met with their consultant for an individual session. The curriculum drew on our previous work as well as on the exemplary parent training programs reported by Forehand and McMahon (1981), Barkley (1981), and Patterson, Reid, Jones, and Conger (1975). An outline of the topics covered is shown in Table 9.1.

The early sessions instructed parents about hyperactivity, behavior observation and measurement, and how to understand behavior in the context of antecedents and consequences. At home, parents carried out Forehand and McMahon's (1981) child game; in 15-minute play sessions with the child, parents tried to increase their own positive or encouraging responses and decrease negative or intrusive responses. In subsequent sessions parents developed behavior management programs and learned more about how to modify antecedents and consequences. They also learned about the self-regulation methods being used in the child program (Hinshaw, Henker, & Whalen, 1984), and were helped to examine and reframe their own cognitions regarding their child's behavior. Individual sessions became more variable, attuned to each family's needs related to implementing behavior management programming at home. Four monthly follow-up group sessions were held to review, consult further, and integrate our program with the child's school program. The outcome measures that we will report, however, were taken at the end of the summer program, so they do not reflect possible benefits of follow-up.

Participation

At least one parent in each family met the completion criteria of attending 8 or more of the 12 meetings as well as pre- and post-assessment sessions. Of 33 mothers, 30 completed training and measures. Of 28 fathers, 19 completed training and assessments. Trainers completed a weekly evaluation after the individual consultation session with each family. They rated attendance, homework completed, participation, and mastery of material. At the end of the program, trainers drew on these to complete an overall evaluation for each parent. Table 9.2 shows selected indices of participation from this extensive program evaluation. These indicate a high level of parent participation. In 83% of families, for example, parents took baseline and carried out a program for at least one behavior problem.

Knowledge of Behavioral Principles

A Behavioral Vignettes Test for Hyperactivity (BVT-H) was devised, with 20 items following the format of the BVT (see Chapter 4). Gains in

TABLE 9.1

Irvine Curriculum: Group and Individual Sessions

Week 1   Group:
Introduction, overview, rationale
What is hyperactivity
Specifying and measuring behaviors
A-B-C Model

Individual:
Review group/reading content
Child play session (positive scanning and reinforcement)

Week 2   Group:
B expanded: Targeting and measuring a problem behavior
A expanded: Antecedents
C expanded: Consequences (attention and ignoring)

Individual:
Consult re: target behavior and measurement
Review records on home play session
Child play session (videotaped)

Week 3   Group:
Developing a program
Consequences and encouraging alternative behaviors
Premack principle, contracts, token economy

Individual:
Review data and develop behavior management program
Consult on obstacles as needed
Child play session for families that have not done it well

Week 4   Group:
Compliance training
Punishment: Time out and response cost

Individual:
Consult on behavior management program

Week 5   Group:
Problems with physical punishment
Self-regulation training
Role of parents' cognitions (self-talk) and anger management

Individual:
Consult on behavior management program
Develop second program if possible

Week 6   Group:
Review (videotape of programming errors)
Sharing program examples and successes
Further program development
Goal Attainment Scaling

Individual:
Further consultation
Goal Attainment Scale re: parent and child goals for follow-through

TABLE 9.2

Trainer Post-training Evaluations of Parent Participation

ASSIGNMENT	PERCENTAGE COMPLETING		
	MOTHERS	FATHERS	FAMILIES
1. Read 75% + of assigned book	70	40	76
2. Gave positive attention at rate of 2+ per minute in child game session	86	68	93
3. Gave 75% + positive attention in child game session	62	52	76
4. Kept records of play sessions at home	86	52	86
5. Took baseline for at least one behavior	86	40	86
6. Programmed at least one behavior	83	56	83
Completed 4, 5, and 6 (home program assignments)	83	36	83

Note. The trainer evaluation was missing for 5 families (5 mothers, 4 fathers); $n = 29$ for mothers and $n = 25$ for fathers.

knowledge of behavioral principles from pre- to post-training were significant for mothers (t (29) = 6.21, $p < .001$) and fathers (t (18) = 7.74, $p < .001$). Combined, parents improved from a pre-score of 12.8 to a post-score of 16.8 (t (48) = 9.29, $p < .001$). With the 75% criterion for proficiency that we have used with the BVT, 34% of parents were proficient pre-training and 89% post-training.

Behavior Management Proficiency

To assess application of behavioral principles in mother-child dyads, we modified Barkley's (1981) clinic playroom task into a standardized 15-minute videotaped session. In this Behavior Management Proficiency Test (BMPT), the mother was provided a list of eight simple commands to give her child: (a) Come, sit down. (b) Move these toys off the table and put them over there. (c) Let's play Take Five. (d) I want you to practice your handwriting. Write the alphabet three times here. (e) Let's do the Etch-a-Sketch together. (f) OK, it's time to quit. Put all these materials and those toys in the box. (g) Put the box over on the other side of the room. (h) Put the chairs under the table.''

Patrice Yasuda (1986) developed a scoring system for the BMPT, drawing on our Teaching Profiency Test (see Chapter 4). Raters blind to time of testing scored the videotapes on eight dimensions. Three of these were primary: task presentation, reinforcement, and behavior management. These represented basic aspects of good behavior management and related most closely to training content. Table 9.3 shows pre-scores, post-scores, and significance tests for these scales. Mothers improved

TABLE 9.3

Mothers' Behavior Management Proficiency Test Scores Pre- and
Post-training

SCALE/SUBSCALE	PRE	POST	t
Task presentation	**3.5**	**4.9**	4.75***
Clarity of directions	2.0	2.7	4.79***
Tone of voice	1.5	2.1	3.14**
Reinforcement techniques	**4.6**	**8.6**	4.24***
Choice of reinforcer	2.4	3.1	1.98
Contingency of reinforcer	2.1	3.2	2.81**
Frequency of reinforcer	0.1	2.3	6.08***
Behavior management techniques	**6.8**	**9.3**	3.38**
Choice of behavior management	2.1	3.0	2.40*
Contingency of behavior management	2.5	3.3	2.84**
Frequency of behavior management	2.2	3.0	2.27*
Total Score	**14.9**	**22.8**	4.78***

Note. From *Family variables as predictors of successful parent training outcome with families of hyperactive children* by P. Yasuda, 1986.
* $p < .05$. ** $p < .01$. *** $p < .001$.

significantly on all three scales, and a Behavior Management Proficiency Test sum score had high interjudge reliability and improved significantly.

On the five additional scales, mothers scored significantly higher post-training in efforts to get the child's attention, the frequency and positiveness of their verbalizations, and their flexibility in trying alternative behavior management strategies when necessary. Mothers and children also were rated as enjoying the session significantly more following training. Unfortunately, the only scale where improvement did not reach statistical significance was the key outcome measure: child compliance. In discussing the compliance results, Yasuda (1986) noted that parents placed more demands on the child at the post-assessment than at the pre-assessment and that hyperactive children have been shown to be under better control in novel situations (as in the pre-assessment) and to act out more as the situation becomes familiar (Yates, 1981). In some ways, the child compliance findings increase our confidence in the improvements in mother behavior management proficiency, for these were not simply an artifact of having more manageable children. It would be important, however, to extend observation into the home and over a longer time period.

Parent-child Problem Solving

Valerie Marshall (1986), a doctoral student working with Michael Goldstein, went beyond behavior management to study parent and child problem-solving skills in a conflict resolution task. With 22 of these families she used a clever interaction task adapted from Goldstein, Judd, Rodnick, Alkire, and Gould (1968). The child and parents began in separate rooms. The child was presented a list of six problems that are common in families and was instructed to pick the two that caused the most parent-child conflict in his family. Whenever possible, he was encouraged to pick one that involved his mother and one that involved his father. He explained on audiotape how he felt about each problem. Next, these statements were played to the relevant parent, who gave a taped response to the child's statement. The procedure was also carried out in reverse, with each parent selecting two problems from the list of six and audiotaping their feelings, to which the child subsequently taped a response.

The two statement-response tapes that generated the most affect in family members were chosen as stimuli. The family was assembled in a room, where the experimenter played the first statement-response audiotape and encouraged all three family members to discuss and attempt to resolve the problem. The experimenter left the room for 7 minutes and videotaped the interaction. This procedure was repeated for the second interaction.

The videotapes were coded, with high interrater reliability, for verbal and nonverbal behaviors, although we will consider only the verbal behavior here. Parents showed a significant decrease following the program in coercive behaviors (e.g., ignoring, disagreement, negative self-disclosure, negative solutions, blocking of conversation) and in negative affective style (specific criticism, personal criticism, guilt induction, intrusiveness). There was, however, no change in the amount of prosocial behavior (e.g., acceptance, agreement, positive self-disclosure, praise positive solutions). Child changes paralleled the parent changes. These results were encouraging, because the primary focus of parent training had been behavior management, with only limited coverage of problem-solving. More such training might be fruitful, perhaps using a practice paradigm similar to Marshall's interaction task.

Attitudes

Marshall (1986) also studied parents' attitudes toward the hyperactive child. She measured *expressed emotion (EE)*, originally conceived of as the negative affective attitudes key relatives express about psychiatrically disturbed family members (Brown, Birley, & Wing, 1972). Families are traditionally interviewed about feelings toward the patient; those who make a number of statements that express criticism and/or overprotective-ness are scored high-EE. Numerous studies have shown that high-EE in families predicts poor outcomes in psychiatric patients (Vaughn & Leff, 1976; Vaughn, Snyder, Jones, Freeman, and Falloon, 1984) and even future psychiatric disturbance in disturbed nonpsychotic adolescents (Valone, Norton, Goldstein, & Doane, 1983). Moreover, high-EE parents actually express more negative affective statements during family interactions (Miklowitz, 1985; Miklowitz, Goldstein, Falloon, & Doane, 1984). In short, high-EE in the family is a source of stress for the vulnerable member (Valone, Goldstein, & Norton, 1984).

Because a focus of our parent training was to improve negative parental attitudes, Marshall (1986) reasoned that these might be reflected in lowered expressed emotion. Instead of the traditional 2-hour interview, she used a very brief method of assessing EE, where each parent talks for 5 uninterrupted minutes about his or her relationship with the child and views of the child (Magana et al., 1986). Blind scoring of audiotaped 5-minute speech samples taken before and after the program revealed striking changes. Whereas 12 families were scored high-EE before the program, only 1 family remained in the high-EE catagory after the program.

We have presented the outcomes from this program in some detail, because the measures addressed a variety of dimensions and found positive results whether one looks at participation, knowledge, satisfaction, behavioral proficiency, problem-solving, or attitudes. Some of these changes (e.g., skills) can be directly linked to the parent training experience, while others (e.g., attitudes) likely reflect effects of the total program.

CASE EXAMPLE

Drew Erhardt and I adapted the Irvine curriculum for use with parents of younger hyperactive children (Erhardt, 1987; Erhardt & Baker, 1989). The following case example illustrates parent training further and shows that key child problems were improved, although not eliminated, following a 10-week program.

Calvin, a 5-year, 10-month-old Filipino child from an intact middle class family was representative of the families studied (Erhardt, 1987). Calvin lived with his mother, a registered nurse, his father, a medical technician, and his 4-year-old brother. Calvin had received a diagnosis of attention deficit disorder with hyperactivity from his pediatrician and this had been confirmed by a staffing at the UCLA medical center. Although Ritalin had been recommended, Calvin's mother was opposed to the idea of medicating her son and sought alternative methods to control his behavior.

Calvin's mother, Jan, discussed his behavioral and emotional difficulties at school and home. Although he was progressing well academically, his teachers reported that he was frequently off task, inattentive, noncompliant, and unable to remain still in one place. He was easily frustrated and a sore loser in competitive situations; moreover, he had a tendency to blame and disparage himself when discouraged. The behavior problems that Jan cited as being most salient at home were noncompliance and a tendency to whine, cry, and throw tantrums when frustrated. Jan reported that her responses to Calvin's behavior were inconsistent—she acquiesced, ignored, demanded, yelled, or spanked depending upon her moods.

The parent training program was conducted in 6 small group sessions with 2 other families and in 4 individual sessions. It essentially followed the curriculum we have outlined above except that, because the children were younger, self-control techniques were not included and more emphasis was placed on behavior management. We targeted noncompliance and tantrums for intervention. Figure 9.1 shows the frequency of these two target behaviors, with daily counts averaged across weeks. For noncompliance, a treatment program was initiated in Week 3. It included giving clearer commands, removing reinforcement contingent upon noncompliance, and employing simple contracts to reinforce compliance. Over the 10 weeks noncompliance was reduced to approximately half of the baseline level. Jan noticed the improvement but felt that noncompliance was a problem she would like to reduce further. Calvin's teacher reported that he evidenced improved compliance at school as well as less out-of-seat behavior and improved play with peers.

We intended a multiple baseline design of staggered interventions, and targeted temper tantrums as the second behavior problem for intervention. In Week 5, we formally began a management program of simple contracts, antecedent control, differential reinforcement of desirable behavior, and removing reinforcers. However, Jan had actually begun to employ some of these strategies on her own with Calvin a week earlier. In any event, Figure 9.1 shows a marked drop in tantrums.

The Conners Rating Scale (Conners, 1973) is a widely used scale of 10 behaviors characterizing ADHD, each rated by the parent on a 0 to 3 scale. Calvin's pre to post-training scores decreased from 21 to 13, below the commonly accepted cut-off (15) for hyperactivity on this scale. A variation of this scale, the Iowa Conners Rating Scale (Loney & Milich, 1981), has two subscales tapping aggression and hyperactivity. Jan completed the Iowa Conners each week, and Figure 9.2 shows the decline on this measure that closely parallels the frequency counts of the key target behaviors.

Jan increased on the BVT-H from a score of 7 to 17, indicating good

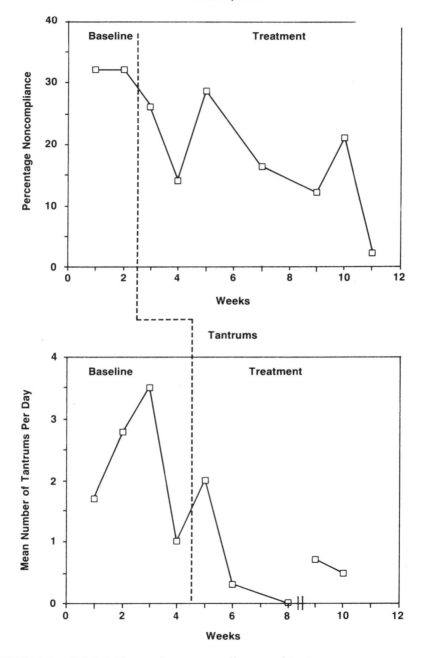

FIGURE 9.1: Calvin's change in non-compliance and tantrums.

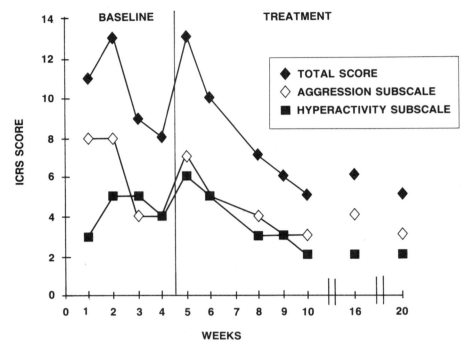

FIGURE 9.2   Calvin's data on the Conners Rating Scale.

behavioral knowledge, and at post-training she rated her own effectiveness in managing Calvin's behavior much higher. She reported
incorporating various behavior management principles and techniques
into her daily parenting, including increased use of praise, simple
contracts, clearer commands, more consistency, removing rewards
contingent upon misbehavior, and incorporating other family members
into behavioral management programs.

CLINICAL ISSUES

Early Intervention

Although parent training shows promise for families whose children
have difficulties with attention, activity, and conduct, there is still much to
be learned. A critical question concerns the child age at which such
programs might be fruitful. Because ADHD is typically diagnosed in
elementary school, the preponderance of research has involved children
between the ages of about 7 and 12. Yet, looking backwards, most families
can trace the behavioral abnormalities into the preschool years and

sometimes even infancy. It seems logical to begin intervention much earlier, when children and perhaps their parents are more pliable and, before the academic and social sequelae of ADHD make intervention more complex and difficult. There have been, however, few reported parent training programs for preschool-aged ADHD children (Pisterman et al., 1989).

One reason for this is that there are few diagnosed preschool children available. The natural high exuberance of preschoolers and the instability of behavioral difficulties in very young children make diagnosis risky. Even when problems are recognized, pediatricians and parents are reluctant to label the child so early, anticipating hopefully that "he'll grow out of it." Longitudinal studies, however, indicate that children at age 4 with ADHD-related behaviors are quite likely to retain these and be clinically diagnosed at age 6 (Campbell, Ewing, Breaux, & Szumowski, 1986).

Child Targets

Another important clinical question concerns the focus of intervention. Is there a key, a pivotal, behavior to target? It seems quite possible that if, within the myriad of behavioral difficulties drawn into the ADHD diagnosis, there is a key behavior to intervene with, then either the behavior or at least the approach to it might differ with child age. Again, we would conjecture that for the preschool child noncompliance may be pivotal and that a program for parents focused on behavior management may be very effective. For the older child, however, cognitive difficulties (e.g., social agendas, problem-solving) may be much more salient and a parent training program would have to concern itself with a much broader array of interventions.

Family Targets

Finally, and again related, we must ask whether behavioral parent training is too narrow an approach to family intervention for ADHD. Is broader intervention desirable, to alter adverse family characteristics that either contribute to the child's problem or may have resulted from it? As we noted earlier, there are some correlational reports of psychological difficulties in families with an ADHD child, but we know very little about how family factors contribute to the etiology or maintenance of ADHD or about how living with a child with such behaviors affects the family. Rather than producing a global therapy prescription for parents with a problem child, a promising strategy is to identify particular family characteristics that relate to parent training outcome and then tailor adjunct treatments to these.

Marital discord, for example, may be one such characteristic that interferes with outcome (Baker, et al., 1981; Cole & Morrow, 1976; Patterson, Cobb, & Ray, 1973), although not all investigators have found this relationship (Brody & Forehand, 1985; Oltmanns, Broderick, & O'Leary, 1977). Marital discord may interfere primarily with follow-through once the program is over (see Chapter 11). In a study that speaks directly to this issue, Dadds, Schwartz, and Sanders (1987) provided individual child management training to families whose preschool children manifested oppositional or conduct disorders. In addition, they designated 12 of the families as having marital discord and 12 as having no marital discord. Half of the families in each group also received 6 hours of partner support training (PST) focusing on marital conflict, communication, and problem-solving. By objective measures and maternal perceptions of child behavior, the conditions improved equally at post-training. At a 6-month follow-up the no-marital discord families sustained gains, whether or not they had had the adjunctive PST. In the high-marital discord families, however, only those with the PST showed sustained improvement, and families that did not have the adjunctive treatment showed some worsening.

A fruitful direction for further research on parent training for hyperactivity and related problems would be to develop and evaluate focused short-term treatments as Dadds, Schwartz, & Sanders (1987) have done. These would be targeted to specifiable child and family problem areas, such as child noncompliance, aggression, or problem-solving skills, and parent marital discord, anger management, or depression. Following a thorough assessment, then, the clinician could put together a package of specific treatments tailored to that family's needs.

Chapter 10

Autism

Stephen R. Anderson
The May Institute

Peter's babbling had not turned into speech by the time he was three. His play was solitary and repetitious. He tore paper into long thin strips, bushel baskets of it every day. He spun the lids from my canning jars and became upset if we tried to divert him. Only rarely could I catch his eye, and then saw his focus change from me to the reflection in my glasses. It was like trying to pick up mercury with chopsticks.

His adventures into our suburban neighbourhood had been unhappy. He had disregarded the universal rule that sand is to be kept in sand-boxes, and the children themselves had punished him. He walked around a sad and solitary figure, always carrying a toy aeroplane, a toy he never played with. At that time, I had not heard the word that was to dominate our lives, to hover over every conversation, to sit through every meal beside us. That word was autism. (Eberhardy, 1967, p. 258)

The rationale for training parents as teachers for their handicapped child is persuasive. There are far too few special education professionals and they are able to provide too few hours of child-centered therapy, often with little demonstration that newly taught skills have generalized to home and community. Possibly an even stronger argument for training parents can be made in the more specific case of autism. Although there is a rapidly growing empirical literature regarding the training of parents, few programs have been directed toward the very special problems of autistic children and their families.

AUTISM

While current definitions differ somewhat (American Psychiatric Association, 1987; Ritvo & Freeman, 1978; Rutter, 1978), the autistic syndrome generally is considered to include one or more of the following characteristics:(a) profound failure to relate to other persons; (b) impaired or delayed language acquisition and comprehension; (c) apparent sensory dysfunction; (d) stereotyped, repetitive mannerisms or self-stimulatory behaviors; (e) failure to develop normal, appropriate play; and (f) obsessive, ritualistic behavior that has been characterized as a profound resistance to change in the environment.

For many years, professionals believed that parents were the cause of their children's autism (Bettelheim, 1967). Parents were reported to be cold, detached, overly intellectual, and not capable of providing the necessary warmth for proper parent-child bonding. Thus, psychotherapy directed toward the parent was the recommended course of treatment. Unfortunately, this approach resulted in few educational services being directly applied to the child and eventually was shown to be without empirical basis (McAdoo & DeMyer, 1978).

A widely accepted alternative explanation is that autism is the result of a neurophysiological defect (Ornitz, 1985; Rimland, 1964). No factors in the social/psychological environment have been shown to cause autism. Moreover, the majority of autistic children earn IQ scores in the retarded range and these scores remain relatively unchanged over time (Freeman, Ritvo, Needleman, & Yokota, 1985). Difficulty in learning for these children is pervasive (Schreibman & Britten, 1984) and the acquisition of even very simple skills may require intensive, systematic intervention (Lovaas, Berberich, Perloff, & Schaeffer, 1966). These problems frequently are exacerbated by a general level of unmanageability (aggression, self-injury, noncompliance, and/or tantrums) that may interfere with the acquisition of adaptive skills. As a result, few autistic children remain in public school placements and many are in out-of-home placements (Rutter, 1970; Sherman, 1988).

Although slow to come, one product of changing views of etiology has been a shift in the focus of treatment from the parents as cause to the role of parents as teacher for the autistic child (e.g., Czyzewski, Christian, & Norris, 1982; Harris, 1982, 1983; Kozloff, 1973). The problems of autistic children and the impact on their families are pervasive, however, and make parent training a particularly difficult undertaking. Parents who would assume the role of teacher must confront the characteristic skill deficits and behavior excesses exhibited by autistic children, including an extreme resistance to change, unresponsiveness to social reinforcement, extreme attention deficits, significant communication delays, and self-stimulation, to name some most commonly present. Obligatory teaching situations often produce severe oppositional behaviors, including tantrums, self-injury, and aggression. Obviously, the degree of the child's disability and his or her resistance to management and instruction are likely to influence the parents' ability to apply and maintain teaching and behavior management skills.

PARENT TRAINING
APPROACHES

Despite these misgivings, there have been notable successes. Two often-cited studies provide support for the role of parents in the education and treatment of their autistic children. Lovaas, Koegel, Simmons, and Long (1973) obtained follow-up measures for two groups of autistic children who had received one year of intensive behavior therapy. The initial group received hospital-based training without parent involvement, and subsequently were placed in residential institutions. Follow-up measures taken 1 to 4 years after termination of treatment indicated that these children had failed to maintain the gains they originally achieved. By contrast, a second group of children whose parents were taught to implement behavior therapy, and who remained in their homes, continued to show improvements at follow-up. Although a number of factors could have influenced outcome here, parent involvement seemed worth pursuing.

Schreibman and Britten (1984) assigned families of autistic children to either a parent training or no parent training group. All children received clinic-based instruction provided by professionals. Although both groups of children improved, the children in the clinic-treatment-only group failed to generalize newly acquired skills to their mothers. A variety of measures designed to determine the impact of training on the families' daily activities also showed a significant difference. Those who participated in parent training expressed improvements in the quality of their leisure time activities. The authors concluded that training the parents as therapists had the potential for alleviating some of the negative impact of the child on the family's everyday lives (DeMyer, 1979).

In recent years, several authors have reported success in teaching parents to use behavioral techniques to address specific problems, but have also noted that parents often failed to generalize to other behaviors of the child (e.g., Koegel, Glahn, & Nieminen, 1978) or maintain skills after training had been discontinued (Harris, 1982). Some authors have suggested models for training parents in the generalized use of behavioral teaching and management methods (Harris, 1983; Koegel et al., 1978; Schopler & Reichler, 1971). They were concerned less with training specific strategies and behaviors and more with training parents in the use of behavioral principles that could be applied to a wide range of behaviors (adaptive and maladaptive) and conditions (McMahon, Forehand, & Griest, 1981). Such generalized applications may be necessary for parents to deal with the often unpredictable and resistant behavior patterns of their autistic child.

Koegel et al. (1978) found that modeling the use of behavioral techniques with an autistic child was effective in training parents how to teach the child; however, generalization to new target behaviors did not occur. For example, modeling how to teach imitation did not enable the parents to teach instruction-following to their children. In a second study, the authors demonstrated that when parent training was directed toward teaching the use of general behavior-modification procedures, the parents could apply the procedures to a wide variety of behaviors targeted for the child.

The one most common training model involves some form of group training with self-guided manuals, such as the Parents as Teachers program described in this monograph. When applied to the parents of autistic children, the group training model typically has been augmented by some level of home training or consultation (Czyzewski et al., 1982; Harris, 1982). Usually one of the group leaders visits the family and provides specific feedback on parent performance consistent with topics discussed in group meetings. This extension of the group training model may be necessary to effectively address the very special needs of autistic children and their families.

Turning to curricula, there are many similarities between those for parents of mentally retarded children (cf. Chapter 2) and those specified for parents of autistic children (Harris, 1983; Kozloff, 1973; Lovaas, 1981; McClannahan, Krantz, & McGee, 1982). On the other hand, with the parents of autistic children there seems to be a stronger emphasis on strategies for dealing with maladaptive behaviors, the need to provide nearly continuous training to the child, and the role of parents as co-therapists for their child's education and treatment (e.g., Schopler & Reichler, 1971).

In general, the more severe the child's handicap (particularly the child's language deficit), the more likely it is that associated features of autism will be present. These include stereotyped behavior, self-injury, aggression, and sleeping, drinking, and eating problems. Most parent training programs include training in the use of specific behavior reduction strategies, typically involving reinforcement of nonspecific alternative behaviors (e.g., absence of aggression) and the delivery of a consequence likely to decrease the occurrence of the problem behavior (punishment). More recently, research with autistic children has focused on variables that might maintain the problem behavior (e.g., escape from instructional demands). The goal of this approach is to replace the problem behavior with socially appropriate behaviors such as functional communication (Carr & Durand, 1985). The newly established verbal response may obviate the child's need to use inappropriate behavior.

Thus, the training curriculum for parents begins to resemble a curriculum for teachers (e.g., discrete trials methods, writing goals and objectives, developing task-analyzed training programs, functionally identifying variables maintaining behavior problems, and obtaining and interpreting data). Harris (1983) has suggested that training to a lesser level of competence could result in considerable ongoing involvement with the trainers.

Two groups of researchers have investigated an alternative model to group training—home-based training for families with autistic children. Their models differ from previously reported parent training efforts along several dimensions: (a) the emphasis on home rather than center-based training, (b) the use of an individual training format rather than group instruction, and (c) the length of the intervention period. Both programs have done considerable evaluation.

INTENSIVE HOME-BASED TRAINING

Lovaas' Young Autism Project

A recently published article by Lovaas (1987) provides a description of an intensive home-based training model for autistic children and their families. Critical features of the program include: (a) early identification and treatment of autistic children, (b) intensive application of behavior teaching technique and treatment procedure, (c) training conducted in the child's natural home, and (d) extensive parent training allowing the parents eventually to serve as primary teachers for their autistic child. The model differs from earlier attempts to educate autistic children primarily in the intensity of the training provided (i.e., 40 hours or more per week) and the length of the intervention (2 years or more). It also differed from other studies in its emphasis on home-based rather than center-based training and its focus on training parents as co-therapists.

Lovaas (1987) assigned preschool-aged, autistic children to one of two groups: an Intensive-Treatment Group that received more than 40 hours of one-on-one treatment per week or a Minimal- Treatment Control Group that received 10 hours or less of one-on-one treatment per week. Each child in the experimental group was assigned several well-trained student therapists who worked with the child and the parents in the home for 2 or more years. Lovaas reported that the child's parents worked as part of the treatment team throughout the intervention and were extensively trained in the treatment procedures, although details of the training for parents were not provided.

Lovaas employed behavioral training and treatment procedures with the children initially to reduce self-stimulatory and aggressive behaviors while simultaneously addressing early development skills such as play with toys, compliance to simple requests, and motor imitation. Later training sessions emphasized expressive language, interactive play with peers, and academic and social behaviors. Pre-treatment measures revealed no significant differences between treatment and control groups. However, post-treatment data indicated that 9 of 19 (47%) children in the experimental group "recovered." These 9 children were reported to have achieved normal intellectual and educational functioning in the first grade. In contrast, only 2% of the children in the control group met this criterion.

Of particular interest is a follow-up study conducted when these children reached a mean age of 13 years (Lovaas, Smith, & McEachin, 1989; McEachin, 1987). The best outcome cases were evaluated on the Wechsler Intelligence Scale for Children-Revised, the Personality Inventory for Children, the Vineland Adaptive Behavior Scales, and a clinical interview. Evaluation was done by clinicians blind to the children's prior history; these cases were intermixed with children who had no history of psychological disturbance. At this point, 8 of the 19 experimental group subjects were indistinguishable from the comparison group.

These impressive results provide encouragement that children with autism, whatever its causes, can be helped. They indicate, though, that progress may only result from a much more structured and intensive effort than one finds in most parent training programs. The model relied on a large population of university students to serve as home therapists, providing massive hours of training over a long intervention period. To make such a model feasible in the service delivery system, one important question is whether similar effects could be realized by using significantly fewer staff, providing fewer hours over a shorter intervention period. Moreover, could parents have involvement sufficient to allow them to eventually take over from the home therapist and themselves serve as home teacher/therapist for their autistic children?

Anderson et al. Intensive Home-Based Model

At The May Institute, we have developed and evaluated a cost-effective model for providing intensive home-based intervention (Anderson, Avery, Dipietro, Edwards, & Christian, 1987). The goal was to replicate the critical features of the Lovaas model (i.e., early identification, home-based training, use of behavioral teaching technique, parent training) and to investigate a possibly more practical application of the model. The most significant changes included greater involvement of parents to provide most of the day-to-day programming for their child at home and fewer home therapists providing fewer hours of in-home service.

Program description

A therapist is assigned to an individual child and his or her family 20 hours a week. Fifteen hours are devoted to direct instruction with parents and child and 5 hours are for program development and planning. The home therapists are individuals with Bachelor's or Master's-level education in psychology, special education, speech, or early childhood education. Prior to working with the children and their families, the therapists receive extensive training in the use of behavioral teaching technique and treatment procedures.

The major focus of the program is to train the parents in the skills necessary to effectively manage maladaptive behaviors and to teach new adaptive skills to their autistic child. Their involvement proceeds gradually from observer to primary therapist for their child's home-based program. As part of their contract with the program, parents agree to be involved in training at least 50% of the time that the therapist is in the home and to devote a minimum of 10 hours per week to training at other times. The total involvement of one or both parents together is 15 to 25 hours per week. Parents also receive one or more training manuals from *Steps to Independence* (or earlier manuals; see Chapter 2) and Lovaas' (1981) *Teaching Developmentally Disabled Children*. These help to acquaint them with basic principles of learning theory, terms, and specific strategies for managing behavior and teaching new skills.

Parent participation begins by helping the home therapist complete a behavioral assessment of the child and to develop specific goals and objectives for training in each of the major developmental areas: language, social/behavioral, pre-academic, play, and self-help. Progress toward the completion of these objectives is monitored continuously through reliably obtained measures collected by therapist and parents.

One area of focus is to train the parents in the use of behavioral techniques to teach adaptive skills to their autistic child, most notably the use of discrete trials methods (Koegel et al., 1978; Koegel, Rincover, & Egel, 1982). This training includes skills that would enable them to (a) correctly arrange the training environment to eliminate extraneous and potentially distracting stimuli, (b) provide clear and concise instructions, (c) use effective prompts, and (d) deliver unambiguous and immediate rewards. This training occurs within the context of teaching readiness skills to the child such as eye contact on command, appropriate sitting in a chair, motor imitation, and compliance with simple instructions (e.g., sit down, come here).

The therapist begins most training sessions by providing a description and rationale for the use of a specific teaching procedure, then modeling its use with the child. The therapist next asks the parent to demonstrate the use of the procedure while the therapist provides verbal feedback regarding the parent's performance. In most instances, these occasions are the child's first exposure to an obligatory teaching situation; thus, oppositional behaviors often occur (e.g., tantrums, out-of-seat, aggression).

In addition, many of these children have persistent, severe behavior problems. The parents are taught the general problem-solving approach outlined in Table 10.1 to address these. An important step in the sequence is the functional analysis of variables (antecedent and consequence) that may set the occasion for or maintain the problem behavior. Based upon this assessment, the parents develop specific programs designed to teach acceptable alternative responses and to discourage the problem behavior. The therapist helps the parents design programs that first evaluate the use of the least intrusive methods (e.g., differential reinforcement of other behavior, teaching acceptable forms of communication) before considering more intrusive interventions (e.g., punishment). The use of corporal punishment methods is strongly discouraged and never modeled by the therapist.

Modified versions of the Parent and Child's Games described by Forehand and McMahon (1981) are also used to teach attending and praising skills. During the Child's Game, the parents are instructed to provide a variety of toys and materials and to describe the child's actions

TABLE 10.1

Steps in Behavior Problem Management

1. Specify the behavior problem
2. Define the behavior in observable terms
3. Determine a measurement strategy
4. Obtain a baseline measure
5. Analyze the A-B-C pattern
6. Change antecedents

   Establish clear rules
   Provide concise instructions
   Develop a schedule of activities
   Teach alternate forms of communication
   Teach prerequisite skills
   Reinforce acceptable behavior
7. Change consequences

   Add a reinforcer
   Remove a reinforcer (e.g., timeout, response cost)
   Add a punisher (e.g., positive practice, overcorrection)
8. Continue to evaluate

(e.g., You're picking up the blue block). They are also asked to restrict the use of questions and instructions and to ignore inappropriate behaviors by removing toys, containing the child in the defined area, and turning away until the child is quiet. After modeling the appropriate procedures, the therapist gives the parents an opportunity to conduct the session and provides feedback. When a specified performance criterion is achieved, the therapist begins the Parent's Game. In these sessions, the parents learn to add praise to their descriptive statements, to give clear and concise instructions, and to provide effective consequences for inappropriate responses. In the Parent's Game, unlike the Child's Game, the parents attempt to structure the content and pace of the training sessions for the child.

As the parents demonstrate the ability to use the teaching and management strategies correctly, they are instructed to apply the procedures whenever appropriate throughout the child's day and night. The parents and therapist also agree upon a small group of programs that the parents are to conduct outside of the time that the therapist is in the home. The parents are required to maintain a record of these sessions and to share that information with the therapist during the next home visit.

Evaluation Sample

Although over 50 children have participated in the program during a 4-year period, we will consider here the first 14 children and their families, which were studied extensively. The primary source for the identification of participants for the program was the Developmental Evaluation Clinic at Children's Hospital in Boston. Criteria for acceptance were based on a diagnosis of autism (or autistic-like behavior), age (less than 6 years), parents' willingness to participate, and geographic proximity to the clinic (within a 35-mile radius). The mean age of the child at the time of admission was 43 months (range: 18 to 64 months).

The children exhibited behaviors representative of the definition of autism provided by the American Psychiatric Association in *Diagnostic and Statistical Manual* (III-R) (1987) including the following primary and associated features: (a) lack of responsiveness to other people (93% exhibited gaze aversion); (b) impairments in communication (43% were nonverbal and 50% exhibited echolalia); (c) bizarre responses to the environment (86% resisted change and 86% engaged in self-stimulatory behaviors); (d) aggression (43%); (e) self-injury (50%); (f) noncompliance with instruction (93%); and (g) severe tantrums (100%). The children all lived at home with their natural parents. Eleven of the children also participated in preschool programs provided by their local public schools.

An analysis of the socioeconomic level of the families suggested that the major provider was likely to be engaged in a supervisory or professional occupation, had at least a high school degree, and lived in an area in which the per capita income was average or above. All but one of the children were from two-parent families. Mothers were the primary participants for 11 of the 14 families and fathers and mothers participated equally in the remaining families. Each child and family participated a minimum of 1 year in the study. Six of the 14 children had finished a second year at the time that the study was completed.

Parent Outcomes

The parents' ability to use behavioral teaching techniques was measured prior to intervention, after 6 months of participation in the study, and again after 12 months of participation. Trained observers viewed 5-minute videotaped samples of the parents conducting a specific training program (e.g., training motor imitation). The observers coded in 30-second intervals whether the parents provided clear and concise instructions, effective prompts, and immediate consequences (Koegel et al., 1977). The performance of the mothers only was evaluated.

Figure 10.1 shows the dramatic improvement in parents' ability to use behavioral teaching techniques correctly from baseline to 6 months in the program; all gains were significant by t-tests ($p < .01$). Parents maintained their correct use of the techniques at the second evaluation after 12 months of participation.

Another measure of the effectiveness of parent training was an assessment of the parents' knowledge of behavioral teaching principles as measured by the Behavioral Vignettes Test (see Chapter 4 and Appendix B). After a year or more in the program parents averaged a score of 15.4—they chose the correct course of action over 77% of the time. These scores were slightly higher than those parents obtained following the shorter Parents as Teachers group program (see Chapter 4).

Child Outcomes

Measures were also collected on a variety of behaviors exhibited by the children. One measure of child performance was gains in standardized test scores yielded by annual psychological and speech and language evaluations. Mental-age, social-age, and language-age scores were obtained for each child before the program began and after 1 year; for some children 2-year scores were also obtained. The children gained significantly ($p < .01$) on all measures after 1 year of participation. On the mental-age scores, for example, 46% of the children gained at least 12 months, although the range of scores varied significantly (see Anderson et al., 1987, for a complete analysis of these data). Significant changes were also obtained between the first and second year scores on all measures for

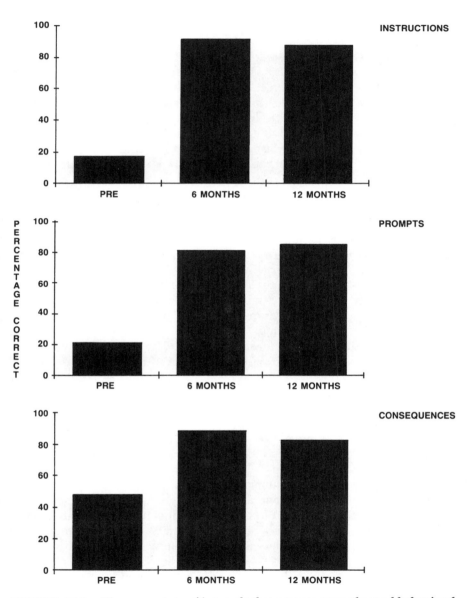

FIGURE 10.1:   The percentage of intervals that parents correctly used behavioral teaching procedures: clear instructions, effective prompts, and immediate consequences.

the children who completed a full second year and for whom test scores were available.

Another measure of program effectiveness was the children's progress on the Uniform Performance Assessment System (UPAS) (White, Edgar, Haring, Afflick, & Hayden, 1978), a norm-referenced assessment instrument that lists skills in a normal developmental sequence. Performance was assessed by determining where in the sequence each child fell. The results of the communication, social/self-help, and pre-academic sections were used to evaluate treatment effects. Scores obtained by the completion of the UPAS also indicate that the intervention produced statistically significant changes ($p < .005$) in the children's performance between pre- and Year 1 scores (Anderson et al., 1987).

Although changes were statistically significant, we could not conclude with confidence that positive changes in the children's test scores were a result of the treatment intervention. Therefore, the data were subjected to further analysis to determine whether the children exhibited more rapid development during the intervention period. Developmental ratios were established by dividing changes in test scores by the number of months elapsed since birth or last assessment. A higher developmental ratio score following a period of intervention (typically 12 months) would indicate an accelerated period of learning. Figure 10.2 provides a summary of developmental ratio scores (group means). The figure shows higher developmental ratios for the first year of intervention when compared to pre-intervention ratio scores. Second year gains by this measure were less impressive but still somewhat greater than pre-intervention developmental ratio scores.

A third area of potential improvement was progress made by the children on their individualized sequence of behavioral objectives. The trainers and parents recorded correct and incorrect responses of the children across trials or steps of each program, as well as frequency, duration, or time sampling of maladaptive behaviors. A summary of these data indicate that 274 behavioral objectives were achieved by the 14 subjects during the first year of participation (mean: 20 per child; range: 7 to 29 per child). Similar results were obtained after two years of intervention with 85 objectives achieved (mean: 17 per child; range: 10 to 30 per child).

Although most of the children clearly improved and several achieved partial integration with nonhandicapped peers, none of the children "recovered" as defined by Lovaas (1987) (i.e., tested in the normal range of intelligence and were fully integrated in a classroom with nonhandicapped peers). This disparity may be attributable to three distinct features of this program when compared to Lovaas' program: (a) the children were on the average older and exhibited lower mental age scores at entry; (b)

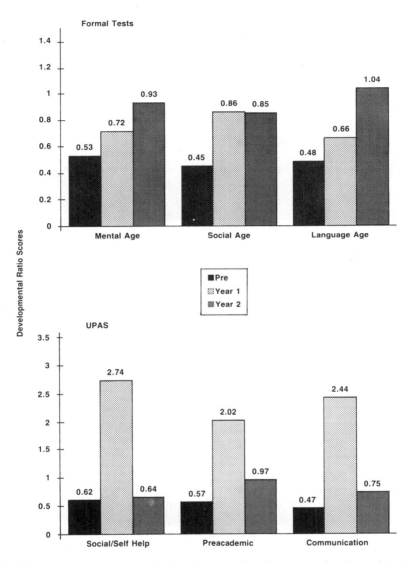

FIGURE 10.2: A summary of developmental ratio scores for formal tests of mental, social, and language development, as well as progress on the Uniform Performance Assessment System. Bars represent group scores for all subjects prior to intervention and after 1 and 2 years of participation in the study.

children received fewer hours of training provided over a shorter intervention period; and (c) strong aversive procedures were not used to control maladaptive behaviors (Lovaas reports using some physical aversives to control interfering behaviors). It is possible that one or more of these differences may explain the discrepancy between the results of the two studies.

A CASE STUDY OF AMBER

Amber was first seen by our agency when she was 4 years, 1 month old. Amber had been a full term baby and there were no unusual circumstances surrounding the prenatal period or delivery. She seemed to develop normally until about age 18 months, when her mother became concerned about Amber's poor eye contact, social unresponsiveness, and delayed language development. Amber was referred to our agency by her teacher who was not able to manage her in the classroom.

When we first observed Amber in our clinic setting, she was extremely resistant to our prompts to engage her in play activities or social interactions. She frequently echoed words or phrases that she had previously heard and rarely used language in an appropriate, clearly functional manner. At home, she refused to sit down to eat, would spend long periods of time gazing at lights, played in a perseverative, nonfunctional manner with strings, and ran repeatedly back and forth across the house. She was often aggressive toward her mother, who primarily used sharp reprimands and strong physical prompts in an attempt to control Amber's disruptive behaviors.

Initially, most training sessions were conducted in Amber's bedroom. The home therapist and Amber's mother began by conducting short training sessions to improve Amber's ability to remain seated in a chair, to provide eye contact on command, to follow several simple instructions, and to imitate motor demonstrations of an adult. During these sessions, Amber's mother was taught to use behavioral teaching techniques, including giving clear and concise instructions, using effective prompts, and providing immediate reinforcing consequences. During the initial days of Amber's training, her mother correctly applied behavioral teaching methods on only 11% of the opportunities observed. After 6 months of training her accuracy had improved to 93% of the opportunities and this level was maintained at a 12-month follow-up observation.

During the initial weeks of her participation, Amber's mother began to understand that she needed to clearly establish limits for Amber's behavior and to consistently enforce those limits. By the end of a few weeks, Amber exhibited a marked improvement in her behavior (more compliance with instruction) and her mother began to apply teaching and management strategies in less structured situations (e.g., mealtimes). Amber's mother developed and introduced programs to teach a variety of adaptive skills, including dressing and undressing, object identification and matching, and labeling.

To illustrate the session-by-session observations that were taken during all programs, Figure 10.3 provides a multiple baseline analysis of Amber's acquisition of simple motor imitation. The figure represents the percentage of trials that Amber correctly matched the motor demonstra-

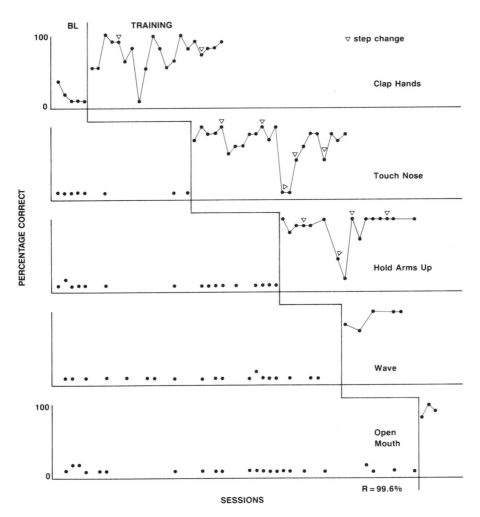

FIGURE 10.3: A multiple baseline analysis of Amber's acquisition of motor imitation. Points represent the percentage of correct responses by session. The arrows note the points at which program step changes occurred. The staggered vertical line indicates the point at which training was introduced for each modeled response.

tion modeled by her mother or the therapist. The staggered vertical line indicates the point at which intervention occurred for each item. The therapist and mother consulted regularly with Amber's teacher about the programs that were being conducted at home and provided advice about strategies to be applied at school.

DISCUSSION

There remains little argument among researchers regarding the important role parents have in the education and treatment of autistic children. Furthermore, there seems to be a general concensus that parent education can also lessen the often debilitating effects of an autistic child on the family system. Nevertheless, many questions remain unanswered.

What training model is best? The literature suggests that the group training model has been effective in teaching parents (see Chapter 4), although some authors have pointed to the possible significance of also incorporating home visits (e.g., Harris, 1983). Unfortunately, studies that have compared teaching formats most often have assessed gains in knowledge (i.e., results on a paper and pencil test) rather than actual teaching competencies with the child. Furthermore, these studies typically provided outcome data only on parent behavior and did not examine the impact of their training efforts on the child's behavior, obviously the ultimate training goal.

The individualized home training format has many distinct advantages over group training because of the potential flexibility of the model and the opportunity to observe directly the interactions between the parent and child. It is easier to teach some behaviors as the situation arises rather than to rely on simulated, highly contrived conditions. Individual instruction also affords an opportunity for the parent to participate in the application of behavior training and treatment procedures across a broad range of skill deficits and behavioral excesses of the child, thus increasing the possibility of generalization (Stokes & Baer, 1977).

In the home-based training studies described herein, parents and children participated in the program a minimum of one year and in some cases several years (Lovaas, 1987). Further analysis will be required to determine the ideal length of the intervention period and the potential risks and benefits to the family. Long intervention periods may be important for children with significant developmental delays. However, there are the dual risks of overburdening the parents and/or unwittingly fostering parental dependency.

At what age should training begin? Many authors have emphasized the importance of early identification and treatment of autistic children (Christian, 1981; Fenske, Zalenski, Krantz, & McClannahan, 1985). They argued that it is easier to teach social and language skills effectively to younger children, as well as to manage undesirable behaviors that compete with the acquisition of new skills. It might also be argued that the parents of younger autistic children may be more willing to devote the amount of time and energy needed to ensure the development and elaboration of skills at home and to recognize that their training efforts are making a difference in the child's development. Many parents of older autistic children have experienced years of unsuccessfully managing and teaching their children. This history has made some of them wary of professionals and pessimistic about their ability to parent their children effectively.

Should parents be educated in the use of physical punishment to control maladaptive behavior? Although most professionals would agree that reduction of behavior problems is an important step in the education of autistic children, there has been considerable recent debate over the use of physical punishments. Some psychologists argue that brief aversive stimuli may be justified for children who have not responded to nonaversive techniques. Others believe that the use of such aversives under any circumstances is dehumanizing and unethical. No doubt, most professionals would agree that parents should receive training adequate to allow them to select and effectively use nonaversive techniques. Unfortunately, much additional research and development will be necessary before one can safely conclude that punishment should never be used. Until such time, parents should be equipped with a clear understanding of the risks and benefits of all available treatment strategies. Again, the individual home training format may have distinct advantages in its opportunity to observe and provide immediate feedback to parents regarding their treatment decisions.

The recent programs by Lovaas and Anderson and their colleagues that we have described provide encouraging support for the impact of intensive home-based training on the development of young autistic children. Although both programs report very positive results, the effects reported by Lovaas are greater. Age at admission, mental age levels, and the intensity of the training program (number of hours and length of the intervention period) are possible reasons for the differential effects. Further study will be required to experimentally isolate the critical variables.

Unit IV

Broader Issues

"Sometime after Nicholas had started nursery school, I saw a videotape that demonstrated what Dr. [Berry] Brazelton calls the irresistible responsiveness of a premature baby. I almost cried while I watched as a 3 lb. preemie slowly followed a ball with his eyes, looking for the sound of his mother's voice, and with heroic effort, finally turned his head and even reached for her. A nurse practitioner had taught that mother to read the subtle clues that would have drawn me to my son so much earlier. It was a piece of information, a teachable skill, that might have changed the course of our lives." (Ann Oster, 1984, p. 31).

───────────────

This mother's reflections highlight two critical issues. She muses about the impact on her and her family that might have been—had she learned a particular "teachable skill." But, sadly, she notes that for her the right service simply was not there when she needed it. These are the issues that we will address in Unit 4: the broader impact of parent training on the family and the availability of such services to families.

In Chapter 11 we widen our lens a bit to examine the impact of parent training programs on the family. Thus far we have concentrated on describing programs and examining whether they deliver what they promise to deliver. We have found encouraging evidence that parents learn not only a new vocabulary but also an array of teaching skills to go along with it, and that their children take small but valued steps toward independence. But, we wonder, in the words of the song: Is that all there is? It seems reasonable that parent training might have a broader impact on the family for better or even, perhaps, for worse. In Chapter 12, we explore the role that fathers, brothers, and sisters play in training programs, for despite our discussion of "parents" and "families," our focus in the preceding chapters has really been almost exclusively on mothers.

In Chapter 13 we present several efforts to disseminate the Parents as Teachers program to other agencies. Benefits of parent training are of little consequence if these programs are not available to families. We have two concerns here. First, despite the promise of the literature and the mandates of legislation, a typical family with a child who is handicapped often cannot find an accessible program that will teach them instructional and behavior management skills. Second, many programs in this subarea of the mental health field share the unfortunate tendency of the broader field, to provide services that reflect the service provider's personal philosophy and predispositions more than empirical evidence.

In Chapter 14 we conclude the monograph with a summary of our research findings. We have organized these around several critical questions that have implications for service delivery.

Chapter 11

Impact on the Family

With all of the successes we have reviewed, questions linger about parent training and the family. Although we know that most mothers increase in behavioral expertise following training, we know very little about other emanative effects of this experience—on more elusive dimensions like attitudes and adjustment.

There is widespread belief among professionals involved in parent training that these programs benefit families in multiple ways. Beyond the specific gains in parent teaching and child learning that are customarily assessed, generalized effects are assumed. In Chapter 2, for example, we voiced hopeful expectations that parents' attitudes toward the child improve, self-esteem and confidence in the parenting role increase, the family works better together and perhaps communicates with the school better, and other children benefit indirectly. It even seems possible that families with more teaching and behavior management skills would be less stressed and in turn less likely to consider out-of-home placement for the child.

And yet, voices of caution have begun to be raised. Some observers point out that training programs and other parent involvements sometimes make many excessive or inappropriate demands on parents. Perhaps in some cases, they argue, the parent-child relationship becomes disturbed or the perceived burden of raising a handicapped child is increased (Benson & Turnbull, 1986; Featherstone, 1980; Foster, Berger, & McLean, 1981). Turnbull and Turnbull (1982) argued that parents' rights to involvement are being distorted into excessive program demands, and cited interviews with parents who expressed a desire not to be involved in their child's schooling (Winton & Turnbull, 1981).

Speaking specifically about parent training, Allen and Hudd (1987) stated that when parents are placed in the role of direct teacher and expected to carry out a prescribed curriculum, they often feel uncomfortable and may become frustrated if the child does not show progress. More extreme critics draw a picture of parent trainers as all-knowing professionals pushing training upon unwilling parents and acting as if parents are without skills (Lyon & Preis, 1983). These authors also conjecture that preoccupation with training has probably inhibited many parents from other involvements in their child's life, and that parent trainers insensitive to the family system have been intrusive to the family (Lyon & Preis, 1983). The case is summed up by Gallagher, Beckman, and Cross (1983), who advised that "professionals should consider whether asking parents to participate actively in the child's treatment by carrying out specific program activities may not, in fact, impose additional stress on the family" (p. 16).

There is actually very little evidence available on either side of this issue. Critics' arguments have been based upon personal opinions and observations or interviews with selected parents. Proponents' arguments also have been based upon limited data. The behavioral tradition and its emphasis on assessing specific behaviors has eschewed measures that take a broader look at constructs such as attitudes, mood, or stress, although we have noted the recent attention to the social validity of interventions and to parents' satisfaction with them (Chapter 4).

Griest and Forehand (1982) used the term *family generalization* to refer to changes that occur in the areas of parents' personal and marital adjustment as well as extrafamilial interactions when the focus of treatment is strictly on parent-child behavior. The several studies that have examined family generalization have trained parents with conduct-problem children and usually employed a one-on-one model. These studies have been consistent in noting *positive* post-training changes, among them positively changed attitudes (Forrest, Holland, Daly, & Fellbaum, 1984; Omizo, Williams, & Omizo, 1986; Tavormina, 1975), decreased depression (Forehand, Wells, & Griest, 1980; Webster-Stratton, 1985b), and increased family cohesion (Karoly & Rosenthal, 1977).

There is virtually no evidence, however, about generalized changes in families with a child who is developmentally disabled. Unlike families coping with problem behaviors and reacting to the successful modification of one salient target behavior, these families must cope with a more complex and lifelong adjustment to disability. Generalized changes may be less clear. We have begun to study family generalization following parent training by obtaining psychological measures in two programs: our Parents as Teachers program for families with a child who is retarded, and the program considered in Chapter 9 for families with a child who is hyperactive.

GENERALIZATION: FAMILIES
WITH A CHILD WHO IS
RETARDED

We assessed 49 primary parents (all but 4 were mothers) before and after the 3-month training program on measures of depression, family stress, family adaptability and cohesion, and satisfaction with the family (Baker, Landen & Kashima, 1989). We will examine each in turn.

Depression

Parents of retarded children are thought by some to be at heightened risk of depression (Cummings, Bayley, & Rie, 1966). Olshanksy (1962), in an often-cited paper, even posited a lasting state in these families that he called *chronic sorrow*, which can be exacerbated by significant lifestages or stressors. Following the critics of parent training, it seemed possible that for some families teaching requirements would increase the burden of care, or that less-than-ideal outcomes would elicit feelings of failure or pessimism, contrasting the optimistic goals of the program with less successful realities. These stresses might lead in turn to increased depression.

A self-report mood inventory can give only a limited perspective on depression, but we felt that it would at least be indicative if major changes occurred. We employed the Beck Depression Inventory (BDI) (Beck, Ward, Mendelson, Mock, & Erbaugh, 1961), a 21-item self-report questionnaire in a multiple choice format that assesses cognitive, affective, and physiological symptoms of depression. In this sample, Beck Depression Inventory scores were reasonably stable (r pre-post $= .65$) but decreased significantly, from 7.0 to 5.0 (t (40) $= 2.58$, $p < .05$). Considered another way, 4 parents before and only 1 parent after training scored 16 or above, the cutoff commonly used to designate moderate depression. On the BDI, then, changes in mood following parent training were small but in a positive direction, consistent with findings in families with conduct disordered children cited above.

Stress

There is considerable evidence of chronic heightened stress in families with a retarded child, especially around issues related to the child (Blacher, 1984a; Crnic, Friedrich, & Greenberg, 1983). Holroyd (1974) developed the Questionnaire on Resources and Stress, a widely researched self-report measure of stress and attitudes related to a developmentally disabled child. Several authors have derived shorter forms, most notably the 53-item QRS-F by Friedrich and his colleagues (Friedrich, Greenberg, & Crnic, 1983). The QRS-F yields a total score and four subscales derived from factor analysis: parent and family problems, pessimism, child characteristics, and physical incapacitation.

We reasoned that this measure would directly tap the iatrogenic effects of parent training that have been posited. Perceived burden and stress on the family is reflected in the first factor, pessimism about the child's progress and future is reflected in the second factor, and frustration about teaching the child is reflected in the third factor. When we examined QRS-F scores, however, they were very stable, with pre-post correlations ranging from $r = .73$ to $r = .86$ for the subscales. Parents' mean scores decreased slightly on all scales except pessimism, which remained the same. The decreases were significant for the parent and family problems subscale (t (42) = 2.75, $p < .01$) and for the total QRS-F score (t (40) = 2.44, $p < .05$). In sum, on this measure that is frequently used with families of handicapped children, our parents reported lower levels of stress following their training experience.

Cohesion and Adaptability

In addition to the negatively toned dimensions of depression and stress, we wanted to assess normal family processes that might be impacted upon by parent training. We were particularly interested in a conceptualization by Olson, Russell, and Sprenkle (1983; Olson, Sprenkle, & Russell, 1979), who clustered more than 50 family systems concepts and postulated two salient dimensions: cohesion and adaptability. They define cohesion as the emotional bonding family members have toward one another. Adaptability is the capacity of the family system to change its power structure, role relations, and relationship rules in response to situational and developmental stress.

Olson and his associates developed the 30-item Family Adaptability and Cohesion Evaluation Scales (FACES) that gives separate scores for adaptability and cohesion (Olson et al., 1982). They hypothesized curvilinear relationships between each of these dimensions and optimal family functioning, so the best adjusted, or balanced, families would fall in the middle of each scale. On the cohesion dimension, families need a balance between too much closeness (enmeshed system) and too little closeness (disengaged system). On the adaptability dimension, families need a balance between too much change (chaotic system) and too little change (rigid system). There is some validation of this measure; for example, in a study of single-parent families with teenagers, those with a delinquent child were much more likely to score at the extreme on one or both FACES dimensions, while families with a nondelinquent child were practically all balanced in the middle (Rodick, Henggeler, & Hanson, 1986). However, there has been very little study of pre-post intervention changes on these dimensions of family functioning.

Although we felt that parent training might impact on the family system, FACES scores were, in fact, highly stable from pre- to post- for both adaptability ($r = .86$) and cohesion ($r = .76$). Moreover, pre- and post- group means were almost identical. On this measure, though, stable means could reflect no change, movement from both extremes toward the balanced middle, or movement toward the extremes. We analyzed individual difference scores from the midpoint in Olson's norms (1982) and found no consistent movement of families toward greater or lesser balance.

Satisfaction with the Family

A related dimension of interest is the parent's satisfaction with the family. We did not assess marital satisfaction after training. However, Olson et al. (1982) proposed an index of family satisfaction derived from the FACES. They advised having family members complete the measure twice at each administration, to describe first how they perceive the family (Actual) and then how they would like the family to be (Ideal). The discrepancies between actual and ideal scores provided indices of satisfaction with the family's adaptability and cohesion. We analyzed the absolute difference between actual and ideal scores for parents. This "satisfaction index" improved significantly for adaptability (t (39) = 2.54, $p < .05$). In sum, then, while parents did not perceive family adaptability or cohesion differently following training, they were more satisfied with the family's level of adaptability.

Satisfaction with Training

Finally, in the event that parents were harmed or helped by parent training in ways not detected by our other measures, we wanted to more globally assess satisfaction with the training experience. We reported consumer evaluations from this group of parents in Chapter 4 (Table 4.1), and will recall them just briefly here. In their self-assessment of participation, almost all parents responded that they had met most or all of the home teaching requirements, but fewer than half had met most or all of the requirements for recordkeeping. It would seem that, in a voluntary program such as this one, some parents avoid becoming burdened by assignments by simply not doing them! At the end of training, most parents reported feeling confident or very confident in their ability to teach their child. Every parent rated the approach used as appropriate or very appropriate for their family and every parent said she or he would recommend the program much or very much to other families.

GENERALIZATION: FAMILIES
WITH A CHILD WHO IS
HYPERACTIVE

In Chapter 9 we described a training program for parents of schoolaged hyperactive children. We assessed these mothers and fathers pre and post-training on the Beck Depression Inventory, FACES, and Locke-Wallace Marital Adjustment Test. We have combined data from both parents here because the group and individual training program was directed as much toward fathers as toward mothers.

Scores on the psychological measures either remained the same or showed small positive changes, as they had for families with retarded children. Depression scores decreased slightly, but not significantly. On the FACES, there were significant increases in both adaptability (t (45) = 4.10, $p < .001$) and cohesiveness (t (45) = 2.17, $p < .05$). Parents' scores changed in the direction of moving toward the normative sample mean—toward more balance. As in the mental retardation sample, the satisfaction index for adaptability improved significantly (t (43) = 2.16, $p < .05$). The marital adjustment test scores were stable (r pre-post = .84) and the means did not change.

CONSIDERATIONS

Our studies of generalized effects turned up no evidence of adverse effects, such as experiencing increased family stress or perceiving greater burden. The programs for parents of retarded children and hyperactive children had good social validity; parents evaluated the behavioral approach employed as very appropriate for their families and evaluated the program very highly on a number of dimensions. Post-training psychological measures either remained the same or changed in a positive direction. In one or both samples there were small but statistically significant improvements in reports of symptoms of depression, parent and family problems, overall family stress, family adaptability and cohesion, and satisfaction with the family's adaptability.

These findings are only suggestive, however. Three factors limit their generalizability. First, these studies did not assess untrained control parents to determine whether scores on these psychological measures tend to improve with repeated testing. Although we must await a controlled study to determine whether the improvements found were real and not a measurement artifact, we can at least conclude that families did not change for the worse.

Second, we only examined families that had completed training. A reasonable argument would be that the casualties of a voluntary parent training program are to be found not in the completers but in dropouts—that those who find the program burdensome would leave it. We did not retest dropouts, but this would seem advisable if possible. We should note, however, that practically all dropouts in voluntary parent training programs leave early, after one or several sessions (Dangel & Polster, 1984), before any or much home teaching has taken place. Although some of these families may not feel comfortable with the training approach, it is unlikely they have suffered any significant burden from such brief involvement. Moreover, in the hyperactivity sample all families completed training, and the results were comparable to those of the Los Angeles III sample.

Third, our evaluation has been limited to two rather similar, time-limited group parent training programs that did not make heavy demands on families. They met for only 9 and 12 sessions. Instead of lengthy formal teaching, homework for parents involved about 10 or 15 minutes with the child for 3 or 4 days a week, as well as some reading and record keeping. Attendance did not interfere with jobs, because the groups met in the evenings or at several optional times throughout the day, and the Los Angeles III program provided child care. Participation in this program was voluntary. Although we might have hypothesized more negative effects in the required hyperactivity program, this did not occur. The group nature of both programs and the accompanying individual sessions may have facilitated generalized gains, because parents could share ideas with other parents in the group and work on personal concerns in individual sessions.

We would cautiously conclude from the present data that families who complete a voluntary group parent training program derive a range of benefits and no demonstrable ill effects. The arguments about iatrogenic effects of parent training are overdrawn. However, it may be important to distinguish between voluntary and required programs, and to consider the response cost to families of their involvement. Required and time-consuming programs may well produce more variable results. We certainly agree with Turnbull and Turnbull's (1982) general argument that families with a handicapped child are as different from one another as any families, and must not be force fit into any programmatic model. Families must be given options, and allowed to pursue them, including the option not to be involved—without guilt. When this is done, generalized effects to the extent that they occur seem to be positive.

PREDICTORS OF OUTCOME
REVISITED

In Chapter 6 we presented several studies predicting outcome. We return to this topic briefly here, because in the Los Angeles III sample we were able to broaden the predictor variables and examine the relationship between the psychological measures we have considered in this chapter and outcome, especially follow-through implementation. We reasoned that, whereas demographic variables such as socioeconomic status predict post-training proficiency rather well, the continued implementation of teaching at home might relate more to family factors. One year after training, we obtained Teaching Interviews covering the previous 3-month period, by telephone (Baker, Landen, & Kashima, 1989).

Follow-up Teaching Interview scores were related to several pre-training psychological scores. In families with lower TI scores, on the Locke-Wallace the primary parent had reported lower marital adjustment (r (34) = .29, p < .05). On the QRS-F, she had reported higher stress related to the child's behavior (r (37) = −.41, p < .01) and the child's physical problems (r (37) = −.31, p < .05). On the FACES, she had viewed the family lower on adaptability (r (37) = .35, p < .05) and she had been less satisfied with the family on both the adaptability (r (36) = −.62, p < .001) and cohesion (r (36) = −.40, p < .01) dimensions. In general terms, then, the initially more stressed and less satisfied parents were less likely to follow through after training with teaching at home. This supports the view considered in Chapter 9, that for maximum benefits parent training might fruitfully be broadened to intervene also at the level of psychological problems in the family (Berger & Fowlkes, 1980; Cunningham, 1988; Dadds, Schwartz, & Sanders, 1987).

CONCLUSION

Noting that most reports of parent training have focused rather narrowly on measures of parent skills and child behaviors, we cast a broader net. We examined measures of psychological dimensions, including depression, stress, marital adjustment, cohesiveness and adaptability of the family, and satisfaction with the family. As predictors, these measures indicated that parents with more stress and less satisfaction were less likely to continue to implement programs at home. As indicators of outcome, these measures either remained quite stable or showed some improvement following training. Moreover, parent evaluations of the approach and the program were consistently quite positive. We have found no empirical evidence to support the views expressed by some writers that parent training is harmful. Our understanding of this issue would be increased by less attention in the literature to selected personal opinions and more study of representative samples of parents, perhaps delineating the effects on families of a greater range of parent training programs.

Chapter 12

Fathers and Siblings

Although the whole family is sometimes engaged in intervention programs, most of the focus of measures has been on mothers. We know little about how fathers, brothers, and sisters are involved in training programs, and what difference their involvement makes.

FATHERS

We have structured our programs to encourage and facilitate father participation. We found high father completion rates in the Boston sample at a time when services to families were more novel. Here 59% of fathers in the group conditions met completion criteria of attending more than half of the meetings and both assessment sessions. Father attendance was also high in the hyperactivity program, where attendance by at least one parent was required and there was considerable latitude in scheduling appointments. Here, 62% of fathers met the more stringent completion criteria of attending at least two-thirds of the meetings and both assessment sessions. In our Los Angeles samples, fathers typically attended and met the completion criteria in from one-third to one-half of intact families.

How do fathers relate to our group training when they attend? Generally, fathers are active, albeit circumscribed, participants. The majority defer to the mother to speak about the child's skills and learning needs. Although they attend meetings and learn the principles being taught, most fathers do not share many responsibilities for home teaching or recordkeeping, even during training. We have found that fathers participate more consistently in behavior management programs than in teaching ones. In teaching, while few fathers do consistent self-help, speech and language, or academic teaching, more are engaged with incidental teaching of play.

Benefits of Participation

What are the benefits of father participation? This question has received considerable attention from parent training researchers. We have seen (Chapter 3) that the most consistent predictor of dropouts from parent training is being a single parent. Yet, while having a spouse is predictive of completion, the literature, with one exception, suggests that it does not seem to matter much whether or not he is involved in the intervention program, a finding that seems at odds with theories of family process. The exception is Webster-Stratton's (1985a) finding of more behavioral improvement a year following training in families where the father was involved in training. However, this result is not readily interpretable, because her father uninvolved group had lower socioeconomic status and also included many single-parent families where there was no father.

Behrendt (1978) found that families with child management problems did equally well on all measures of outcome after parent training, whether or not the father participated. In studies where father participation was controlled by the researcher, who assigned some families to mother-only and some to mother-and-father conditions, father involvement made no difference (Adesso & Lipson, 1981; Firestone, Kelly, & Fike, 1980; Martin, 1977). These studies all involved children of normal intelligence who had behavior problems. One would expect that father involvement would be helpful in carrying out a consistent behavior management program. In families with a child who is developmental disabled, however, father involvement would seem even more crucial, because programming aims not at one troublesome behavior but at ongoing teaching needs.

Perhaps interested fathers in the above-cited studies learned new teaching methods from their wives, although they did not participate directly. Adubato, Adams, and Budd (1981), for example, demonstrated that a mother who had completed training was then able to train her husband, so that in a few sessions he too was an effective teacher for their child with severe disabilities. Reisinger (1982) even found that in four families whose training involved only mothers in the clinic, fathers' use of differential attention with their children at home improved. Sandler, Coren, and Thurman (1983) found contrary results, though; training involved only mothers, and fathers' knowledge of teaching principles did not change. Despite the scarce empirical support, it does seem possible that there are unmeasured delayed benefits of having both spouses involved, if only to prevent such a strong alliance between the teaching parent and handicapped child that the rest of the family is excluded. Perhaps the place to look for effects is in continuing teaching at home after the formal program ends.

Evaluating Benefits of Father Participation

We first asked about benefits of training for fathers who met completion criteria. These fathers consistently showed significant gains in knowledge of teaching principles and in actual teaching skills. We saw in Chapter 5 that fathers in the Boston group programs increased in knowledge of behavioral principles as much as mothers. In the Los Angeles III sample, the nonprimary parent (who was the father in all but 4 cases) increased on the Behavioral Vignettes Test from 9.2 to 13.1 ($p <$ .001) and on the Teaching Proficiency Test from 17.9 to 27.0 ($p < $ .01). These gains were comparable to the primary parents' scores shown in Table 4.2. In addition, fathers who completed the program evaluated it quite highly. Of the 21 fathers in the Los Angeles III sample who completed the program evaluation, for example, 100% said they would recommend the program to others.

We next considered whether the fathers' participation had been beneficial to the mother, to the child, and to continued teaching at home. We examined the proportion of married families in which the second parent attended training and whether that person's attendance related to outcome. There were 57 intact families in the Los Angeles III sample. In 15 (26%) the spouse never attended. In 23 (40%) the spouse attended some sessions but not enough to be designated as a completer. In only 19 (33%) the spouse completed the program, attending at least 5 of 8 meetings and both assessments.

It did not seem to matter on outcome measures whether the spouse never attended or attended some, so we combined these as noncompleters. There was a significant relationship to primary parent attendance: single parents had the lowest attendance (4.2 meetings), as expected from our dropout findings. This was followed by married parents with noncompleter spouses (5.6 meetings) and then married parents where both completed (7.3 meetings). The three conditions differed significantly by analysis of variance ($F(2,69) = 9.45$, $p < .001$), and the married conditions also differed significantly ($t (55) = 4.23$, $p < .001$).

We compared one-completer and two-completer married families on the primary parent's post-training scores and pre-post gains for the Behavioral Vignettes Test, Teaching Proficiency Test, and Teaching Interview. We also compared them on the 1-year follow-up Teaching Interview and pre- to follow-up gains. The post- and follow-up levels were quite similar for the two groups, and the gain scores actually were higher on every measure for the one-completer families, although these differences were not statistically significant. They certainly are consistent with previous findings, however, in that we could not detect immediate or delayed benefits of the spouse's participation either on the primary parent's outcome scores or on the total family teaching implementation.

We next compared one-completer and two-completer families on the measures of generalized benefits that we discussed above. We reasoned that the positive changes primary parents reported on variables like depression, family stress, and family satisfaction might be accounted for mainly by families where both parents worked together and completed the program. We also reasoned that primary parents would evaluate the program more highly when the spouse was also involved. In fact, however, neither changes in the psychological variables nor program evaluation related to completion status.

SIBLINGS: RISK OR RESOURCE?

We know that a retarded child can profoundly affect the life of a sibling and that a sibling, in turn, can influence the attitude and decisions of his parents and the behaviour of the [retarded child] (Wolfensberger & Kurtz, 1969, p. 432).

Siblings in families with a handicapped member are variously seen by the professional community as *at risk* for psychiatric disorder, and as *resources* for the handicapped child's development. These two not necessarily contradictory perspectives have driven intervention efforts. Researchers' interest in siblings of retarded children initially derived from the assumption that siblings are "at risk" psychologically (Lobato, 1983; Rodger, 1985; San Martino & Newman, 1974). In turn, programs of individual and group counseling for siblings have been designed to provide an opportunity for sharing experiences that will hopefully ameliorate negative effects (Schreiber & Feeley, 1965; Grossman, 1972). There are two cautions, however (Lobato, 1983). These interventions have not been well evaluated, and the evidence for risk status upon which these programs are based is mixed.

Numerous studies, beginning with Farber's (1959) classic efforts, have pointed to negative effects of growing up with a handicapped brother or sister (Breslau, Weitzman, & Messenger, 1981; Fowle, 1968; Gath, 1973). Farber (1959), for example, found that older girls from low-income homes were especially affected, because much of the childrearing fell to them. Other researchers, though, have found few adverse effects and even reported some positive outcomes such as increased compassion, sensitivity, and maturity (Cleveland & Miller, 1977; Grailiker, Fishler, & Koch, 1962; Grossman, 1972; Simeonsson & McHale, 1981; Wilson, Blacher, & Baker, 1989). It is interesting to note that studies finding greater psychological difficulties have tended to interview the parents, while those finding more benign outcomes have interviewed the siblings themselves.

Most of these studies were conducted before the increased services of the past decade were in place. We recently interviewed 24 children aged 9 to 13, drawn from Blacher's (1984) longitudinal sample of families with a severely handicapped child. We asked detailed questions about life with their younger, severely handicapped siblings, and we found a consistently high level of involvement, strong feelings of responsibility, and an emphasis on positive aspects of family life (Wilson, Blacher, & Baker, 1989). Hardships were not denied, but these children seemed to be faring better than children studied in earlier research, before schooling for handicapped children and other supports for their families were mandated.

Alternatively, some individual and group training programs for siblings have been developed on the assumption that siblings are resources "with an unusually high therapeutic potential if it can be tapped constructively" (Adams, 1967, p. 311). Programs have been designed to train siblings to conduct behavior change programs with their brothers or sisters who are retarded (Schreibman, O'Neill, & Koegel, 1983) or, more typically, to work in conjunction with parents instead of undermining parents' programs because of ignorance or jealousy (Brown-Miller & Cantwell, 1976; Laviguer, 1976).

We have carried out a number of group sibling training programs, usually in conjunction with parent training programs. We have grappled with the risk and resource perspectives, especially when they would lead in opposite directions. Do we emphasize sharing experiences or learning how to teach better? If some siblings suffer from excessive burdens of caring for the handicapped child, might not a typical behavioral program exacerbate the situation by further increasing demands for involvement? Or would learning better teaching and coping methods make caretaking easier? Is it desirable to encourage siblings to relate as teacher and learner? Does this happen anyway, and so might more skilled teaching not make it a better experience? We have not resolved these contradictions, and consequently we have organized programs that are more flexible and less demanding than those for parents, programs that provide siblings with information and enhance siblings' teaching skills but do not press for increased teaching. (For a well-integrated approach to intervention with siblings, see also Powell & Ogle, 1985).

Initial Programs

We initially conducted programs for siblings aged 10 to 18 in conjunction with Camp Freedom, a summer residential program for retarded children. Siblings either spent 6 days at camp (Pasick, 1975; Weinrott, 1974) or attended an intensive weekend program (Pasick, 1975). One program component that we do not typically include in parent training was information about developmental disabilities; this combination of didactic presentation and discussion of personal experiences, conducted over several sessions, was very important to dispel myths and to normalize the siblings' experience. The majority of the program taught them behavioral skills by workshops, observation, supervised practice, and viewing videotapes of their teaching. In this setting, siblings as young as 12 showed significant gains in teaching skills as assessed by the Behavioral Vignettes Test and an earlier version of the Teaching Proficiency Test (Pasick, 1975).

Two months after the program, parents reported moderate or vast improvements in the quality of interactions between the siblings and their retarded brother or sister. Parents in two-thirds of the families reported that the siblings were spending more time with the mentally retarded child. Of particular interest are some unintended "spin-offs." Parents reported that the siblings, after training, gave them feedback on their interactions with the handicapped child and that this promoted consistency in the family. Moreover, the parents reported that they themselves were now more willing to discuss problems related to the handicapped child (Weinrott, 1974).

Bilingual Sibling Program

A sibling program developed by Sandra Landen was unique in that it ran concurrently with a Spanish-speaking parent training program (which involved the families recruited in Shenk's, 1984 study, described in Chapter 3). Siblings in these families play critical roles. The families are often large, and typically poor, and siblings are very likely to be involved with child care responsibilities. Moreover, where the parents speak little or no English, the siblings have the role of translator/spokesperson with English-speaking service providers (e.g., the special education teacher).

We offered participation to all siblings who met the criteria of being 8 to 17 years of age, older than the developmentally disabled child, and making adequate progress in an age-appropriate classroom. Twenty siblings voluntarily joined groups that met 1 evening a week for 7 weeks; groups were conducted in English and Spanish by 2 bilingual Hispanic women who had considerable experience with developmentally disabled children and behavioral programming (Landen, 1984; Landen & Baker, 1986). Incentives (lottery tickets, small prizes) were given for participation and completion of measures. Program goals were to improve behavioral teaching and behavior management techniques, provide accurate information about mental retardation, and provide the opportunity to share feelings and concerns.

Fully 18 of 20 siblings (90%) completed the program. All measures were administered by bilingual staff who were not involved with the training; siblings were given the option of completing the measures in

English, Spanish, or any combination thereof. We found significant improvements ($p < .001$) in participants' knowledge about mental retardation (adapted from Hazzard, 1981), knowledge about behavioral principles (adapted from the Verbal Behavior Vignettes Test, see Chapter 7), and ability to apply behavioral techniques in a teaching session (the play skills portion of the Teaching Proficiency Test, see Chapter 4) (Landen, 1984).

Siblings were very positive in their evaluation of the training program. Most reported after training that they had greater understanding of (94%) and were "less frustrated" with (72%) their brother or sister. In identifying the "worst thing about the program," 83% responded "nothing." Others said the group ended too soon or that other kids in the group were too shy. This latter observation highlights an area that was less successful— these groups did not share feelings as freely as the leaders had expected they would. Landen (1984) noted that the lack of expressiveness may have been attributable to the wide age range, cultural practices, and/or language barriers.

CONCLUSIONS

Our experience with training programs for fathers and siblings has been generally encouraging. Fathers have been less likely to complete parent training than mothers, but those who did complete it showed comparable gains to mothers in knowledge acquired and satisfaction with the program. Siblings who are at least 10 or so years old have become quite involved in training, with high completion rates and satisfaction with the program and with considerable gains in knowledge and teaching skills. We do not, however, have much evidence that father or sibling involvement in training either enhances the handicapped child's development or benefits the mother, who remains the person in most families assuming the major responsibility for teaching the child. These are issues that must be addressed by further studies and perhaps different measures, such as the mothers' perceptions of benefits.

Chapter 13

Program
Dissemination

The fate of most innovative social service programs is the same— non-use. Often, despite evidence that a new program effectively meets a need, it is ignored, rejected, or only partially attempted by the service system. A case in point: Parent training has been demonstrated to be effective by researchers, endorsed enthusiastically by many human service providers, and even mandated in certain programs by legislators (see Chapter 1). But all this may be news to the typical family, for whom no appropriate program has been available.

We do not actually know much about the availability of parent training programs. The majority of programs offered by agencies are never reported in the professional literature. And the literature is replete with descriptions of one-shot demonstration programs, one session analogue programs for research, or programs for one or just a few families. The program that sounds just right may be in England, a long way to travel from the U.S. for weekly meetings.

We do know from informal surveys that most agencies serving children with developmental disabilities provide some counseling for parents but do not have a well-conceived and systematic way of relating to parents. Practice derives little from what has come to be known about parent training. I have noted my own casual survey of 19 students in a seminar I was teaching in 1981 (Baker, 1983). Each student was placed in a different public or private agency in Southern California serving developmentally disabled children or adults. After the students had read articles on parent training, they expressed puzzlement, for despite these promising reports, not one of their agencies was offering a systematic program to its families.

SUCCESSFUL DISSEMINATION

There is, however, some reason for optimism, because successful dissemination of parent training programs has occurred. The most notable is the Portage Guide to Early Education, originally developed in rural Wisconsin in 1969 as a home based training program for families with developmentally delayed pre- school children dispersed throughout a large geographical area (Shearer & Shearer, 1976). In 1972 the Office of Special

175

Education funded a replication and evaluation project, and in 1975 the Joint Dissemination and Review panel designated Portage as a model program. In 1976 two pilot programs were set up in the United Kingdom, and since then in the U.K. over 100 Portage services have developed and a national Portage Association has been established (Sturmey & Crisp, 1986). We do not know why this program has been disseminated so widely, but we note several possible reasons in addition to concerted staff efforts. Portage is a total service program and it targets children in the critical preschool years. It embraces a wide range of developmental disabilities and continues for several years. It has produced extensive written guides for training home visitors and facilitating selection and teaching of skills. Last, and probably least, although the program has not been extensively evaluated, the outcomes that have been reported are encouraging.

An area of more circumscribed but still successful program dissemination has been the utilization by parents and parent training programs of self-instructional books and manuals. Among those most widely employed are *Living with Children* (Patterson & Gullion, 1976), *Families: Application of Social Learning to Family Life* (Patterson, 1977), *Between Parent and Child* (Ginott, 1965), *Parents Are Teachers* (Becker, 1971), *Toilet Training in Less Than a Day* (Azrin & Foxx, 1974) and, with developmental disabilities, our *Steps to Independence Series* (see Chapter 2). While there has been no study of the extent of use, sales figures indicate wide utilization. It seems that most self-instructional books reach parents through professionals, whether they are incorporated into a parent training curriculum or just given to parents who express a particular need. There have been several reviews of self- instructional materials (Andraisik & Murphy, 1977; Bernal & North, 1978). Two reservations expressed are that many of these books, including ours, are written at too difficult a reading level for many parents, and that there has been very little systematic study of their effectiveness. We can conclude that there is some evidence of successful dissemination of whole programs and program aids. The process of dissemination, though, has not received much attention.

DEMONSTRATION IS NOT ENOUGH

McClelland (1978), discussing the failure of solidly researched social programs to take root, argued that a central fallacy is the assumption that "knowing how to do something will motivate people to do it. . . ." (p.207). Indeed, it does seem that information about programs, even effective ones, is not enough. Fairweather, Sanders, and Tornatzky (1974) encountered this phenomenon in their program of experimental social innovation, "The Lodge," a community living program for previously hospitalized psychiatric patients (Fairweather, Sanders, Cressler, & Maynard, 1969). The researchers had found that Lodge residents were significantly more able than controls to remain in the community and to maintain employment at a program cost of less than one-third that of the usual ward treatment. Yet even the setting within which the demonstration project was conducted failed to incorporate the program!

WHEN SUCCESSFUL ADOPTION OCCURS

In predicting successful adoption of an innovation, relatively static variables, such as size and funding of the agency, professional affiliations of the innovators, and personality and sociodemographic attributes of potential users, have not consistently predicted very well (Corwin, 1972; Kimberly, 1976). Dynamic variables, those describing characteristics of the change process, have had more utility. A review of process variables (Berlin, 1980) highlighted the following three: active stimulation of a setting's members by an outside agent who catalyzes group cohesion and problem-solving; staff perception of involvement in making decisions about a new program; and staff perceptions of the need for change and of a match between the particular innovation and their own needs, values, experience, and expectations. The last two of these involve staff members' perceptions or expectations.

DISSEMINATION STUDIES

During the 1980s, we conducted two studies where the intent was to disseminate the Parents as Teachers program in agencies throughout the greater Los Angeles area, a region that includes about 10 million people and hundreds of schools and agencies that provide services to persons with developmental disabilities. The first study aimed to have selected agency staff initiate parent training programs based generally on the Parents as Teachers program but adapted to fit their own setting and clients. We took the above-mentioned findings about successful adoption to heart, providing extensive consultation and measuring a number of staff perceptions that might mediate implementation. The second study aimed to have selected agency staff implement the video-directed program we have described in Chapter 5, with much less consultation from us.

STUDY 1: STAFF TRAINING

This study, carried out by Peggy Henning Berlin (Berlin, 1980; Berlin & Baker, 1983), investigated the extent to which agency staff would implement a parent training program. Berlin hypothesized that two major *cognitive expectancy* variables would relate to implementation: perceived organizational readiness to accept a new program (perceived environment) and perceived discrepancy between the staff member's present role and the new role posed by the innovation (role conflict).

Participants

Participants were staff from children's service agencies in Los Angeles County. We contacted directors of 161 agencies by letter and then telephone, and found 64 that either served children (or families of children) between the ages of 3 and 13 years who functioned at a mentally retarded level, or were clinics with the capacity for serving this population. Two consultants visited the 26 interested agencies to meet with potential participants and explore the utility and feasibility of adopting a parent training program. All but two confirmed participation. The final sample of 24 included 13 private schools, 6 mental health clinics, and 5 regional centers for the developmentally disabled.

There were 83 staff participants (2 to 4 from each setting), including 14 men and 69 women with a median age of 32 years. Most were administrators, counselors, or teachers. Most served developmentally disabled clients and had some informal service contact with the clients' parents. They reported occasional use of behavior modification principles, but none were involved in systematic parent training.

Training

Consultant-trainers were 5 men and 3 women, with degrees ranging from B.A. to Ph.D. in clinical psychology. Each had at least two years of experience in using the Parents as Teachers program. Training was conducted in two phases. Phase I, the more structured segment of the program, included 6 training meetings. It began with two weekly half-day workshops that presented the major tenets, both content and process, of the Parents as Teachers curriculum. Between sessions participants were to read manuals and identify a family with whom to initiate training. Following the two workshops, agencies were divided into six groups of four each according to time availabilities and geographic locations. Four additional weekly 2-hour consultation meetings were held with each small group. These contained progressively fewer components structured by the consultants and relatively more consultation based upon the needs of participants. At the sixth and final session, participants from each agency developed behavioral goals toward implementation that they thought would be achievable during the next four months. Phase II provided ongoing consultation as needed to agencies doing training.

Participation and Initial Achievements

Three agencies discontinued following Phase I workshops and 1 discontinued during Phase I consultation meetings. Thus, 20 agencies completed the consultation. Table 13.1 shows the number of agencies that met selected program objectives by the end of Phase I. At this point, 19 of the 20 agencies had conducted at least one training session with a family and 8 of these had begun training with more than one family.

Follow-up

Four months after training, onsite interviews were conducted with each participant by research assistants experienced in developmental disabilities but neither involved in this training program nor familiar with subjects' prior participation. The interview asked about steps in preparation for and actual implementation of a parent training program. Although the interview was originally designed as a continuous measure, outcomes were such that agencies and staff alike clustered neatly into four achievement categories. Based on the combined achievements of staff members, each agency was classified as a *noncompleter* if all participating staff discontinued the program prior to the last 2 sessions ($n = 4$); a *noninitiator* if 1 or more staff continued to attend but did not institute a viable pilot parent training program (i.e., at least 4 sessions with at least 1 family ($n = 7$); an *initiator* if 1 or more staff conducted a viable parent

TABLE 13.1

Number of Agencies Achieving Representative Steps in Implementing Parent Training with One Family and with More Than One Family by Phase I Meeting 6

	NUMBER OF AGENCIES	
IMPLEMENTATION STEP	1 FAMILY	MORE THAN 1 FAMILY
Recruit family	20	12
Assess family	18	7
Conduct 1 training meeting	19	8
Target 1 skill	15	6
Conduct 2 training meetings	10	6
Consult about teaching	11	5
Conduct 3 training meetings	8	2
Observe teaching	2	0
Target second skill	7	2

Note. Of 24 agencies that began training, 20 remained at this point.

training program but did not institute new training after the consultation program ended ($n = 7$); or an *implementer* if 1 or more staff initiated a viable parent training program and continued to initate new parent training after the consultation program ended ($n = 6$). Implementers and initiators are together referred to as *achievers* (54%) while the other two groups are termed *nonachievers* (46%).

Individual staff members were assigned to a four-group implementation classification roughly paralleling that used for agencies. Staff were classified as *noncompleters* if they attended 3 or fewer sessions and did no parent training ($n = 26$); *noninitiators* if they continued to attend but did no parent training ($n = 15$); *initiators* if they initiated parent training during the consultation program but did not continue after the program's conclusion ($n = 24$); and *implementers* if they initiated parent training during the consultation program and continued thereafter ($n = 18$). Again, as with agencies, initiators and implementers are together referred to as *achievers* (49%) and the other two groups are termed *nonachievers* (51%).

The overall level of parent training implementation achieved in this project was not high. The percentage of settings that continued program adoption after consultation ended (25%: 6 of 24) was comparable to the percentage (20%: 5 of 25) reported by Fairweather et al. (1974), underscoring their conclusion that "experimenting" with a program differs from "incorporating" it. Both programs focused on "active learning," making implementation demands on participants early in training. Such a model may discourage ambivalent persons. Indeed, a number of staff did discontinue participation, and agencies whose participants took early steps toward initiating parent training were more often categorized as achievers at follow-up.

At 8 months an additional phone follow-up of agency implementation revealed a pattern similar to the 4-month follow-up. There was no delayed effect of training: nonimplementers did not become implementers. Four agencies that had been classified as implementers were still conducting parent training. In all four, at least two persons were working together, supporting observations that the viable unit of study may be the small group of people who take responsibility for change within a setting (Sarason, 1972).

Correlates of Achievement Status

To distinguish those agencies and staff who implemented programs from those who did not, we obtained pre-training measures at the individual and agency levels. In addition to staff and agency demographic questionnaires, we employed three self-report measures of the work environment and expectations. The Readiness for Program Change

Survey—Revised is a 96-item Likert format scale drawn from a longer instrument assessing staff perceptions of their agency's receptivity to change (Search Institute, 1978). The Role Description Questionnaire is a list of 24 behaviors noted from experience and the literature to facilitate successful parent training and program innovations (Berlin, 1980). Each staff member completed the items before training (as they would describe their own current role), and after the first training session (as they would describe the role of parent trainer). Absolute discrepancy scores on the 24 items were summed for a measure of role conflict. Expectations Regarding Parent Training is a 22-item Likert format scale assessing past experiences and future expectations regarding involvement in parent training (Berlin, 1980).

Because of the small number of agencies involved, comparisons on the major independent variables were made between achievers and nonachievers. In general, there were few differences at the agency level of analysis. Demographic characteristics did not predict agency outcome, nor did consensual (aggregated) perceptions of the agency's climate for change. In fact, few of the cognitive variables were found to be shared characteristics even among members of the same setting. Perceptions and expectations tended to be individual characteristics. Aggregation of perceived climate data in implementation research may mask predictive relationships existing at the individual level. This finding echoes Barrett and Trickett's (1979) proposal that social climate scales as consensual perception tools may be useful for promoting discussion of feelings and attitudes within organizations, but are less useful when the goal is behavior prediction.

On the other hand, individual staff perceptions of the agency's characteristics did relate to implementation. Achievers perceived in their agencies significantly more openness and less resistance to program change. Achievers also expected *less* comfort in the role of training parents. Only 1 of 25 demographic comparisons was significant: nonachievers had reported that they were doing more individual parent counseling before training.

Discriminant analysis was performed using staff cognitive and demographic variables to predict staff implementation outcome (Dixon & Brown, 1979). A two-group outcome classification was used, discriminating achievers from nonachievers. Four variables entered the predictor equation. Achiever status was predicted from low perception of the agency as resistant to program change, low expectation of comfort in the role of teaching parents, high prior knowledge and use of behavioral principles, and low role conflict vis-à-vis the role of parent trainer. None of the demographic variables entered the equation. Using the "leaving-one-out" validation procedure (see Chapter 6), this formula correctly classified 30 of 42 achievers (71%) and 29 of 41 nonachievers (71%) (χ^2 (1 df) = 13.1, $p < .001$).

Static, demographic characteristics did not predict well. Rather, individuals' perceptions of the agency's resistance to change and of their own role conflict in relation to the program change combined with related experience (prior knowledge and use of behavioral principles) to predict implementation behavior.

Throughout the analyses at individual and agency levels, face-valid statements of expectations with regard to parent training were negatively associated with outcome and often not associated with other measures presumed to tap an open posture vis-à-vis parent training. It seems that staff already involved with counseling parents were more likely to predict comfort in the role of parent trainer, but in the end less likely to adopt this somewhat new way of relating to parents. As others have noted, positive attitudes do not necessarily predict actual behavior (Fairweather et al., 1974).

Why was implementation not greater? One question that naturally arises: Did staff become proficient in the necessary skills to implement parent training? The Behavioral Vignettes Test was administered prior to training and after the last Phase I meeting to determine how much those still in attendance had gained in their knowledge of behavioral principles. The gain was highly significant ($t = 8.48$, df $= 48$, $p < .001$) and after training 71% (compared with 45% before) reached a previously established proficiency criterion for staff of 80% correct (Brightman, 1974). Nonetheless, the consultants felt that most participants could have profited from more training in behavior modification, especially in applying techniques in direct work with children. Had we assessed participants' skills in other areas necessary for implementing parent training (e.g., planning a program, speaking in front of a group), additional training might have been indicated.

STUDY 2: MEDIA-DIRECTED PARENT TRAINING

We developed the media-directed training program (see Chapters 2 and 5) to facilitate dissemination. Four videotapes and a self-instructional manual guided a group of parents through four training sessions focused on applying behavioral methods to teaching self-help skills. There may be advantages to families in receiving training through media, as they can see a variety of well-chosen models and receive a standardized program presented by highly experienced individuals. Our primary motive in developing this program, however, was to increase the likelihood that agency staff would implement parent training. We reasoned that social service personnel might be more inclined to utilize a packaged training program, just as they have been receptive to utilizing self-instructional books. Staff would not have to be highly familiar with behavioral methods to implement such a program, and much of the group presentation pressure would be eased. Accordingly, staff would not need as extensive training and supervision. Hence, even if only a minority of staff who were exposed to the program implemented it, the training effort would still be cost-effective.

Participation

We sent a brochure describing the program to schools, clinics, parent associations and other agencies in Los Angeles County that serve children with mental retardation. We screened interested participants on the phone, making clear that our aim was to have participants facilitate at least one small parent group using our video package in the ensuing six months. Thirty-five potential facilitators, representing 18 agencies (1 to 7 per agency), each attended a 3-hour orientation meeting in groups of 6 to 10. Each indicated that he or she would facilitate at least one group. They completed measures of demographics and their current job responsibilities, knowledge of behavioral principles, and expectations about problems in implementing parent training.

These facilitators were predominantly female (71%) and well educated: 74% had a Master's or doctoral degree. Their average age was 40 years and they had been on the job for an average of 8 years. Positions included special education teachers (43%), other service providers (e.g. counselors) (29%), administrators (20%), and psychologists (9%). Half (49%) worked in public schools and the other half were distributed among private schools (14%), state regional centers (23%), and other agencies (14%).

Implementation

Three months following the orientation workshop, a staff member not involved in the workshops conducted follow-up interviews by phone. At that time, 8 (23%) of the participants had implemented at least one parent training group with our media package. Of the remaining 27, 6 had taken some steps to implement, 12 still professed plans to, and 9 reported that they had decided not to implement.

The 9 who indicated a clear decision not to implement at the 3-month follow-up were given a list of reasons and asked which applied. None indicated that they did not like the program. The most frequent response was that "I find that implementing the program does not really fit with my job responsibilities." Most of these participants indicated that there had been changes in their positions, or duties, or the population they worked

TABLE 13.2

Facilitator Family Sample (N = 19): Parent and Child Demographics

Parent Demographics	
Age (Primary parent)—Mean years	38.9
Education (Primary parent)—Mean years	13.5
Marital status—Percent single	26.3
Employment (Primary parent)—Percent Full	15.8
Family Income—Percent	
Less than $24,999 (US)	23.5
$25,000–34,999	17.6
$35,000–49,999	47.0
More than $50,000	11.8
Child Demographics	
Age—Mean years (Range: 2.0 to 14.4)	5.3
Sex—Percent boys	57.9
Child diagnosis—Percent	
Mental retardation, cause unknown	36.8
Down syndrome	21.1
Autism	26.3
Cerebral Palsy	10.6
Other	5.3

with. In several cases, the agency had designated another participant as the person to conduct the parent training.

Six months following orientation, an additional follow-up found several more persons taking steps to implement but no evidence of any additional participants completing a training group. It is possible that some of these participants later facilitated a group, but this seems unlikely, as they had to obtain the tapes from us. Hence, we conclude that only 23% of participants facilitated a group and, as in our previous study, if a potential facilitator did not begin almost immediately, he or she did not begin at all.

We examined correlates of implementation at both the agency and individual levels. Of the 18 agencies, the 5 that implemented were not of any particular type. One notable correlate, however, was whether more than one staff member had attended the orientation. Of the 7 agencies with two or more participants, 4 (57%) implemented. Of the 11 agencies with one participant, only 1 (9%) implemented, and she was a special case, having been sent as a representative of an out-of-state agency. The 8 implementers were contrasted with the 27 non-implementers, in a search for distinguishing characteristics. The groups did not differ by demographic characteristics such as age, sex, education, position, or years on the job, although with this small a sample a difference would have to be quite striking to reach statistical significance. We did find that implementers were generally better prepared to conduct behavioral parent

TABLE 13.3

Primary Parent Program Evaluation: Facilitator
Replication Sample (N=19)

A. *Program Evaluation*	
1. Appropriateness of approach	95%[a]
2. Helpfulness of group	100
3. Helpfulness of leader	100
4. Competence of leader	100
5. Recommend program	100
6. Overall feeling (6 or 7 on 7-point scale)	95
B. *Self-evaluation*	
1. Attending meetings	100[b]
2. Completing readings	100
3. Teaching	94
4. Keeping records	47
5. Understanding material	100
6. Confidence in teaching (6 or 7 on 7-point scale)	89

[a] Percentage of parents in each condition who reported much (4) or very much (5) on a 5-point scale. [b] Percentage of parents in each condition who reported most (3) or all (4) on a 4-point scale.

training. Their pre-score on a 10-item form of the Behavioral Vignettes Test was 8.4, compared with 6.3 for nonimplementers (t (33) = 2.78, $p <$ .01), and fully 88% of implementers reported that they personally used behavioral principles extensively in their work, as compared with 33% of nonimplementers (χ^2 (1) = 5.28, $p < .05$).

Impact on Families

An important question not addressed in our previous study was whether the results for parents trained by agency professionals were comparable to those found in our own program. Facilitators were given an evaluation packet for each participating family. Before training, the primary parent completed a demographic questionnaire and the 10-item Behavioral Vignettes Test; after training, the same parent repeated the Behavioral Vignettes Test and completed a slightly simplified version of the Consumer Satisfaction Questionnaire. We report here on results obtained from the first 19 families (trained in 5 groups) on which we received complete data. The parent and child demographics are shown in Table 13.2. They were quite similar to those reported for parents trained directly by us.

The 10-item Behavioral Vignettes Test scores increased modestly, although significantly, from a mean of 4.9 to 6.1 (t (18) = 3.45, $p < .01$). Parents' responses to the Consumer Satisfaction measure were, as in the UCLA sample, highly positive, as shown in Table 13.3. Once again, though, most parents truthfully admitted that they had not done the recommended recordkeeping.

These measures indicate comparability in the sample and the results between UCLA-sponsored groups and those conducted by agency facilitators. While this is encouraging, the gains in knowledge were only modest; moreover, in this study we were not able to examine the extent to which parents actually implemented programming and how well they followed through over time.

CONCLUSIONS

We are left with several conclusions and, typically, even more uncertainties about program dissemination. We can conclude that some agency staff can be trained to implement parent training successfully and that potential implementers can to some extent be identified in advance, based on their perceptions of their agency and their roles, and based on their preparation. We can conclude for the media-directed training that parents evaluate it highly. We can conclude, again for media-directed training, that with only brief orientation some agency personnel can be effective facilitators, and that the parents they train benefit.

On a more pessimistic note, we must conclude that the majority of professionals who go through either a training program or a brief orientation do not fully implement the program. We do not know whether this is particular to our program—perhaps with another type of program more staff would have implemented. Despite our efforts to draw out this response, however, the nonimplementers consistently spoke highly of the program. There is a clear need for greater attention to the dissemination of effective human service programs. We need to know much more about what types of programs can be most readily disseminated, which service providers to enlist as potential implementers, and how best to help them carry out the program.

Chapter 14

Practice and Policy Implications

The program of applied research on parent training reported in this monograph had one overarching purpose: to improve services to families with children who are developmentally disabled. The studies involved about 500 families with children who were retarded, autistic, hyperactive, or abused. Obviously their needs differed, perhaps even in 500 ways. Nonetheless, it seems best to conclude by attempting to draw from our research and clinical experiences some implications, organized around several common but critical questions raised by those who serve families or are responsible for service delivery policy.

IS PARENT TRAINING A SERVICE THAT FAMILIES WANT?

Every parent of a young child seeks information, advice, guidance, and a sympathetic ear—often. And parents of children who do not grow up according to the norms worry more, and ask more, and more often find their questions unanswered. In the words of one of our parents, with a sidelong glance at her very active son who was mentally retarded: "These kids don't come with instructions." The question is not whether to provide information to families, but how best to do it.

There is much evidence that parents of children who are developmentally disabled welcome the guidance they can receive from books, ranging from the sharing of personal experiences (Featherstone, 1981; Greenfeld, 1973; Turnbull & Turnbull, 1985) to advice about aspects of child rearing (Baker & Brightman, 1989; Carr, 1980; Lovaas, 1981; Goldfarb, Brotherson, Summers, & Turnbull, 1986). We have received hundreds of letters from parents thanking us for our instructional manuals, sometimes with the message: I wish they had been available sooner.

There is now also good evidence that many parents welcome clinical/educational training in teaching and behavior management. In Chapter 1 we listed 11 criteria for addressing the question: Did the program work? The first five of these asked about social validity, enrollment, completion, participation, and consumer satisfaction—criteria that generally speak to whether parents like the service. Our Parents as

Teachers programs, the Active Parenting Curriculum (Chapter 8), and the May Institute's home-based program (Chapter 10) seem to do well against these criteria.

Although the *social validity* of our programs has been assessed thus far only from information given by parents who completed them, they almost universally agreed that the behavioral approach employed was appropriate for the children. Ambrose (Chapter 8) noted less social validity in the child-abuse program, however, as these parents often disagree with the antipunishment stance taken by leaders. These parents are typically court-referred and many quite likely would not want parent training, given the choice.

In the two studies where we assessed *enrollment* rates, 18% of families enrolled when notices were sent home from school and 63% enrolled when invited personally by someone they knew. These rates certainly indicate interest, given that parents did not have choices about meeting times, or places, or content, options that would presumably increase enrollment. Of families that began our programs, over 80% met *completion* criteria of attending more than half the meetings and completing post-assessment. Anderson's home-based program maintained 100% of families, and the completion rate was 81% even in Ambrose's child-abuse program.

Parent *participation* throughout the programs has generally been very high. Virtually all families completed home assignments to assess their child's skills, target a skill, carry out a teaching program, and keep some records of progress, although records were not usually as complete as we asked for. The reading and teaching assignments in our program, if carried out fully, would take about an hour-and-a-half each week. In contrast, Anderson's program requires parents to teach for 10 hours and be present to observe during additional hours each week. Still, most comply. On *consumer satisfaction* measures, our parents have evaluated all aspects of the program highly. Virtually all parents felt they had learned something of value and said they would recommend the program much or very much to other families.

These data convincingly show that the parent training we have studied is a service that families—at least some families—definitely want and make good use of. This seems to contrast with the observation voiced by some writers that parents of children with handicaps would rather avoid such teacher roles and parent training involvements. For example, Benson and Turnbull (1986) concluded that "a review of the literature suggests that enthusiasm for the intervenor role has emanated more from professional sources than from parent sources" (p. 133). Sadly, this thin and not very empirical literature about parent needs and desires relies heavily on the opinions of only a few articulate parents who have found satisfactory ways to cope with their child's retardation without a consultation and/or who perceive the "intervenor role" as something quite different and intrusive. In truth, every parent is a teacher, every day of the year. It is understandable that parents may not be too enthusiastic about a required and very time-consuming program that makes extensive teaching demands without sensitivity to their other needs, but such a program is in many ways a straw man. We have seen that many parents express high enthusiasm for more information and for some ways to make the natural teaching they do go more smoothly. We have also seen that many programs can fit very well with the time and energy that parents have available.

HOW DO FAMILIES BENEFIT?

Beyond liking the program, do families benefit in the ways that service providers intended? Let us continue with the list of criteria in Chapter 1 that address the question: Did the program work? The last six of these ask about parent proficiency, child gains, maintenance of gains, maintenance of teaching at home, family generalization, and advocacy—criteria that speak to whether the service benefitted families.

Parents' *proficiency* in behavior modification clearly increases with training. In knowledge of behavioral principles, families increased significantly from pre- to post-training in every study we have reported. We have assessed knowledge as it is applied in teaching and behavior management vignettes, either written or verbally presented. In actual teaching skills demonstrated in a clinic-based videotaped session, parents have consistently shown significant gains by several different scoring systems. In some controlled comparisons, however, gains have not surpassed those of delayed training control parents. We have also noted that when proficiency is measured not by gains but by attaining a predetermined criterion, a sizable minority of families do not achieve proficiency. We will consider these further below.

Concerning *child gains*, the Parents as Teachers program has been oriented primarily toward self-help skills and behavior problems, and it is fair to say that when parents have carried out programs, children have consistently shown gains. Anderson's programs included a wider range of skill areas and also demonstrated significant child gains. When we have assessed the *maintenance of child gains*, we have found that skills once learned are maintained. We have not assessed this area as much, however, because the more critical question with children who are developmentally disabled is whether families go on to teach new skills. This *maintenance of teaching*—parents' putting what they have learned into practice at home months or years later—is in many ways the most important of the outcome criteria.

The evidence about continued implementation is mixed. We have measured the extent and quality of teaching at home at various points (six months, one year) following training. It has not been feasible to continue a no-training control group for this long, so we have compared each family's home teaching at follow-up with that family's home teaching before training. By this procedure, we have typically found an increase in home teaching (extent and quality) during training, but a decline at follow-up. In most studies, though, the follow-up mean has still been higher than the pre-training mean. This is a difficult area to assess, and requires more attention in the future.

By *family generalization* we have meant changes in attitudes or adjustment that were not directly targeted by the parent training program. The thrust of the evidence is that parent training programs either produce no measurable family generalization or trigger a benign cycle, where other areas of family functioning improve as well. In our programs we found some evidence for lower post-training depression and stress, and higher family adaptability and cohesion as well as satisfaction with the family's adaptability. When we measured attitudes in the Boston sample (Baker, Heifetz, & Murphy, 1980) the second biggest increase parents reported was in self-confidence, followed by increased ability to handle problems, decreased frustration, and better communication with the spouse about the child.

The final criterion we have listed is *advocacy*; whether parents who become better teachers of their children also become better able to advocate for their children. Returning to the attitude survey noted above, the biggest change parents reported was an increase in "my ability to evaluate the quality of school services he receives." (By way of control, we had also asked parents about their ability to evaluate medical services—an area that should not be affected by our program—and, indeed, change here was ranked lowest.) We have received reports from schools about how parents that we have trained stand out later for their proactive involvement in their children's IEPs, but we have not looked systematically to see if this is the case and, if so, whether the parent training program contributed. Both family generalization and advocacy are potential outcomes that require much more study.

HOW CAN AGENCIES SERVE
MORE FAMILIES MORE
EFFECTIVELY?

From our studies that have compared different training approaches, we can state one general conclusion: more is not necessarily better. Parent training that is done in individual consultation sessions is much more costly in staff time than is group parent training. Yet we found no short-term or long-term differences in outcomes when we compared individual and group training. Parent training through written instruction alone produced gains in parent knowledge of behavioral principles and child self-help skills that were comparable to much more expensive models employing groups and home visits. Media-directed parent training in groups oriented around written instruction and videotapes produced results comparable to groups with highly experienced leaders. One exception to this rule was parent training that supplemented written instruction with telephone consultation. We reasoned that this model might be a viable alternative for rural areas, where distances preclude regular center visits. However, staff did not like this type of training, and it proved less effective than even written instruction alone.

Agencies should, then, be encouraged to explore ways of providing information and guidance to families that are alternatives to the individual counseling typically offered. One difficulty with the individual counseling model, especially when it is open-ended and crisis-driven, is that a small number of clients occupy a large percentage of agency resources. Wiser service provision would allocate significant resources to prevention and early intervention, making training programs available to all families when their children are quite young and focusing on parents' roles in skill development rather than just on behavior management. We are encouraged that cost-efficient formats, such as groups, books, and videotapes, can reach a large number of families with good success.

HOW CAN AN AGENCY CONDUCT A SUCCESSFUL PROGRAM?

Despite the apparent simplicity of parent training, it takes many good decisions to make a program truly successful. We will not presume to condense the points throughout the monograph into a list of suggestions for success, because it would be very long, with many caveats. On the other hand, our research and experiences do underscore a number of points at which a program can practically ensure its *failure*. Table 14.1 lists suggestions for failure—13 in all (for bad luck)! If you want a successful program, go over the list to make sure that you are not following any of our suggestions. While these pertain a bit more to group programs, there are many good ways here to make programs of individual behavioral counseling fail as well.

TABLE 14.1

How to Make a Parent Training Program Fail

1. *Assign just one staff member to parent training.* A staff member working alone, without the social support and collaboration of a colleague, is much less likely to actually implement parent training.

2. *Create role conflict.* Select staff whose other roles within the agency are quite different from the role of parent trainer. It also helps not to give staff sufficient preparation time; this way, they will feel ill-prepared when they begin the program.

3. *Select inexperienced leaders.* It is particularly important to select those who do not have good behavior modification problem solving skills. They will be less likely to implement the program at all; if they do implement it, they will do so less well. Some programs also have ensured failure by selecting staff who are skeptical about the aims and strategies involved.

4. *Select leaders who cannot teach children.* This is a common strategy for failure, for as soon as parents see that the leader cannot get down on the floor with a child and put teachings into practice, they may lose faith.

5. *Tie parent training to a poor school program.* Schools must in some way involve parents. In a school where children are not taught very well, however, a parent training program may be a formula for failure, for it will not have legitimacy. Moreover, parents who complete the program may become sophisticated critics of the school.

6. *Recruit impersonally.* You may be able to avoid ever having to start the program if you recruit through the mail or through notices sent home with children. If you do not make personal contact with parents, especially if you are working with low-income, ethnic minority parents, they will be much less likely to join.

7. *Make participation required.* This will not always insure failure; if parents are desperate enough for their children to be enrolled in a special program, they will participate successfully.

8. *Make access difficult.* Schedule the meetings only during the day, when it is convenient for staff but inconvenient for working parents. Also, do not provide child care, bilingual staff when needed, telephone reminders, and make-up sessions to facilitate involvement.

9. *Follow too tight a curriculum.* Go into each session with such a strict game plan that there is no room to address individual parent concerns. Take the position that you know just what parents need. Follow a tight time schedule—if a topic requires more time to be really helpful, cut it short in the interest of time. Don't consider adapting your plan. Some parents will feel they are not benefitting and will drop out.

10. *Follow too loose a curriculum.* Go into each session with only a vague sense of what you want to accomplish. In a group, be receptive to any parent who would like to use up most of the meeting time discussing his or her child's problem. Better still, let the discussion drift to other topics. Some parents will feel they are not benefitting and will drop out.

11. *Go over parents' heads.* Failure can be assured by being overly didactic, giving long lectures at a high level of abstraction, or insisting on tiresome recordkeeping. Failure will be more certain with parents whose education is limited, and who would benefit more from action-oriented approaches.

12. *Focus on behavior problems.* Begin with behavior problem management and make this the main focus of your consultation. Do not begin with skill building, where parents can get a better understanding of their child's learning needs and become comfortable teachers before they tackle the more emotionally charged area of behavior problems.

13. *Select measures that are too general.* If you get to the end of the program and the parents have participated and liked it, you can still seize failure from the jaws of success. Evaluate the program's success with broad developmental scales rather than measures that specifically tap the skills targeted. In this way, the children, especially if they have severe handicaps, will seem not to have benefitted.

WHAT ARE THE LIMITS OF
PARENT TRAINING?

Although we have found that most training formats seem to produce comparable outcomes, we have also found considerable variability in outcome within each format. First, we should note that about one family in five does not complete the program. Second, even for completers we should look beyond the good group outcomes to individual cases. Here we find that, although most families feel that they have benefitted, a sizable minority do not reach our criteria for success. About one parent in three does not achieve sufficient knowledge of behavioral principles and skill in actual teaching for us to classify him or her as proficient. Moreover, by various criteria, from 25% to 39% of families were doing little or no useful teaching at follow-up.

HOW CAN PARENT TRAINING
BE ADAPTED FOR BROADER
IMPACT?

We know some predictors of less successful outcome, and these have implications for program adaptations. Parents who drop out of the program have been more likely to be single parents and initially very low in knowledge of behavioral principles. We have found it beneficial for single parents to attend training with someone (e.g., friend, relative). We also have suggested scheduling several pre-training sessions with the leader, to establish a relationship and to introduce the behavioral framework gradually, before beginning any formal training with demands for home assessment or teaching.

Parents who complete the program but do not achieve proficiency have been lower on various socioeconomic indices (e.g. education, income), have had less previous exposure to behavior modification, and have entered the program expecting more problems in teaching that they cannot overcome. Parents who do not continue to teach after the program has ended achieved lower levels of proficiency during the program.

These findings have suggested two adaptations. We have directly countered low expectations with a more cognitive approach (see Chapter 2). We have sought to increase proficiency by simplifying the program and using more action-oriented approaches: parents observe teaching and teach their own children throughout the program (see Chapter 7). Anderson's intensive home-based program takes participant modeling further and it works well with families who otherwise would be predicted to do poorly in our group program. We have also made efforts to increase parents' access to the program by meeting in community settings as close as possible to their homes, conducting meetings in the evening so as not to conflict with work schedules, providing child care, and the like. The encouraging outcomes we have reported with lower income families, Spanish-speaking families, and even child-abusive families indicate the promise of these program variations.

WHERE CAN PARENT TRAINING
FIT INTO A CONTINUUM OF
SERVICES?

An agency concerned with families and developmental disabilities might take to heart several implications of these studies. There is no single service that will fit all families' needs and desires, so multiple offerings are a necessity. Services should be concerned with prevention of future difficulties as well as meeting present crises, and parent training programs can serve well here. Parent training programs can entertain diverse aims (e.g., to help parents teach better, cope better with problems, advocate for services) and they can be effectively offered in a variety of formats (e.g., individual, group, home visits). Parents should be made aware of the range of services available and counseled as to when a parent training program may be helpful for them.

A focus of increased attention has been changing service needs across the life span of the person with developmental disabilities (Fewell & Vadasy, 1986) and across the lifecycle of the family (Turnbull, Summers, & Brotherson, 1986). Parent training has heretofore been thought of primarily as a service for families with young children, concentrating on early skill development and behavior problem management. We would encourage service providers to consider adapting what we have learned about conducting systematic parent training programs to develop programs for families at later points in the lifecycle. We can imagine, for example, programs presented through media and/or small groups with topics such as collaboration with schools, peer group problems of adolescence, emerging sexuality, letting go in late adolescence, transitioning from school to work, transitioning from living at home to out-of-home placement, assisting adult offspring, and estate planning. For these and many other areas, rather than relying solely on counseling by individual staff whose expertise in any one area may be wanting, the agency could develop programs with planned curricula and offer repeated series of these. Counselors could then supplement and individualize these programs when necessary. Parents could take, and even retake, programs as they felt the need.

We will end on a related and cautionary note. Recent conceptualizations of the family with a child who is developmentally disabled have stressed complexity. Writers draw up lengthy lists of family needs and remind us that these needs fluctuate over the life cycle. All this is, of course, true and, at a conceptual level, helpful. A possible service consequence, however, is a devaluing of any specific intervention (e.g., parent training in language teaching) because it addresses only one of a host of needs. The situation is similar to what the clinician encounters in a microcosm when a parent, overwhelmed by the enormity of her child's problems and deficiencies, finds it impossible to target any one key behavior and try to do something about it. Being absorbed with the complexity can lead to spinning one's wheels.

Moreover, some family needs are not ours to address. Mental health and education professionals should distinguish between an awareness of the complexity of family needs and an inflated belief that we have, or should have, something to offer that meets them all. We must maintain our concentration on developing focused services that have a sound empirical basis. It is more honest to be clear about what a professional and an agency can do for families—and then do it well.

Appendix A

Parents As Teachers Group Curriculum

_____

PARENTS AS TEACHERS GROUP
CURRICULUM

Below is an outline of the 10 session group parent training curriculum, followed by forms parents use for planning and record keeping. Please see chapter 2 for details about format and program variations. No one (not even the author) will follow the program exactly as it is described; you will need to adapt the content and pacing of what we present here to your particular leaders and families. A complete curriculum guide may be obtained from the author (c/o Department of Psychology, UCLA, Los Angeles,CA 90024). The curriculum is designed to be used with our book, *Steps to Independence: A Skills Training Guide For Parents and Teachers of Children with Special Needs* (Baker & Brightman, 1989).

MEETING 1

Aims

That parents are introduced—to one another, to program parameters, to behavioral observation, and to a cognitive-behavioral perspective. That they target a skill to teach.

Timetable

0:00   Introductions—Spend 2–3 minutes with each family, learning about the child.
0:25   Program overview—What program aims to do and how we will do it.
0:40   Behaviors vs. Interpretations—Parents view a child on videotape and describe him; leaders list behaviors (specific, observable, measurable) and interpretations in 2 columns on the board, and then discuss distinctions.
0:55   Break—We provide coffee (decaff), tea, and cookies; sometimes parents will bring something for the group.
1:05   Teaching tape (optional)—Show a tape of good teaching and have parents note what teacher is doing, as introduction to concepts that follow.
1:15   Discuss why and why not to teach—Elicit two lists (on board)—reasons why a parent might want to assume the teacher role, and reasons why not. Discuss
1:30   Introduce problem solving vs. interfering thoughts and problem-solving scheme—introduce cognitive behavioral ideas. Discuss how some thoughts can interfere with teaching and others promote problem solving.
1:45   Target a skill—Considerations in targeting one skill to teach.

Homework

Read *Steps to Independence*, Chapters 1–6, and Chapter 9: Self-help Skills. (If possible, give parents the book *before* Meeting 1, and have them begin reading.) Complete Skill Teaching form. Complete Self-help Inventory if not already done. Teach 3 sessions (or hold until next week).

Notes

The teaching tape can be omitted if none is available or if there is not sufficient time. Alternatively, use the tape and cut the cognitive behavioral discussion short, to be elaborated in the next session. If self-help skills are very high for some older children, you may want to have their parents read Chapters 12 and 13: Toward Independent Living.

MEETING 2

Aims

That parents understand Antecedents in teaching, including their own thoughts, the steps of a skill, setting the stage, and presenting the task. That they design a teaching program for the skill they have targeted.

Timetable

0:00 Individual progress report—For every meeting, as each family arrives one trainer reviews with them their homework, progress, and problems.

0:15 Group discussion of obstacles and problem solving—List obstacles to teaching or to doing homework on board and generate problem-solving thoughts and strategies.

0:30 Task analysis exercise—Breaking a skill into component steps; use a live demonstration, with parents giving instructions (e.g., buttoning); break a skill down on the board.

0:50 Break

1:00 A-B-C Model: Antecedents—Explain and discuss A-B-C. Review Behaviors, and then focus on Antecedents. Describe setting the stage, and use video segments.

1:25 Backward chaining—Review concept from book. Demonstrate with teaching puzzle. Show backward chaining video segment. Discuss application to parents' target behaviors.

1:45 Instruction: Tell, show, and guide—Briefly introduce these.

1:55 Get ready skills—Mention priority of coming, sitting, looking, waiting. Coverage depends upon level of children. If necessary, set aside more time for this.

Homework

Review *Steps to Independence,* Chapter 4: Picking Rewards. Teach targeted skill for 5–10 minutes each day, for at least five days. Log progress.

Notes

There is always too much to cover in Meeting 2. If parents have read the book well, you can rely more on discussion and may get through most of it. Plan to carry some over into the discussion of Meeting 3.

MEETING 3

Aims

That parents understand Consequences in teaching, and further develop their ability to problem-solve around obstacles. That they decide what rewards they will use in teaching.

Timetable

0:00   Individual progress report.
0:15   Discussion of teaching programs—Break into 2 groups if 6 or more families. Each family describes teaching program (skill, setting stage, step child began with, progress, problems etc). Use as review of behavioral specificity and antecedents. Work in material you did not get to in Meeting 2.
0:40   Cognitive Review—Review Problem Solving Scheme. Note feelings during teaching and consider automatic thoughts that may lead to them.
1:00   Break
1:10   A-B-C: Consequences (Rewards)—Generate list of rewards. Solicit rewards that work best for their children. Discuss appropriateness, immediacy, consistency, and contingency. View video segments on rewards.
1:35   Rewards, role plays—Cover shaping, fading, and ending with a success. Leaders role play good and faulty teaching, with each other and/or with parents.
1:50   Self-rewards—How will parents reward themselves for teaching?

Homework

Read *Steps to Independence*, Chapter 7: Observing Progress and Troubleshooting, and Chapter 10: Toilet Training, if appropriate. Continue to teach 5–10 minute sessions at least 5 days and log progress.

Notes

This is a good time to start any families that will be working on toilet training. Consult for a few minutes after the meeting. Assign the chapter. If there are only one or two families and there is time, decide whether they will begin with urine or bowel training and have them begin charting.

MEETING 4

Aims

That parents integrate what they have learned about antecedents, consequences, and cognitions and see how these can improve their own teaching. That they troubleshoot their program.

Timetable

0:00 Schedule Meeting 5—Schedule individual appointments for Meeting 5. Four families per hour (two with each leader). Remind them to bring teaching materials—and the child!

0:05 Troubleshooting: "Coping" loop of Problem Solving Scheme

0:15 Divide into two groups:
Group A: Critique screening tapes.
Take 10 minutes or so per family. Show a few minutes of each family's teaching tape made pre-training; have parent recount thoughts, indicate positives, and critique. Encourage group to share positive aspects and to make suggestions for improvement.
Group B: Troubleshoot home teaching.
Discuss home teaching programs. Parents report problems, and leaders and other group members consult to develop coping strategies.

0:50 Break

1:00 *Group A & B reverse*

1:40 Incidental teaching—Reassemble to consider ways to make use of opportunities throughout the day to teach.

1:55 Self-help and toilet training consultation (as needed).

Homework

Continue teaching original self-help skill; if mastered, move to a new skill. Continue to log progress. Continue (or begin) charting toileting.

Notes

Some parents understandably may be embarrassed for the group to see them on video tape (and they should have the right to refuse). This exercise works very well, though. Keep the atmosphere supportive, with ample praise and gentle criticism.

MEETING 5

Aims

That parents demonstrate self-help skill teaching, receive feedback, and plan next steps.

Timetable

A recommended format is to schedule four parents each hour. Each trainer works with two families for that hour. Each family will have 15 minutes or so to teach, while the other family and the trainer observe. Feedback can be provided by the second family as well as the trainer. The families then switch roles. If time permits, have parents also teach a game or puzzle that you've brought. Also consult with families about their next self-help teaching program and develop a toilet training program if appropriate.

Homework

Read *Steps to Independence*, Chapter 15: Behavior Problems, pp. 161–178. Continue self-help and toileting programs, as before.

MEETING 6

Aims

That parents target a behavior problem and learn how to take baseline measures.

Timetable

0:00   Obstacles to behavior management—List parent reactions to behavior problems and their management; discuss those that interfere and those that facilitate. Show behavior problem video if possible; have parents guess what thoughts or reactions the child's teacher or parent might have, and consider problem-solving thoughts.

0:25   Introduce Behavior Management Guides

0:30   Define and measure behavior problems—Criteria for behavior problems, and frequency/duration measures. Look again at video and have parents take data, perhaps on one general problem and one specific one.)

0:55   Break

1:05   Re-introduce A-B-C model—Illustrate with several behavior problem examples.

1:15   Antecedents—If possible, show a video tape example; have parents define problem behaviors and then indicate antecedents (where, with whom, when, under what demands?). Pair families; role-play consulting, where each determines the Antecedents for the other's target behavior and then reports back to the group.

1:35   Individual targeting of problem behavior—Have each family target a behavior problem and decide how to measure it; leaders circulate to consult. If time, parents then report to the group.

1:55   Toilet training consultation/self-help consultation

Homework

Finish reading Behavior Problems chapter, pp. 178–191. Keep baseline data on targeted behavior problem. Continue self-help/toileting programs.

Notes

For this and subsequent meetings, rather than take initial meeting time for consultations about self-help programs, review progress individually before the meeting with parents who arrive early and then consult at the end of the meeting with the remaining parents. Demands on parent time are now increased, so you may want to make self-help teaching logs optional.

MEETING 7

Aims

That parents understand ways to respond to problem behaviors and to encourage alternate behaviors. That parents develop a management strategy of the behavior problem that they have targeted.

Timetable

0:00   Individual review of data—As each family arrives, spend a few minutes checking data sheets. If not done, assess why.

0:15   Locating better consequences—List all the consequences that parents have seen in response to problem behaviors. Discuss why some methods are ineffective (e.g., they give attention). Review A-B-C, and discuss removing the reward, ignoring, and forced compliance. Show video taped examples if possible. Role play with cognitive modeling of interfering and problem solving thoughts.

1:00   Break

1:10   Encouraging alternate behaviors—Emphasize importance, discuss differential reinforcement of incompatible behaviors (DRI: also DRL). If possible show a brief behavior problem video and have parents pose several alternative behaviors to reward.

1:25   Develop behavior management programs—Break into two groups. For each family, review targeted behavior and baseline, establish the A-B-C pattern, and *make certain they leave with a program to carry out.* For parents who did not take baseline, do not develop a program yet.

Homework

Begin behavior management program; continue to keep data. Reread Behavior Problems chapter as necessary. Continue self-help/toileting programs.

Notes

Behavior problems is an emotionally charged area, and can elicit considerable response. Avoid long stories or having one or two parents dominate the meeting. Encourage parents to share brief observations, but keep on task.

MEETING 8

Aims

That parents learn about time out, contracting, troubleshooting, and ways to manage their own feelings of frustration and anger. That parents develop their own programs further.

Timetable

0:00 Review behavior management program—Review data, review programs and principles, and problem-solve about obstacles. Break into two groups if group is large or if some parents are behind.

0:30 Time out & contracting—Discuss and role play time out; model cognitions. Consider contingency contracts and simple token systems.

1:00 Break

1:10 Troubleshooting management programs—Show video tape of behavior problems and ask parents to function as consultants: how would they change As and Cs? Alternatively, describe behavior problem vignettes verbally to the group and discuss solutions.

1:35 Anger control/cognitive role plays—Solicit problem behaviors and related thoughts that elicit parents' frustration and anger, and as a group discuss ways to cope better.

Homework

Continue behavior management programs and data keeping. Continue self-help and toileting programs.

Notes

The plan for this meeting assumes that parents have kept data and begun their programs with some success. If parents require more didactic input on the basics, use this meeting for review. Structure the meeting around the extensive practice of identifying A-B-C patterns, reviewing components. Then follow this meeting's plan in the next meeting.

MEETING 9

Aims

That parents troubleshoot their behavior management programs and apply behavioral principles to another skill teaching area: play. That parents begin to plan for follow-through after the program ends.

Timetable

0:00 Individual review of management programs—As parents enter, check data and ascertain progress; put each family's data since beginning baseline on board.

0:15 Group discussion of management programs—In one or two groups, have each family describe progress and problems. Talk about data on board. If some families are ready to modify another problem, prompt them to formulate A-B-C patterns and develop a program. Encourage others to persist.

0:45 Parent role plays of coping strategies—Have parents report, and perhaps role-play, strategies they found useful to overcome obstacles and/or cope with anger (optional if covered well in group discussion).

1:00 Break

1:10 Introduce follow-through—Discuss problems of following through after program is over. Solicit possible obstacles to follow-through and problem solve about them.

1:25 Play skills—Introduce play skills as another area for teaching. Solicit examples of play skills from group and consider how behavioral teaching principles would be applied. View videos of play skill teaching, if possible.

Homework

Read *Steps to Independence*, Chapter 11: Play Skills. Target a play skill and teach it two or three few times. Continue with behavior management programs and data keeping.

Notes

If the group is progressing well, with high understanding, then it will be informative to move into a new area such as play skills, but this is optional. Play skills is a good area for fathers and/or siblings to take primary responsibility for teaching.

MEETING 10

Aims

That parents consolidate what they have learned and plan for the future.

Timetable

0:00   Behavior management progress—In one or two groups, review behavior management progress, chart on board. Also review self-help skill progress.

0:30   Play skill teaching—Discuss and role-play parents efforts to teach a play skill, using this as an opportunity to review teaching principles.

1:00   Break

1:10   Individual development of follow through plans—Distribute Follow-Through Planning Sheets. Have parents consult with each other (perhaps in pairs) about programming objectives over the next several months, projecting obstacles and deriving coping strategies. Leaders circulate as needed.

1:35   Discuss follow through obstacles—Discuss overcoming obstacles to follow through.

Notes

Leave parents with a clear schedule for any follow-up meetings, either individual or group. A group meeting in a month or so is usually helpful. Also, an individual post-training session with each family, to collect post-measures and do future planning, has always been part of our program.

SKILL TEACHING FORM

Note: Complete one form for each skill that you target. Refer to it as you teach and complete the Daily Teaching Log.

Possible skills to teach: _____

_____

_____

GOAL Skill targeted: _____

(Why? _____)

Steps to teach: 1. _____

2. _____

3. _____

4. _____

5. _____

6. _____

7. _____

PLANS *Where* will the teaching be done? *When* will I teach?

What *materials* do I need?

What *rewards* do I need?

How will I *reward myself* for a good session?

Other plans to consider:

Are distractions eliminated?
Does this skill require backward chaining?
Am I using clear and simple directions?
Do I model (show) him/her what to do?
Do I guide him/her through the steps at first?
Am I remembering to reward frequently with praise?
Am I rewarding the GET READY SKILLS (coming, sitting, looking, waiting)?

DO (Record each session on a Daily Teaching Log)

STEPS TO PROBLEM SOLVING

I. Set a GOAL

What will I focus on?

↓

II. Make PLANS

What steps will I take to get there?

↓

III. Go ahead and DO IT!

↓

IV. Throughout CHECK YOURSELF carefully

How am I doing? Are the plans working?

↙   ↘

Possibility A: *Possibility B:*
Things are going   Not so great; plans
according to plan   aren't getting me there

↓   ↓

REWARD YOURSELF   **KEEP COOL**

All right! If I   It's not the end of the world
teach in short
sessions I can do it!   Don't blow up; think about
Etc.   specifics and change them

↓   ↓

FINISH THE SESSION &   **FIGURE OUT NEW PLANS &**
KNOCK OFF TILL TOMORROW   **STRATEGIES**

Use your Skill Teaching Form to
review your old plans & make
changes

↓

TRY AGAIN

DAILY TEACHING LOG

Date: _____

Time & place of session: _____

First, check the skill teaching form to be clear on your **GOAL** and your specific **PLANS** for the session. Skill: _____

Now, **CHECK** yourself carefully:
What happened in the session? For example, which steps did you work on? Did he succeed? What problems did you encounter?

What were your thoughts and feelings during the session? For example, "I'm too tired to teach today"; "It's helpful to use short sessions"; etc., etc.

How did you reward yourself for the good parts of the session?

What did you do when things didn't work according to plans?

Suggestions for next sessions:

FOLLOW-THROUGH PLANS

Name: _____

Date: _____

1. *First major area or problem to teach or manage:*

   What will likely get in the way of doing so?

   How can I work around these problems?

2. *Second major area to teach or manage:*

   What will likely get in the way of doing so?

   How can I work around these problems?

3. *Third major area to teach or manage:*

   What will likely get in the way of doing so?

   How can I work around these problems?

BEHAVIOR PROBLEM DATA SHEET

Behavior problem: _____

How to measure: Count how many? _____   Time to measure: All day? _____
how long? _____   Certain times (when _____)

Week #: _____
Baseline? _____   Program type (e.g., ignoring, time out): _____

Date: _____	S	M	T	W	T	F	S
1. Data							
2. Antecedents							
3. Consequences							
4. Your thoughts/ feelings/ reactions							
5. How to cope with and manage the behavior better next time							

Appendix B

_____Measures

UCLA PROJECT FOR DEVELOPMENTAL DISABILITIES

DEMOGRAPHIC QUESTIONNAIRE

Parent _____   Child _____   Date _____

I. Family Identifying Information

1) Child's relation to family:
    a) Natural Child _____   c) Foster Child _____
    b) Adopted Child _____   d) Other (specify) _____

2) Present Marital Status of Parents: _____

3) Who lives with child? (Mother and/or Father) _____

4a) Other children in the family:

Name	Sex	Birthdate	Age	Relationship*	Living at home?
_____	___	_____	___	_____	_____
_____	___	_____	___	_____	_____
_____	___	_____	___	_____	_____
_____	___	_____	___	_____	_____

    * Relation: Natural, Step, Adoptive, Foster, Other

4b) Other persons living at home (Please specify): _____
_____

5) Mother's Date of Birth: _____

6) Highest Grade of School Completed by Mother: _____

7a) Current Occupation of Mother: _____

7b) Mother is employed: _____ hours per week _____ not employed

8) Father's Date of Birth: _____

9) Highest Grade of School Completed by Father: _____

10a) Current Occupation of Father: _____

10b) Father is employed: _____ hours per week _____ not employed

11) Total Family Income (Before Taxes):

    _____ Less than $6,000   _____ $17,000–24,999   _____ $50,000 +
    _____ $ 6,000–10,999   _____ $25,000–34,999
    _____ $11,000–16,999   _____ $35,000–49,999

II. Child Identifying Information

1) Child's Date of Birth: _____

2) Child's Sex: _____ Female   _____ Male

3) Child's age at first diagnosis of disability: _____

4a) Child's Diagnosis (Check which most accurately describes child's most recent diagnosis):

_____ Brain Damage
_____ Down Syndrome
_____ Cerebral Palsy
_____ Autism or Childhood Schizophrenia
_____ Organic/Genetic Syndrome (please specify) _____
_____ Retardation, cause unknown
_____ Learning Disabled
_____ Educationally Handicapped
_____ Other (please specify) _____

4b) Child's Current Level of Retardation:

_____ profound
_____ severe
_____ moderate or trainable
_____ mild or educable
_____ borderline
_____ not retarded
_____ no information as to level

5a) Regional Center at which child is registered: _____

5b) Name of Regional Center caseworker: _____

6) Child's Present School Placement (check placement that applies best):

_____ none
_____ lives in residential setting for part or all of the
            week (describe: _____)
_____ day care
_____ pre-school or nursery program
_____ regular-education class (grade: _____)
_____ Resource room part of day
_____ Special-education (S.E.D.)
_____ Special-education (L.D.)
_____ Special-education (other: _____)
_____ Tutoring

7) Child's Present School Placement Is:

_____ Public
_____ Private

III. Experiences with Services

1) Parents' Consultation Experience (please indicate with M (Mother) and/or F (Father) which of the following programs each parent has participated in):

Program	Participated in past	Currently participating
Parent Organizations (specify:_____)	_____	_____
Parent Support Group	_____	_____
Parent-training Group (behavioral)	_____	_____
Parent-education Program	_____	_____
Individual consultation with mental-health professional	_____	_____
Family Therapy	_____	_____
Couples Therapy/Marital Therapy	_____	_____
Other Regional Center service (specify: _____)	_____	_____

2) Parents' familiarity with behavior modification before present program—indicate M (Mother) and/or F (Father):

_____ Had not heard of approach
_____ Knew a little about it
_____ Had read book or talked with professional about it
_____ Had seen it practiced in child's school
_____ Had participated in behavior modification training program

3) Please identify yourself:

_____ Asian
_____ Black
_____ Caucasian
_____ Hispanic
_____ Other (please specify): _____

Self-Help Checklist

Please check the box that most appropriately describes your child's ability to perform the following self-help skills.

SKILL	NONE	SOME	ALL
1. Drinking from a cup	☐	☐	☐
2. Eating with a spoon	☐	☐	☐
3. Eating with a fork	☐	☐	☐
4. Spreading with a knife	☐	☐	☐
5. Cutting with a knife	☐	☐	☐
6. Removing pants	☐	☐	☐
7. Putting on pants	☐	☐	☐
8. Putting on socks	☐	☐	☐
9. Putting on a pullover shirt	☐	☐	☐
10. Putting on a front-button blouse, shirt, or coat	☐	☐	☐
11. Putting on shoes	☐	☐	☐
12. Threading a belt	☐	☐	☐
13. Buckling a belt	☐	☐	☐
14. Zipping up	☐	☐	☐
15. Buttoning	☐	☐	☐
16. Starting a zipper	☐	☐	☐
17. Tying shoes	☐	☐	☐
18. Hanging up clothes	☐	☐	☐
19. Drying hands	☐	☐	☐
20. Washing hands	☐	☐	☐
21. Brushing teeth	☐	☐	☐
22. Washing face	☐	☐	☐
23. Bathing—drying	☐	☐	☐
24. Bathing—washing	☐	☐	☐
25. Brushing hair	☐	☐	☐
26. Hair washing	☐	☐	☐
27. Making a bed	☐	☐	☐
28. Table setting	☐	☐	☐
29. Changing a bed	☐	☐	☐
30. Sweeping	☐	☐	☐

Note. The Self-Help Checklist is reprinted from *Steps to independence: A skills training guide for parents and teachers of children with special needs* (2nd ed.) (p. 54) by B. L. Baker and A. J. Brightman, 1989. Baltimore: Brookes Publishing. Copyright 1989 by Paul H. Brookes Publishing Co. Reprinted by permission.

SELF HELP INVENTORY

Parent _____ Child _____ Date _____

The purpose of this inventory is to determine exactly what your child is presently able to do. This will allow us to plan together an appropriate teaching program for your child. While children often vary in their performance of skills, we want to know how much of each skill your child usually can do.

Circle the highest step your child can do. *Circling a step means he can do that step and ALL the steps before it.* For example, if your child can do Steps 1, 2, and 4 of a skill and cannot do Step 3 then you circle 2.

Note: Circle the highest number step if your child can perform the skill completely on his own - this means that he can do it while you are out of the room.

SKILLS

1) *Drinking from a cup*
   0 — Cannot hold cup at all.
   1 — Holds cup and drinks, with your physical guidance throughout.
   2 — Places cup on table after you assist him to drink and to bring cup partway down.
   3 — Places cup on table after you assist him to drink.
   4 — Drinks from cup after you help him to raise cup partway; replaces cup on table on his own.
   5 — Drinks from cup after you help him pick it up; replaces cup on table on his own.
   6 — Drinks from cup completely on his own.
   7 — Drinks from a variety of cups and glasses, completely on his own.

2) *Eating with a spoon*
   0 — Cannot do any part of eating with a spoon.
   1 — Brings spoon to mouth, with physical guidance from you.
   2 — Brings spoon to mouth after you fill it and lift it partway.
   3 — Brings spoon to mouth and replaces it in food, after you fill it and lift it partway.
   4 — Brings spoon to mouth on own, after you fill it; replaces it in food.
   5 — Eats on his own with your assistance only in scooping food.
   6 — Uses spoon independently with soft solids (e.g., mashed potatoes, squash, oatmeal).
   7 — Uses spoon independently with soup.

Note. The Self Help Inventory is reprinted from *Steps to independence: A skills training guide for parents and teachers of children with special needs* (2nd ed.) (pp. 217–224) by B. L. Baker and A. J. Brightman, 1989. Baltimore: Brookes Publishing. Copyright 1989 by Paul H. Brookes Publishing Co. Reprinted by permission.

3) *Eating with a fork*
   0 — Cannot do any part of eating with a fork.
   1 — Uses fork like a spoon, i.e., scoops with fork.
   2 — Stabs food with fork, with your guidance.
   3 — Stabs food with fork, with your directions.
   4 — Eats *soft foods* with fork completely on his own.
   5 — Eats a *variety of foods* with a fork completely on his own.

4) *Spreading with a knife*
   0 — Cannot do any part of spreading with a knife.
   1 — Spreads part of a piece of bread, with your physical help.
   2 — Spreads a whole piece of bread with your help.
   3 — Spreads part of a piece of bread with you telling him where to spread.
   4 — Spreads a whole piece of bread with direction, after you have put jam on it.
   5 — Puts jam on bread with your help and spreads it on his own.
   6 — Puts jam on bread and spreads it, with your supervision.
   7 — Can get jam and bread, and spread it completely on his own with no supervision.

5) *Cutting with a knife*
   0 — Cannot do any part of cutting with a knife.
   1 — Finishes cutting through meat or a similar food with your help after you have started the cut.
   2 — Cuts all the way through meat or a similar food, with your help.
   3 — Finishes cutting through started food on his own.
   4 — Cuts all the way through meat on his own (you help him hold the food steady with the fork).
   5 — Positions fork in the food and cuts entirely on his own, when you tell him to.
   7 — Uses knife for cutting completely independently; no reminders.

6) *Removing pants*
   0 — Cannot remove pants.
   1 — Pulls pants off one leg after you remove pants from other leg.
   2 — Pulls both pant legs off from ankle, while sitting.
   3 — Pulls pants off from below knees, while sitting.
   4 — Pulls pants down from above knees, then sits and pulls them off.
   5 — Pulls pants down from mid-thigh, then off.
   6 — Pulls pants down from hips and off.
   7 — Removes pants completely, with your supervision.
   8 — Removes pants completely on his own.

7) *Putting on pants (does not include fastening)*
   0 — Cannot put pants on.
   1 — Pulls pants up to waist after you put them on up to hips.
   2 — Pulls pants up to waist after you put them on to middle of thighs.
   3 — Pulls pants up to waist after you put them on up to knees.
   4 — Stands and pulls pants up to waist after you put them over both feet.
   5 — Puts pants on one foot and pulls up to waist after you put them on other foot.
   6 — Puts pants on both feet and pulls up to waist after you hand them to him.
   7 — Puts pants on completely by himself.

8) *Putting on socks*
   0 — Cannot put on socks.
   1 — Pulls socks up from ankle.
   2 — Pulls socks up from heel.
   3 — Pulls socks up from toes.
   4 — Puts socks on completely, with heel in the correct position.

9) *Putting on a pullover shirt*
   0 — Cannot put on a pullover shirt.
   1 — Pulls shirt down over his head after you place it on his head.
   2 — Pulls shirt down to waist after you put arms in.
   3 — Pulls the shirt over his head, and puts one arm in.
   4 — Pulls the shirt over his head, and puts both arms in.
   5 — Puts shirt on after you hand it to him.
   6 — Picks up pullover and puts it on completely on his own.

10) *Putting on a front-button blouse, shirt, or coat (does not include buttoning)*
   0 — Cannot put on a front-button blouse or shirt.
   1 — Grasps both sides of the shirt front and brings them together after you put both arms through shirt sleeves.
   2 — Puts one arm in sleeve after you put his other arm in other sleeve.
   3 — Puts both arms through sleeves after you hold the shirt for him.
   4 — Picks up shirt when laid out and puts one arm through.
   5 — Picks up shirt when laid out and puts both arms in.
   6 — Puts shirt on completely when laid out.
   7 — Takes shirt from drawer or hanger and puts on completely.

11) *Putting on shoes (does not include tying)*
   0 — Cannot put on shoes.
   1 — Pushes foot down into shoe after you put the shoe over heel.
   2 — Pulls shoe over heel after you put the shoe over his toes.
   3 — Slips his toes into shoe and finishes after you position shoe in his palm.
   4 — Puts his shoe on after you hand it to him.
   5 — Puts on his sneakers.
   6 — Puts shoes on the correct feet (completely on his own).

12) *Threading a belt*
    0 — Cannot thread a belt.
    1 — Pulls belt through loop after you start it.
    2 — Inserts belt into one or two loops and pulls it through.
    3 — Inserts and pulls belt through all loops, with pants *off*.
    4 — Inserts and pulls belt through all loops, with pants *on*.

13) *Buckling a belt*
    0 — Cannot buckle a belt.
    1 — Threads belt and inserts tab end through buckle.
    2 — Puts tooth of buckle into hole.
    3 — Buckles belt and inserts tab end through pant loop.

14) *Zipping up*
    0 — Cannot zip.
    1 — Pulls zipper up the rest of the way (while you hold the bottom) once you start the zipper and pull it up to chest.
    2 — Pulls zipper all the way up (while you hold the bottom) once you have started the zipper.
    3 — Holds the bottom and pulls up with other hand once you start it.
    4 — Pulls up side zippers.
    5 — Pulls up back zippers.

15) *Buttoning*
    0 — Cannot button.
    1 — Pulls button through buttonhole after you insert it halfway through.
    2 — Inserts button into the buttonhole while you hold buttonhole open.
    3 — Inserts button halfway through button hole and pulls it through.
    4 — Buttons large buttons in view.
    5 — Buttons small buttons in view.
    6 — Buttons an entire shirt or blouse with verbal direction only.
    7 — Buttons an entire shirt or blouse completely on his own.

16) *Starting a zipper*
    0 — Cannot start a zipper.
    1 — Puts insert into slide as you hold the slide of zipper steady.
    2 — Holds slide steady and places insert in, with direction.
    3 — Places insert into slide, holds it steady, and pulls up zipper, with direction.
    4 — Starts zipper completely on own.

17) *Tying shoes*
    0 — Cannot tie shoes.
    1 — Pulls both laces to tighten.
    2 — Makes first knot.
    3 — Makes first loop of bow.
    4 — Makes second loop of bow.
    5 — Ties shoes completely.
    6 — Threads, laces, and ties shoes completely.

18) Hanging up clothes
   0 — Cannot do any part of hanging up clothes.
   1 — Picks up and holds hanger in one hand, holds light coat in other hand.
   2 — Puts both shoulders of coat over hanger with your guidance.
   3 — Puts hanger into one shoulder of coat with your guidance, and puts the other shoulder of coat over the hanger himself.
   4 — Puts entire coat onto hanger when you tell him what to do.
   5 — Puts the coat onto the hanger completely on his own.
   6 — Hangs up other clothes (shirts, pants, dresses, etc.).
   7 — #6, plus does it when necessary, with no reminders.

19) Drying hands
   0 — Cannot do any part of drying hands.
   1 — Wipes palm of hands while you help hold the towel.
   2 — Wipes back of hands while you help hold the towel.
   3 — Wipes palm of hands holding the towel himself.
   4 — Wipes back of hands holding the towel himself.
   5 — Dries hands completely on his own.

20) Washing hands
   0 — Cannot do any part of washing hands.
   1 — Rinses soap off hands.
   2 — Puts soap on and lathers hands with your help.
   3 — Puts soap on and lathers hands himself.
   4 — Turns on water.
   5 — Turns off water.
   6 — Washes hands completely on his own.

21) Brushing teeth
   0 — Cannot do any part of brushing teeth.
   1 — Brushes teeth with your hands guiding his.
   2 — Brushes front teeth.
   3 — Brushes back teeth.
   4 — Brushes teeth once you have put toothpaste on brush.
   5 — Brushes teeth entirely on his own (puts toothpaste on).

22) Washing face
   0 — Cannot do any part of washing face.
   1 — Washes all parts of his face when you guide him with your hand on his.
   2 — Washes parts of his face when you point to or tell him where to wash.
   3 — Washes all parts of his face.
   4 — Washes and rinses face completely on his own.

23) *Bathing-Drying*
- 0 — Cannot do any part of drying.
- 1 — Dries upper body with your physical guidance.
- 2 — Dries lower body and back with your physical guidance.
- 3 — Dries upper body with you telling him where to dry.
- 4 — Dries lower body and back with you telling him where to dry.
- 5 — Dries upper body on his own.
- 6 — Dries himself completely on his own.

24) *Bathing-Washing*
- 0 — Cannot do any part of bathing.
- 1 — Rinses soap off with your physical guidance.
- 2 — Rinses soap off on his own.
- 3 — Washes upper body with your physical guidance.
- 4 — Washes lower body and back with your physical guidance.
- 5 — Washes upper body with you telling him where to wash.
- 6 — Washes lower body and back with you telling him where to wash.
- 7 — Washes upper body on his own.
- 8 — Washes completely on his own.

25) *Brushing hair*
- 0 — Cannot do any part of hair brushing.
- 1 — Brushes hair with your hands guiding his.
- 2 — Brushes hair with you telling him where to brush.
- 3 — Brushes hair completely on his own.

26) *Hair washing*
- 0 — Cannot do any part of hair washing.
- 1 — Dries hair with your help.
- 2 — Wets and dries hair with your help.
- 3 — Rinses soap from hair with your help.
- 4 — Lathers hair with your help.
- 5 — Rinses soap from hair on his own.
- 6 — Lathers hair on his own.
- 7 — Puts shampoo in hand and on hair on his own.
- 8 — Dries hair on his own.
- 9 — Completely washes hair on his own.

27) *Making a bed*
- 0 — Cannot do any part of making a bed.
- 1 — Pulls the bedspread over pillow, after you have made rest of bed.
- 2 — Folds the sheet and blanket down to make a cuff, puts the pillow on and pulls the spread over the pillow.
- 3 — Pulls up the blanket and finishes making the bed, after you have pulled up the top of the sheet.
- 4 — Pulls up the top sheet and makes bed completely on his own.
- 5 — Makes bed completely on own and does it daily, without reminders.

28) *Table setting*

0 — Cannot do any part of setting the table.

1 — Puts the glasses on the table with direction once the rest of the table is set.

2 — Puts the glasses on the table on his own once rest of table is set.

3 — Puts the spoons on the table with direction once the rest of the table is set, and puts the glasses on by self.

4 — Puts the spoons and glasses on the table by himself.

5 — Puts the knives and forks on the table with direction, and puts the spoons and glasses on by himself.

6 — Puts the knives, forks, spoons, and glasses on by self.

7 — Puts the napkins next to the plates with directions; puts forks, knives, spoons, and glasses by self.

29) *Changing a bed*

0 — Cannot do any part of changing a bed.

1 — Places bedspread on the bed after you have done the rest.

2 — Tucks the top sheet and blanket in at the bottom of the bed with your physical guidance.

3 — Tucks the top sheet and blanket in at the bottom of the bed on his own.

4 — Places the blanket on the bed with your guidance.

5 — Places the blanket on the bed on his own.

6 — Places the top sheet on the bed with your guidance.

7 — Places the top sheet on the bed on his own.

8 — Places the bottom sheet on the bed and tucks it in all around the bed with your guidance.

9 — Places the bottom sheet on the bed and tucks it in, on his own.

10 — Changes the whole bed completely on his own.

11 — Changes the whole bed completely on his own; knows when it needs to be done and does it with no reminders.

30) *Sweeping*

0 — Cannot do any part of sweeping.

1 — Holds broom and makes a sweeping motion with your guidance.

2 — Holds broom and makes a sweeping motion on his own.

3 — Sweeps easy-to-see dirt (large particles of food, paper, etc.) with your guidance.

4 — Sweeps easy-to-see dirt on his own.

5 — Sweeps floor, getting any dirt that is there into a pile, when you tell and show him where to sweep.

6 — Sweeps dirt into a dustpan while you hold the dustpan.

7 — Sweeps floor, getting any dirt that is there into a pile on his own.

8 — Sweeps the dirt into the dustpan, holding it himself.

9 — Sweeps the floor and uses the dustpan completely on his own.

10 — #9, plus recognizes when the floor needs sweeping.

11 — #10, plus assesses work and corrects it until job is acceptable.

31) Toilet training: Urine training
   0 — Never tried toilet training.
   1 — Never urinates in toilet and will not sit on toilet.
   2 — Never urinates in toilet but will sit on toilet.
   3 — Rarely urinates in toilet (1 time out of 10).*
   4 — Sometimes urinates in toilet (2-3 times out of 10).
   5 — Half the time urinates in toilet (4-6 times out of 10).
   6 — Usually urinates in toilet (7-9 times out of 10).
   7 — Always** urinates in toilet but is taken at regular times.
   8 — Always** urinates in toilet but has to be reminded some.
   9 — Always** urinates in toilet without reminders.

32) Toilet training: Bowel training
   0 — Never tried toilet training.
   1 — Never has a bowel movement in toilet and will not sit on toilet.
   2 — Never has a bowel movement in toilet but will sit on toilet.
   3 — Rarely has bowel movements in toilet (1 time out of 10).*
   4 — Sometimes has bowel movements in toilet (2-3 times out of 10).
   5 — Half the time has bowel movements in toilet (4-6 times out of 10).
   6 — Usually has bowel movements in toilet (7-9 times out of 10).
   7 — Always** has bowel movements in toilet but is taken at regular times.
   8 — Always** has bowel movements in toilet but has to be reminded some.
   9 — Always** has bowel movements in toilet without reminders.

* Means one urination/bowel movement in toilet out of every 10 urinations/bowel movements.
** Always — with an occasional accident (1 a month or so) still score as always.

UCLA PROJECT FOR DEVELOPMENTAL DISABILITIES

BEHAVIOR PROBLEM INVENTORY

Parent _____ Child _____ Date _____

For each problem listed, put a check in the first column if you feel it is not a problem at home. If it *is* a problem at home, put a check in the appropriate column indicating how much of a problem.

I. Acting Out Problems

A = Not a problem at home
B = 1 a week or less
C = 2–6 a week
D = 1–3 a day
E = 4–10 a day
F = More than 10 a day

	A	B	C	D	E	F
1) Screaming/crying/whining						
2) Yelling/swearing						
3) Talking back						
4) Hitting, hurting other children						
5) Hitting, hurting adults						
6) Spitting						
7) Throwing, tearing, or breaking things						
8) Biting						
9) Disobeying commands						
10) Inappropriate undressing						
11) Leaving house or yard						
12) Running away in public places						

II. Mealtime Problems

A = Not a problem at home
B = 1 a week or less
C = 2–3 a week
D = 4–6 a week
E = 1–2 a day
F = More than 3 a day

	A	B	C	D	E	F
1) Throwing food	——	——	——	——	——	——
2) Stealing food	——	——	——	——	——	——
3) Putting hands in food	——	——	——	——	——	——
4) Refusing food	——	——	——	——	——	——
5) Spilling food	——	——	——	——	——	——
6) Overeating	——	——	——	——	——	——
7) Undereating	——	——	——	——	——	——
8) Leaving the table during mealtime	——	——	——	——	——	——
9) Eating very fast	——	——	——	——	——	——
10) Eating very slowly	——	——	——	——	——	——

III. Sleeping

A = Not a problem at home
B = 1 a week or less
C = 2–3 a week
D = 4–6 a week
E = Every night

	A	B	C	D	E
1) Refusing/stalling at bedtime	——	——	——	——	——
2) Getting up at night or in early morning	——	——	——	——	——
3) Wetting bed	——	——	——	——	——

IV. Fears

A = Not a problem at home
B = Slightly upset (frightened but will approach)
C = Upset (will approach with parents' help)
D = Very upset; won't approach, seeks parents' protection/help
E = Terrified

	A	B	C	D	E
1) Animals	___	___	___	___	___
2) Water	___	___	___	___	___
3) Darkness	___	___	___	___	___
4) Strangers	___	___	___	___	___
5) Separation from mother	___	___	___	___	___
6) Noise	___	___	___	___	___
7) Other: _____	___	___	___	___	___

V. Repetitive Behaviors

A = Not a problem at home
B = Not daily
C = Less than 10 minutes/day
D = 10–60 minutes a day
E = 1–3 hours a day
F = More than 3 hours/day

	A	B	C	D	E	F
1) Headbanging and/or backbanging	___	___	___	___	___	___
2) Rocking	___	___	___	___	___	___
3) Biting self	___	___	___	___	___	___
4) Picking at self	___	___	___	___	___	___
5) Hitting self	___	___	___	___	___	___
6) Holding hands in strange position	___	___	___	___	___	___
7) Bizarre gesturing	___	___	___	___	___	___
8) Spinning objects	___	___	___	___	___	___
9) Nailbiting	___	___	___	___	___	___
10) Thumb-sucking	___	___	___	___	___	___

VI. Withdrawal

A = Not a problem at home
B = Rarely
C = Occasionally
D = Sometimes
E = Usually
F = Constantly

	A	B	C	D	E	F
1) Avoiding eye and/or physical contact with others	___	___	___	___	___	___
2) Seeming indifferent to others	___	___	___	___	___	___
3) Getting upset/crying in a new situation	___	___	___	___	___	___
4) Not playing with other kids	___	___	___	___	___	___
5) Engaging in aimless activity	___	___	___	___	___	___

VII. Behavior When Being Taught

If you try to teach your child something is he:

	A	B	C	D	E	F
1) Distractable	___	___	___	___	___	___
2) Uncooperative	___	___	___	___	___	___

Please go back and circle the three of your child's problems *from this whole inventory* that you feel are most serious.

UCLA PROJECT FOR DEVELOPMENTAL DISABILITIES

BEHAVIORAL VIGNETTES TEST IIIa

Parent _____ Child _____ Date _____

For each situation below, circle the letter of the response you think would be best. Please circle *only one* letter.

1. You have just started a program to reduce a child's temper tantrums. After following the program for 2 days, you find the tantrums are occurring *more often* than before. You should:
   a. continue the new program for a week, then change the program if there is still no improvement.
   b. abandon the program since it is clearly ineffective.
   c. put the program aside and try it again in a week or two.
   d. change the program somewhat and see if it works any better.

2. Although Jackson knows how to speak properly, he deliberately talks silly very often when he's at home. A lot of the times the things he says make no sense at all. In order to reduce this behavior, his family should:
   a. ignore him at these times and talk to him when he makes sense.
   b. make fun of his silly talk.
   c. scold his silly talk and tell him to talk sense.
   d. try to understand his silly talk, translate it into normal talk, and encourage him to imitate it.

3. You are beginning to teach Alan to name colors. During teaching sessions, especially the first one or two minutes, he looks away and often leaves his chair and walks around the room. You should:
   a. offer him a large reward for naming a color correctly.
   b. forget it for now but promise him a reward for working later.
   c. reward him at first for sitting quietly and looking at you.
   d. try to interest him by pointing at objects in the room and naming the various colors.

4. Twelve-year-old Lisa has some grooming skills and usually dresses herself. Yet she has never made a bed, and you want to teach her how. On the *first teaching day* you would:
   a. offer her a reward for making the bed.
   b. make the bed completely, except for pulling the spread over the pillow, then have Lisa complete the task and reward her.
   c. make the bed completely and explain each step. Then ask Lisa to do the first step, rewarding her for her success.
   d. have Lisa unfold the sheet and reward her for doing it.

5. Darryl's mother is teaching him to button his pajamas. One of the following suggestions is *wrong*. Which one?
   a) start by placing her hands on his to guide him.
   b) use small buttons to fit his small hands.
   c) start by teaching him the last step involved in buttoning.
   d) teach where there are no distractions.

6. You are going to teach 10-year-old Sarah to throw a ball. Which of the following would be the best reward to use?
   a) food, such as popcorn or M&Ms.
   b) affection, such as a hug or praise.
   c) activity, such as watching TV.
   d) cannot say.

7. You are working on Mary's speech. You show her common objects (a ball, a stuffed dog, etc.), name them, and reward her with M&Ms for repeating the name of each object. During the *first teaching session* which of the following should you *not* do?
   a) give her an M&M reward at the beginning of the session for sitting down and paying attention.
   b) reward her with praise as well as an M&M for every correct imitation.
   c) give her M&Ms to keep her interest when she seems to be getting frustrated.
   d) play her favorite game with her after the teaching session ends successfully.

8. Sylvia's mother has been teaching her to drink from a cup. Today, for the first time, Sylvia is able to handle a cup that is 3/4 full. Then a few minutes later Sylvia fumbles the cup, spills some milk and gets upset. Her mother should:
   a) end the session for the day.
   b) calm her down and have her try the 3/4 full cup again.
   c) calm her down and have her drink from a 1/2 full cup, praise her, and then end the session.
   d) calm her down, praise her for doing as well as she did, and end the session.

9. Debby has learned that you will punish her by putting her in her room for two minutes if she spits. When would it be appropriate to give her a second chance?
   a) when she promises not to do it again.
   b) when you know she did it just to see what you would do.
   c) when you think she has forgotten what would happen if she spits.
   d) none of these.

10. Peter often gets up and leaves the table during meals. The *best* time to begin a program to reduce this behavior would be:
    a) right away, since his parents know what the problem is.
    b) right away, keeping records of how often he leaves the table after the program starts.
    c) after keeping records of how often Peter leaves the table for 3 meals.
    d) after keeping records of how often Peter leaves the table for a week.

11. Melda often tries to attract the attention of her sisters by pinching or slapping them. When this does not work she pinches and slaps harder. To eliminate this behavior:
    a) isolate her (put her in her room) for 3 minutes. If she pinches or slaps again, isolate her for another 3 minutes.
    b) isolate her (put her in her room) until she calms down.
    c) ignore her so she won't be rewarded by your attention.
    d) scold her.

12. Billy is constantly out of his seat in class. A new program is introduced that gives Billy a star every time he stays in his seat for five minutes. Which of the following would most clearly show that a star is a good reward for Billy?
    a) Billy stays in his seat longer on each of the next three days.
    b) Billy proudly shows his stars to teachers and visitors.
    c) Billy trades his stars at the class store for candy.
    d) Billy asks his teacher for extra stars.

13. Which of these would *always* be a punishment for any child?
    a) placing him in his room alone.
    b) spanking him.
    c) scolding him.
    d) none of these.

14. Joe, age 4, is able to sit and pay attention for a brief period of time. He can imitate simple actions, like clapping. He makes a variety of infant-like babbling noises, but he does not say any words. The best way to begin teaching him to speak is to:
    a) make sure he is present during conversations between members of the family; involve him by asking him questions that require him to say a simple YES or NO answer.
    b) teach him to imitate simple sounds, rewarding him for increasingly good imitations of the sounds.
    c) wait for him to say simple words and reward him when he does.
    d) teach him to imitate simple words and reward him for correct imitations.

15. Michael is constantly getting out of his seat during his class. He usually wanders to the same cardboard clock. How would you reduce this wandering while motivating him to stay seated and work?
    a) reduce opportunities to leave his seat.
    b) put the clock out of reach.
    c) tell him if he sits down and works for 5 minutes, then he can play with the clock for 5 minutes.
    d) use all three of these methods.

16. Cheryl, age 7, knows the names of several common objects ("cup," "ball," etc.) and you want to teach her more. If you are going to put four objects in front of her and ask for one, you should start with:
    a) 3 new objects and 1 old object.
    b) 2 new objects, 2 old.
    c) 1 new object, 3 old.
    d) depends upon how fast Cheryl learns.

17. Elena's parents say that she is an aggressive child. The first step in changing Elena's aggression is to:
    a) find out why Elena is so aggressive.
    b) teach her to express her aggression in more appropriate ways.
    c) specify what the behaviors are that lead Elena's parents to call her "aggressive."
    d) ignore the aggression and praise Elena when she is not aggressive.

18. Maria has begun to fight with her brothers. In order to get her to stop when she is fighting, her father promises Coke or candy, which Maria enjoys. In the future, Maria's fightly will likely:
    a) occur *less* often.
    b) occur *more* often.
    c) occur about the same amount.
    d) there is no way to predict.

19. Juan has been learning to tell time and is doing very well. For the last two days, though, he is making more errors and is easily distracted from the task. In troubleshooting your program you would want to consider:
    a) may need to switch to different rewards.
    b) may need to advance more slowly, or more quickly.
    c) may need to quit teaching time-telling until he's older.
    d) two of the above.

20. Whenever his teacher reads a book in front of the class, Ross looks at the book for about 30 seconds and then gets up and wanders around the room. Also, when playing circle games, Ross will pay attention for about four minutes and then stand up and leave the circle. In setting up a program for Ross, he can best be described as:
    a) a hyperactive child.
    b) a child whose attention span is limited to 30 seconds when looking at books and four minutes when playing circle games.
    c) a restless child.
    d) an easily bored child who is also hyperactive.

Correct answers:

1. a	6. d	11. a	16. c
2. a	7. c	12. a	17. c
3. c	8. c	13. d	18. b
4. b	9. d	14. b	19. d
5. b	10. d	15. d	20. b

UCLA PROJECT FOR DEVELOPMENTAL DISABILITIES

TEACHING INTERVIEW

Parent _____ Child _____ Date _____

Interviewer _____
Audiotape labeled _____ Taperecorder tested _____

Formal Teaching

(Formal teaching: at least 3 planned teaching sessions per week with repeated trials)

Thinking back over the last three months, what if any, skills have you specifically set out to teach your child? (If you do not meet criteria for formal teaching, list under incidental teaching.)

SKILL #1 _____

SKILL #2 _____

SKILL #3 _____

For each skill:
  a) What made you decide to work on this particular skill?
  b) How long have or had you been working on this particular skill (duration, e.g., days, weeks, months)?
  c) When and how often do or did you work on this skill (frequency and length of teaching sessions)?
  d) Parents often have different approaches to teaching their children. To understand *specifically* how you go about teaching this skill, it would be helpful for you to describe to me *step by step* a typical teaching session on this skill.
  e) What, if any, progress has your child made?
  f) What, if any, obstacles have or had you encountered? How have you tried to deal with them?
  g) Have you kept any written records?

Notes

SKILL #1 _____

SKILL #2 _____

SKILL #3 _____

SCORING FOR FORMAL TEACHING

0 = No formal teaching
1 = Program initiated but discontinued after less than one month;
    no mastery achieved
2 = Mastery achieved in less than one month
3 = Formal teaching for more than one month; discontinued before
    mastery
4 = Formal teaching for more than one month; ongoing or until mastery

SKILL #1 _____ Score: 0 1 2 3 4
SKILL #2 _____ Score: 0 1 2 3 4
SKILL #3 _____ Score: 0 1 2 3 4

TEACHING SOPHISTICATION   Score: + _____
   (+ 1 for each, check if used)

_____ physical guidance   _____ small steps
_____ modeling   _____ special materials
_____ backward chaining   _____ daily lesson plans
_____ ending on a success   _____ fading
_____ other: _____

TEACHING ERRORS   Score: − _____
   (− 1 for each, check if used)

_____ inappropriate attention
_____ inappropriate skill choice
_____ inappropriate reward choice
_____ inappropriate punishment
_____ failure to reward appropriate behaviors
_____ other: _____

Incidental Teaching

   Are there times during the week when someone in the family teaches _____,
as the opportunity arises? (Are there other skills you are working on?) Further
probe: For example, what does _____'s morning routine look like . . . getting
dressed, brushing teeth, etc? How much help do you need to give? Do you try to
teach at these times? What skills?

Notes

SKILL #1 _____

SKILL #2 _____

SKILL #3 _____

SCORING FOR TEACHING

0 = No or minimal evidence of incidental teaching
1 = Report of incidental teaching of skills as opportunity arises during day
    but with little or no regularity or clear goals
2 = Report of incidental teaching of skills where parent has some sense of
    goal, where there is some regularity, where there is some reason to
    believe that it has benefitted the child, when it has been done at least
    one month, or until mastery
4 = Two such reports
6 = Extensive incidental teaching, appropriate and seemingly effective, for
    more than 2 skills from at least 2 skill areas

Incidental Teaching Score: 0 1 2 4 6

Future Teaching Plans

Have you thought about what skills you would like to teach next?

SKILL #1 _____

SKILL #2 _____

SKILL #3 _____

How did you decide upon these skills?

Have you talked with anyone about these plans?

When do you think you might implement them?

SCORING FOR FUTURE TEACHING PLANS

0 = Not sure what to do next or plans seem inappropriate
1 = Seems to be making up plans on the spot; no evidence of forethought
2 = Plans to continue present programs; has not planned beyond this
3 = Articulates one specific new teaching goal; gives clear indication that it
    has been thought about prior to the interview. Commitment evidence
    which makes follow-through likely

Future Teaching Plans Score: 0 1 2 3

Family Involvement

Have any other family members been involved in teaching?

How involved? How helpful?

SCORING FOR FAMILY INVOLVEMENT

NA = No significant other at home
- 0 = An obstacle, discourages primary teacher or doesn't follow-through on programs
- 1 = Generally uninvolved
- 2 = a) encourages primary teacher, specific examples of support
    b) plays some role in teaching, carrying out behavior problem program, or dispensing rewards
    c) both a and b
- 3 = a) conducts incidental teaching apart from primary teacher's programs
    b) conducts formal teaching sessions

Family Involvement Score: NA 0 1 2 3

Rewards

What rewards do you generally use with _____? (Note: some of this information probably has been covered during Formal Teaching)

REWARD #1 _____   REWARD #2 _____

REWARD #3 _____   REWARD #4 _____

When do you use them? _____

How do you use them? _____

How effective are they? _____

SCORING FOR REWARDS

- 0 = No rewards used or praise mentioned with no sense of contingencies or parents' rationale for choice of reinforcers unclear
- 1 = Reward(s) chosen appropriately but administration occasionally lapses in consistency
- 2 = Reward(s) chosen appropriately and given contingently

3 = Parent(s) demonstrate mastery of knowledge on rewards and can apply the knowledge generally

Rewards Score: 0 1 2 3

Written Records

Include diaries, teaching logs, charts, follow-up manual record sheets, etc. Do not include toilet training records.

SCORING FOR WRITTEN RECORDS

0 = No data kept
1 = Data kept on a program and aided their teaching or behavior problem management
+1 = For each additional useful record up to a maximum of 5

Written Records Score: 0 1 2 3 4 5

Behavior Problems

Looking back over the last three months again, has _____ had any behavior problems that you have wanted to decrease or eliminate?

BEHAVIOR PROBLEM #1 _____

BEHAVIOR PROBLEM #2 _____

BEHAVIOR PROBLEM #3 _____

For each behavior problem:
    a) How long has this been a problem
    b) In what situations does it usually occur?
    c) With whom?
    d) How often does it occur?
    e) As specifically as possible, please describe *step by step* what you usually do when it does occur. (Note: any written records)
    f) Does everyone in the family respond the same way?
    g) Any progress so far?
    h) If appropriate, what obstacles have come up?
    i) In the past have you tried anything else?

Notes

BEHAVIOR PROBLEM #1 _____

BEHAVIOR PROBLEM #2 _____

BEHAVIOR PROBLEM #3 _____

SCORING FOR BEHAVIOR PROBLEMS

0 = Excessive physical punishment, yelling or isolation reported in response to this behavior problem

1 = No consistent approach or parents disagree about approach, report not knowing what to do, or obviously reinforce inappropriate behavior

2 = Have made some effort to restructure environment but program is insufficient

3 = Generally consequate behavior problem appropriately with occasional lapses in consistency

4 = Appropriate, systematic use of time-out, ignoring, forced compliances, response cost, or restructured environment and significantly reduced the behavior problem

+1 = If parents report direct reinforcement of incompatible behavior (DRI)

BEHAVIOR PROBLEM #1 _____ Score: 0 1 2 3 4 5
BEHAVIOR PROBLEM #2 _____ Score: 0 1 2 3 4 5
BEHAVIOR PROBLEM #3 _____ Score: 0 1 2 3 4 5

PROBLEM MANAGEMENT SOPHISTICATION   Score: _____
(check if used)

_____ Time-out   _____ Ignoring
_____ Other: _____

PROBLEM MANAGEMENT ERRORS   Score: _____

_____ inappropriate behavior management procedure
_____ inappropriate punishment
_____ appropriate behaviors not rewarded
_____ other: _____

SCORING SUMMARY

Extent of Teaching   Formal Teaching (0–12)   _____

Incidental Teaching (0–6)   _____

Behavior Problem Management (0–15)   _____

SUM: (0–33) _____

Quality of Teaching   Teaching Sophistication

minus errors (−6 to 9)   _____

Future Teaching Plans (0–3)   _____

Rewards (0–3)   _____

Written Records (0–5)   _____

Problem management sophistication

minus errors (−4 to 3)   _____

SUM: (−10 to 23) _____

Teaching Interview Score: Extent & Quality

SUM: (−10 to 56) _____

UCLA PROJECT FOR DEVELOPMENTAL DISABILITIES

PROGRAM GROUP EVALUATION QUESTIONNAIRE

Parent _____ Date _____

Please give us your evaluation of the parent training program.

Section I.   General Evaluation

1)   I feel the approach to teaching my child self-help skills and managing behavior problems that was presented in this parent training program is:

_____ Very inappropriate
_____ Inappropriate
_____ Slightly inappropriate
_____ Neutral
_____ Slightly appropriate
_____ Appropriate
_____ Very appropriate

2) I feel that for me the parent training program and my leader were:

GROUP MEETINGS	MY GROUP LEADER(S)' HELPFULNESS	MY GROUP LEADER(S)' COMPETENCE
_____ Very helpful	_____ Very helpful	_____ Very competent
_____ Helpful	_____ Helpful	_____ Competent
_____ Slightly helpful	_____ Slightly helpful	_____ Slightly competent
_____ Neutral	_____ Neutral	_____ Neutral
_____ Slightly unhelpful	_____ Slightly unhelpful	_____ Slightly incompetent
_____ Unhelpful	_____ Unhelpful	_____ Incompetent
_____ Very unhelpful	_____ Very unhelpful	_____ Very incompetent

3) I feel that for me the amount of material that has been covered in the program was:

_____ Much too little
_____ Too little
_____ Slightly too little
_____ Just right
_____ Slightly too much
_____ Too much
_____ Much too much

4) Considering my confidence *at this point* in teaching my child self-help skills and managing behavior problems, I feel:

_____ Very confident
_____ Confident
_____ Somewhat confident
_____ Neutral
_____ Somewhat unconfident
_____ Unconfident
_____ Very unconfident

5) My best estimate of how much teaching and/or carrying out behavior problem management programs I will be doing 3 months from now is:

_____ Very much: Several programs on an almost daily basis
_____ Much: One or more programs regularly
_____ Some: As the opportunity arises, but not regularly
_____ Supporting my spouse who will be doing it
_____ Very little or none

6) Would you recommend the parent training program to a friend or relative?

_____ Strongly recommend
_____ Recommend
_____ Slightly recommend
_____ Neutral
_____ Slightly not recommend
_____ Not recommend
_____ Strongly not recommend

7) My overall feeling about the parent training program at this point is:

_____ Very positive
_____ Positive
_____ Somewhat positive
_____ Neutral
_____ Somewhat negative
_____ Negative
_____ Very negative

Comments: (optional)

What have you liked most about the program?

What have you liked least, or suggest that we change?

Section II.   Usefulness

We'd like to get your ideas of how useful each of the following types of teaching has been to you. Please rate each one on the following scale:

7 = Extremely useful
6 = Useful
5 = Somewhat useful
4 = Neutral
3 = Somewhat *not* useful
2 = *Not* useful
1 = Extremely *not* useful

a) _____ Lectures by leader
b) _____ Videotapes
c) _____ Group discussions
d) _____ Group exercises (e.g., role plays)
e) _____ Reading the manuals
f) _____ Carrying out observations/teaching at home

Section III.   Self Assessment

We would also like you to evaluate your own participation in and learning from the program. Please rate each activity on the following scale:

4 = All   (of what was recommended)
3 = Most (of what was recommended)
2 = Some (of what was recommended)
1 = None (of what was recommended)

a) _____ Attending meetings
b) _____ Completing the assigned readings
c) _____ Carrying out teaching a self-help skill at home
d) _____ Keeping records of teaching
e) _____ Carrying out a behavior problem management (or toilet training) program at home
f) _____ Keeping records of behavior problem (or toilet training) progress

How would you summarize your own participation in the program and your understanding of the program content?

_____ Very involved	_____ Very high understanding
_____ Involved	_____ High understanding
_____ Somewhat involved	_____ Somewhat high understanding
_____ Uninvolved	_____ Low understanding
_____ Very uninvolved	_____ Very low understanding

THANK YOU!

References

Abikoff, H. (1987). An evaluation of cognitive behavioral therapy for hyperactive children. In B. B. Lahey & A. E. Kazdin (Eds.), *Advances in clinical child psychology* (pp. 171–216). New York: Plenum Press.

Acosta, F. X. (1979). Barriers between mental health services and Mexican Americans: An examination of a paradox. *American Journal of Community Psychology, 7,* 503–520.

Adams, M. E. (1967). Siblings of the retarded: Their problems and treatment. *Child Welfare, 46,* 310–316.

Adesso, V. J., & Lipson, J. W. (1981). Group training of parents as therapists for their children. *Behavior Therapy, 12,* 625–633.

Adubato, S. A., Adams, M. K., & Budd, K. S. (1981). Teaching a parent to train a spouse in child management techniques. *Journal of Applied Behavior Analysis, 14,* 193–205.

Allen, D. A., & Hudd, S. S. (1987). Are we professionalizing parents? Weighing the benefits and pitfalls. *Mental Retardation, 25,* 133–139.

Alvy, K. T. (1987). *Black parenting: Strategies for training.* New York: Irvington Publishers.

Alvy, K. T., Myers, H. F., Arrington, A., Marigna, M., Huff, R., Richardson, M., & Main, M. (1988). *Effects of a culturally-appropriate black parent training program on parental attitudes and practices, parental mental health, and on child behavior outcomes in inner-city black families.* Unpublished manuscript, University of California, Los Angeles.

Ambrose, S. (1983). *An evaluation of a cognitive-behavioral parent training program for abusive and neglectful parents.* Unpublished doctoral dissertation, University of California, Los Angeles.

Ambrose, S. A., & Baker, B. L. (1979). *Training parents of developmentally disabled children: Follow-up outcome.* Paper presented at American Psychological Association Annual Meeting, New York.

Ambrose, S. A., Hazzard A., & Haworth, J. (1980). Cognitive-behavioral parenting groups for abusive families. *Child Abuse and Neglect, 4,* 119–125.

American Psychiatric Association (1980). *Diagnostic and Statistical Manual of Mental Disorders,* (3rd ed.) Washington, DC: Author.

American Psychiatric Association (1987). *Diagnostic and Statistical Manual of Mental Disorders* (3rd ed.–Revised). Washington, DC: Author.

Anderson, S. R., Avery, D. L., Dipietro, E., Edwards, G. L., & Christian, W. P. (1987). Intensive home-based early intervention with autistic children. *Education and Treatment of Children, 10,* 352–366.

Andraisik, R., & Murphy, W. D. (1977). Assessing the readability of thirty-nine behavior modification training manuals and primers. *Journal of Applied Behavior Analysis, 10,* 341–344.

Azrin, N. H., & Foxx, R. M. (1974). *Toilet training in less than a day.* New York: Simon & Schuster.

Baker, B. L. (1973). Camp Freedom: Behavior modification for retarded children in a therapeutic camp setting. *American Journal of Orthopsychiatry, 43,* 418–427.

Baker, B. L. (1980). Training for parents of developmentally disabled children. In S. Salzinger, J. Antrobus, & J. Glick (Eds.), *The ecosystem of the "sick" child.* New York: Academic Press.

Baker, B. L. (1983). Parents as teachers: Issues in training. In J. A. Mulick & S. M. Pueschel (Eds.), *Parent-Professional participation in developmental disability services: Foundations and prospects.* Cambridge, MA: Ware Press.

Baker, B. L. (1984). Intervention in families with young severely handicapped children. In J.B. Blacher (Ed.), *Severely handicapped young children and their families: Research in review*. New York: Academic.

Baker, B. L. (1986). Parents as teachers: An illustration of one programme. In D. Milne (Ed.), *Training behaviour therapists: Methods, evaluation, and implementation with parents, nurses, and teachers*. London: Croom Helm.

Baker, B. L. (1988). Evaluating parent training. *Irish Journal of Psychology, 9* (2), 324–345.

Baker, B. L. (in press). Video-directed parent training: Effectiveness and dissemination. In Frazer, W. (Ed.), *Proceedings of 8th Congress of the International Association for the Scientific Study of Mental Deficiency*.

Baker, B. L., & Brightman, A. J. (1989). *Steps to independence: A skills training guide for parents and teachers of children with special needs*. 2nd ed. Baltimore: Brookes.

Baker, B. L., Brightman, A. J., & Blacher, J. B. (1983). *Steps to independence series: Play skills*. Champaign, IL: Research Press.

Baker, B. L., Brightman, A. J., Carroll, N. B., Heifetz, B. B., & Hinshaw, S. P. (1978a). *Steps to independence series: Speech and language: Level 1*. Champaign, IL: Research Press.

Baker, B. L., Brightman, A. J., Carroll, N. B., Heifetz, B. B., & Hinshaw, S. P. (1978b). *Steps to independence series: Speech and language: Level 2*. Champaign, IL: Research Press.

Baker, B. L., Brightman, A. J., Heifetz, L. J., & Murphy, D. (1976a). *Steps to independence series: Advanced self-help skills*. Champaign, IL: Research Press.

Baker, B. L., Brightman, A. J., Heifetz, L. J., & Murphy, D. (1976b). *Steps to independence series: Behavior problems*. Champaign, IL: Research Press.

Baker, B. L., Brightman, A. J., Heifetz, L. J., & Murphy, D. (1976c). *Steps to independence series: Early self-help skills*, Champaign, IL: Research Press.

Baker, B. L., Brightman, A. J., Heifetz, L. J., & Murphy, D. (1976d). *Steps to independence series: Intermediate self-help skills*, Champaign, IL: Research Press.

Baker, B. L., Brightman, A. J., Heifetz, L. J. & Murphy, D. (1977). *Steps to independence series: Toilet training*. Champaign, IL: Research Press.

Baker, B. L., Brightman, A. J., & Hinshaw, S. P. (1980). *Steps to independence series: Toward independent living*. Champaign, IL: Research Press.

Baker, B. L., & Brightman, R. P. (1984). Training parents of retarded children: Program specific outcomes. *Journal of Behavior Therapy and Experimental Psychiatry, 15*, 255–260.

Baker, B. L., & Clark, D. B. (1987). Intervention with parents of developmentally disabled children. In S. Landesman & P. M. Vietze (Eds.), *Living environments and mental retardation*, pp. 269–292. Washington, DC: American Association on Mental Retardation.

Baker, B. L., Clark, D. B., & Yasuda, P. M. (1981). Predictors of success in parent training. In P. Mittler (Ed.), *Frontiers of knowledge in mental retardation*. Baltimore: University Park Press.

Baker, B. L., & Heifetz, L. J. (1976). The READ Project: Teaching manuals for parents of retarded children. In T. D. Tjossem (Ed.), *Intervention strategies for high risk infants and young children*. Baltimore: University Park Press.

Baker, B. L., Heifetz, L. J., & Murphy, D. (1980). Behavioral training for parents of retarded children: One-year follow-up. *American Journal of Mental Deficiency, 85*(1), 31–38.

Baker, B. L., Landen, S. L., & Kashima, K. J. (1989). *Family characteristics and parent training outcomes*. Unpublished manuscript, University of California, Los Angeles.

Baker, B. L., & McCurry, M. C. (1984, December). School-based parent training: An alternative for parents predicted to demonstrate low teaching proficiency following group training. *Education and Training of the Mentally Retarded, 261–267*.

Baker, B. L., Prieto-Bayard, M., & McCurry, M. C. (1984). Lower socioeconomic status families and programs for training parents of retarded children. In J. M. Berg (Ed.), *Perspectives and progress in mental retardation, Vol. I–Social, psychological, and educational aspects*. Baltimore: University Park Press.

Baker, B. L., & Ward, M. H. (1971). Reinforcement therapy for behavior problems in severely retarded children. *American Journal of Orthopsychiatry, 41*, 124–135.

Ball, T. S., Coyne, A., Jarvis, R. M., & Pease, S. S. F. (1984, February). Parents of retarded children as teaching assistants for other parents. *Education and Training of the Mentally Retarded, 64–69*.

Barkley, R. A. (1981). *Hyperactive children: A handbook for diagnosis and treatment.* New York: Guilford Press.

Barkley, R. A. (1987). *Defiant children: A clinician's manual for parent training.* New York: Guilford Press.

Barna, S., Bidder, R. T., Gray, O. P., Clements, J., & Gardner, S. (1980). The progress of developmentally delayed pre-school children in a home-training scheme. *Child: Care, health and development, 6,* 157–164.

Barrett, D.M., & Trickett, E. J. (1979). Change strategies and perceived environment data: Two conceptual models and their applications. *Journal of Community Psychology, 7,* 305–312.

Beck, A., Ward, C., Mendelson, M., Mock, J., & Erbaugh, J. (1961). An inventory for measuring depression. *Archives of General Psychiatry, 4,* 53–63.

Beck, A. T. (1976). *Cognitive therapy and emotional disorders.* New York: International Universities Press.

Becker, W. C. (1971). *Parents are teachers.* Champaign, IL: Research Press.

Behrendt, W. M. (1978). *The effects of preparation for training and parental characteristics on the outcome of a behavioral parent training program.* Unpublished doctoral dissertation, Washington University, St. Louis.

Benassi, V. A., & Benassi, B. (1973). An approach to teaching behavior modification principles to parents. *Rehabilitation Literature, 34,* 134–135.

Benson, H. A., & Turnbull, A. P. (1986). Approaching families from an individualized perspective. In R. H. Horner, L. H. Meyer, & H. D. B. Fredericks (Eds.), *Education of learners with severe handicaps: Exemplary service strategies.* Baltimore: Brookes.

Berger, M., & Fowlkes, M. A. (1980, May). Family intervention project: A family network model for serving young handicapped children. *Young Children,* 22–32.

Berkeley Planning Associates (1977). *Evaluation of child abuse and neglect projects: 1974–1977. Vol II.* Final Report. Berkeley, CA: Author.

Berlin, P. (1980). *Role conflict and organizational climate as predictors to implementation of a parent training program.* Doctoral dissertation, University of California, Los Angeles.

Berlin, P. H., & Baker, B.L. (1983). *Role conflict and organizational climate as predictors to implementation of a parent training program.* Unpublished manuscript, UCLA.

Bernal, M. E., & North, J. A. (1978). A survey of parent training manuals. *Journal of Applied Behavior Analysis, 11,* 533–544.

Bernal, M. E., Williams, D. E., Miller, W. H., & Reogor, P. A. (1972). The use of videotape feedback and operant learning principles in training parents in management of deviant children. In R. Rubin, H. Fensterheim, J. Henderson, & L. Ullman (Eds.), *Advances in behavior therapy.* New York: Academic Press.

Bettelheim, B. (1967). *The empty fortress.* New York: The Free Press.

Bidder, R., Bryant, G., & Gray, O. P. (1975). Benefits to Down's Syndrome children through training their mothers. *Archives of Disease in Childhood, 50,* 383–386.

Birkel, R., & Reppucci, N. D. (1983). Social networks, information-seeking, and utilization of services. *American Journal of Community Psychology, 11,* 185–205.

Blacher, J. (1984a). A dynamic perspective on the impact of a severely handicapped child on the family. In J. Blacher (Ed.), *Severely handicapped young children and their families: Research in review,* (pp. 3–50). Orlando: Academic Press.

Blacher, J. (1984b). Sequential stages of parental adjustment to the birth of a child with handicaps: fact or artifact? *Mental Retardation, 22,* 55–68.

Blackard, M. K., & Barsh, E. T. (1982). Parents' and professionals' perceptions of the handicapped child's impact on the family. *Journal of the Association for the Severely Handicapped, 7,* 62–70.

Blechman, E. A., Budd, K. S., Szykula, S., Embry, L. H., O'Leary, K. D., Christophersen, E. R., Wahler, R., Kogan, K., & Riner, L. S. (1981). Engagement in behavioral family therapy: A multisite investigation. *Behavior Therapy, 12,* 461–472.

Brassell, W. R. (1977). Intervention with handicapped infants: correlates of progress. *Mental Retardation, 15,* 18–22.

Breslau, N., Weitzman, M., & Messinger, K. (1981). Psychologic functionings of siblings of disabled children. *Pediatrics, 67,* 344–353.

Brightman, A. J. (1974). *Behavior modification in organization development: Toward planned change in five settings for retarded children.* Unpublished doctoral dissertation, Harvard University.

Brightman, R. P. (1984). Training parents as advocates for their developmentally disabled children. *Perspectives and Progress in Mental Retardation, 1,* 451–458.

Brightman, R. P., Ambrose, S.A., & Baker, B. L. (1980). Parent training: A school-based model for enhancing parent performance. *Child Behavior Therapy, 2*(3), 35–47.

Brightman, R. P., Baker, B. L., Clark, D. B., & Ambrose, S. A. (1982). Effectiveness of alternative parent training formats. *Journal of Behavior Therapy and Experimental Psychiatry, 13,* 113–117.

Brody, G. H., & Forehand, R. (1985). The efficacy of parent training with maritally distressed and nondistressed mothers: A multi-method assessment. *Behavior Research and Therapy, 23,* 291–296.

Brooks-Gunn, J., & Lewis, M. (1982). Affective exchanges between normal and handicapped infants and their mothers. In T. Field & A. Fogel (Eds.), *Emotion and early interaction.* New Jersey: Lawrence Erlbaum Associates.

Brown, G. W., Birley, J. L. T., & Wing, J. K. (1972). Influence of family life on the course of schizophrenic disorders. *British Journal of Psychiatry, 121,* 241–258.

Brown, M. B. (Ed.) (1977). *Biomedical computer programs: P-series.* Los Angeles: University of California Press.

Brown-Miller, N., & Cantwell, D. P. (1976). Siblings as therapists. *American Journal of Psychiatry, 133,* 447–450.

Brunk, M., Henggeler, S. W., & Whelan, J. P. (1987). Comparison of multisystemic therapy and parent training in the brief treatment of child abuse and neglect. *Journal of Consulting and Clinical Psychology, 55,* 171–178.

Buriel, R. (1975). Cognitive styles among three generations of Mexican children. *Journal of Cross Cultural Psychology, 6,* 417–429.

Calvert, S. C., & McMahon, R. J. (1987). The treatment acceptability of a behavioral parent training program and its components. *Behavior Therapy, 18,* 165–179.

Campbell, D. T., & Stanley, J. C. (1966). *Experimental and quasi-experimental designs for research.* Chicago: Rand McNally.

Campbell, S. B. (1973). Mother-child interactions in reflective, impulsive, and hyperactive children. *Developmental Psychology, 8,* 341–347.

Campbell, S. B., Ewing, L. J., Breaux, A. M., & Szumowski, E. K. (1986). Parent-referred problem three-year-olds: Follow-up at school entry. *Journal of Child Psychology and Psychiatry, 27,* 473–488.

Carr, E. G., & Durand, V. M. (1985). Reducing behavior problems through functional communication training. *Journal of Applied Behavior Analysis, 18,* 111–126.

Carr, J. (1980). *Helping your handicapped child.* London: Penguin Books.

Chan, S. (1986a). *The multicultural training-of-trainers project.* Paper presented at 110th Annual Meeting of the American Association on Mental Deficiency, Denver.

Chan, S. (1986b). Parents of exceptional Asian children. In M. Kitano and P. Chinn (Eds.), *Exceptional Asian children and youth.* Reston, VA: Council for Exceptional Children.

Christensen, A. (1979). Cost-effectiveness in behavioral family therapy. *Behavior Therapy, 10,* 418–422.

Christensen, A., Johnson, S. M., Phillips, S., & Glasgow, R. E. (1980). Cost effectiveness in behavioral family therapy. *Behavior Therapy, 11,* 208–226.

Christian, W. P. (1981). Reaching autistic children: Strategies for parents and helping professionals. In A. Milunsky (Ed.), *Coping with crisis in handicapped.* New York: Plenum Press.

Clark, D. B., & Baker, B. L. (1982). *Teaching Proficiency Test.* Unpublished manuscript, University of California, Los Angeles.

Clark, D. B., & Baker, B. L. (1983). Predicting outcome in parent training. *Journal of Consulting and Clinical Psychology, 51*(2), 309–311.

Clark, D. B., Baker, B. L., & Heifetz, L. J. (1982). Behavioral training for parents of retarded children: Prediction of outcome. *American Journal of Mental Deficiency, 87,* 14–19.

Clements, J., Evans, C., Jones, C., Osborne, K., & Upton, G. (1982). Evaluation of a home-based language training programme with severely mentally handicapped children. *Behaviour Research and Therapy, 20,* 243–249.

Cleveland, D. W., & Miller, N. (1977). Attitudes and life commitments of older siblings of mentally retarded adults: An exploratory study. *Mental Retardation, 15,* 38–41.

Cohen, N. J., & Minde, K. (1983). The 'Hyperactive Syndrome' in kindergarten children: Comparison of children with pervasive and situational symptoms. *Journal of Child Psychology and Psychiatry, 24,* 443–455.

Cole, C., & Morrow, W. R. (1976). Refractory parent behaviors in behavior modification training groups. *Psychotherapy: Theory, Research, and Practice, 13,* 162–169.

Conners, C. K. (1973). Rating scales for use in drug studies with children. *Psychopharmacology Bulletin [Special Issue, Pharmacology of Children],* 24–84.

Corwin, R. G. (1972). Strategies for organizational innovation: An empirical comparison. *American Sociological Review, 37,* 441–454.

Crnic, K. A., Friedrich, W. N., & Greenberg, M. T. (1983). Adaptation of families with mentally retarded children: A model of stress, coping, and family ecology. *American Journal of Mental Deficiency, 88,* 125–138.

Crutcher, D. (August, 1986). *Parent perspective of disabilities.* Paper presented at the Annual Meeting of the American Psychological Association, Washington, DC.

Cummings, S. T. (1976). The impact of the child's deficiency on the father: A study of fathers of mentally retarded and of chronically ill children. *American Journal of Orthopsychiatry, 46,* 246–255.

Cummings, S. T., Bayley, H. C., & Rie, H. E. (1966). Effects of the child's deficiency on the mother: A study of mothers of mentally retarded, chronically ill, and neurotic children. *American Journal of Orthopsychiatry, 36,* 595–608.

Cunningham, C. E. (1988). *A Family Systems Oriented Cognitive- Behavioral Program for Parents of ADHD Children.* American Psychological Association Annual Meeting, Atlanta, GA.

Cunningham, C. E., & Barkley, R. A. (1979). The interactions of hyperactive and normal children with their mothers in free-play and structured task. *Child Development, 50,* 217–224.

Czyzewski, M. J., Christian, W. P., & Norris, M. B. (1982). Preparing the family for client transition: Outreach parent training. In W. P. Christian, G. T. Hannah, and T. J. Glahn (Eds.), *Programming effective human services.* New York: Plenum Press.

Dadds, M. R., Sanders, M. R., & James, J. E. (1987). The generalization of treatment effects in parent training with multidistressed parents. *Behavioural Psychotherapy, 15,* 289- 313.

Dadds, M. R., Schwartz, S., & Sanders, M. R. (1987). Marital discord and treatment outcome in behavioral treatment of child conduct disorders. *Journal of Consulting and Clinical Psychology, 55,* 396–403.

Dangel, R. F., & Polster, R. A. (1984). WINNING! A systematic, empirical approach to parent training. In R. F. Dangel & R. A. Polster (Eds.), *Parent training: Foundations of research and practice,* (pp. 162–201). New York: Guilford.

DeMyer, M. K. (1979). *Parents and children in autism.* New York: John Wiley & Sons.

Diament, C., & Colletti, G. (1978). Evaluation of behavioral group counseling for parents of learning-disabled children. *Journal of Abnormal Child Psychology, 6,* 385–400.

Dixon, W. J., & Brown, M. B. (Eds.) (1979). *Biomedical computer programs p-series,* Berkeley: University of California Press.

Donahue, M. J. (1973). *Home stimulation of handicapped children: Parent guide.* (ERIC Document Reproduction Service No. ED 079 921).

Dubey, D. R., O'Leary, S. G., & Kaufman, K. F. (1983). Training parents of hyperactive children in child management: A comparative outcome study. *Journal of Abnormal Child Psychology, 11,* 229–246.

Dumas, J. E. (1984). Child, adult-interactional, and socioeconomic setting events as predictors of parent training outcome. *Education and Treatment of Children, 7,* 351–364.

Eberhardy, F. (1967). The view from the "couch." *Journal of Child Psychology and Psychiatry, 8,* 257–263.

Eden-Pearcy, G. V. S., Blacher, J. B., & Eyman, R. K. (1986). Exploring parents' reactions to their young child with severe handicaps. *Mental Retardation, 24,* 285–291.

Egan, K. J. (1983). Stress management and child management with abusive parents. *Journal of Clinical Child Psychology, 12,* 292–299.

Eheart, B. K. (1982). Mother-child interactions with non-retarded and mentally retarded pre-schoolers. *American Journal of Mental Deficiency, 87,* 20–25.

Elmer, E. (1967). *Children in jeopardy: A study of abused minors and their families.* Pittsburgh: University of Pittsburgh Press.

Embry, L. (1980). Family support for handicapped preschool children at risk for abuse. In J. Gallagher (Ed.), *New directions for exceptional children: Vol. 4.* San Francisco: Jossey Bass.

Emery, R. E. (1982). Interparent conflict and the children of discord and divorce. *Psychological Bulletin, 92,* 310–330.

Erhardt, D. (1987). *The effects of behavioral parent training on families with young hyperactive children.* Unpublished manuscript, University of California, Los Angeles.

Erhardt, D., & Baker, B. L. (1989). *The effects of behavioral parent training on families with young hyperactive children.* Unpublished manuscript, University of California, Los Angeles.

Eyberg, S. M., & Matarazzo, R. G. (1980). Training parents as therapists: A comparison between individual parent-child interaction training and parent group didactic training. *Journal of Clinical Child Psychology, 36,* 492–499.

Fairweather, G. W., Sanders, D., Cressler, D. L., & Maynard, H. (1969). *Community life for the mentally ill: An alternative to institutional care.* Chicago: Aldine.

Fairweather, G. W., Sanders, D. H., & Tornatzky, L. G. (1974). *Creating change in mental health organizations.* New York: Pergamon.

Farber, B. (1959). Effects of a severely mentally retarded child on family integration. *Monographs of the Society for Research in Child Development, 24,* (Whole No. 71).

Featherstone, H. (1980). *A difference in the family: Living with a disabled child.* New York: Basic Books.

Feldman, W. S., Manella, K. J., Apodaca, L., & Varni, J. W. (1982). Behavioral group parent training in spina bifida. *Journal of Clinical Child Psychology, 11,* 144–150.

Feldman, W. S., Manella, K. J., & Varni, J. W. (1983). A behavioral parent training program for single mothers of physically handicapped children. *Child: Care, Health, and Development, 9,* 157–168.

Fenske, E. C., Zalenski, S., Krantz, P. J., & McClannahan, L. E. (1985). Age at intervention and treatment outcome for autistic children in a comprehensive intervention program. *Analysis and Intervention in Developmental Disabilities, 5,* 49–58.

Fewell, R. R., & Vadasy, P. F. (1986). *Families of Handicapped Children.* Austin, TX: PRO-ED.

Firestone, P., Kelly, M. J., & Fike, S. (1980). Are fathers necessary in parent training groups? *Journal of Clinical Child Psychology, 9,* 44–47.

Fleischman, M. J. (1979). Using parenting salaries to control attrition and cooperation in therapy. *Behavior Therapy, 10,* 111–116.

Forehand, R., & Atkeson, B. M. (1977). Generality of treatment effects with parents as therapists: A review of assessment and implementation procedures. *Behavior Therapy, 8,* 575–593.

Forehand, R., & McMahon, B. (1981). *Helping the non-compliant child: A clinician's guide to parent training.* New York: Guilford Press.

Forehand, R., Middlebrook, J., Rogers, T., & Steffe, M. (1983). Dropping out of parent training. *Behaviour Research and Therapy, 21,* 663–668.

Forehand, R., Wells, K. C., & Griest, D. L. (1980). An examination of the social validity of a parent training program. *Behavior Therapy, 11,* 488–502.

Forrest, P., Holland, C., Daly, R., & Fellbaum, G. A. (1984). When parents become therapists: Their attitudes toward parenting three years later. *Canadian Journal of Community Mental Health, 3,* 49–54.

Forsythe, A. B., May, P. R., & Engelman, L. (1971). Prediction by multiple regression: How many variables to enter? *Journal of Psychiatric Research, 8,* 119–126.

Foster, M., Berger, M., & McLean, M. (1981). Rethinking a good idea: A reassessment of parent involvement. *Topics in Early Childhood Special Education, 1,* 55–56.

Fowle, C. M. (1968). The effect of the severely mentally retarded child on his family. *American Journal of Mental Deficiency, 73,* 468–473.

Fredericks, H. D., Baldwin, V. L., & Grove, D. (1974). A home- center based parent training model. In J. Grim (Ed.), *Training parents to teach: Four models* (Vol. 3). Chapel Hill, NC: First Chance for Children.

Freeman, B. J., Ritvo, E. R., Needleman, R., & Yokota, A. (1985). The stability of cognitive and linguistic parameters in autism: A five-year prospective study. *Journal of the American Academy of Child Psychology, 24*, 459–464.

Friedrich, W. N., Greenberg, M. T., & Crnic, K. (1983). A short- form of the Questionnaire on Resources and Stress. *American Journal of Mental Deficiency, 88*, 41–48.

Fry, L. (1977). Remedial reading using parents as behaviour technicians. *New Zealand Journal of Educational Studies, 12*, 29–36.

Gallagher, J. J., Beckman, P., & Cross, A. H. (1983). Families of handicapped children: Sources of stress and its amelioration. *Exceptional Children, 50*, 10–19.

Gallagher, J. J., Trohanis, P. L., & Clifford, R. M. (1989). *Policy Implementation and PL 99-457,* Baltimore: Brookes Publishing.

Gath, A. (1973). The school-age siblings of mongol children. *British Journal of Psychiatry, 123,* 161–167.

Ginott, H. G. (1965). *Between parent and child.* New York: Macmillan.

Gittelman-Klein, R. (1987). Pharmacotherapy of childhood hyperactivity: An update. In H. Y. Meltzer (Ed.), *Psychopharmacology: The third generation of progress* (pp. 1215–1224). New York: Raven Press.

Goldfarb, L. A., Brotherson, J. J., Summers, J. A. & Turnbull, A. P. (1986). *Meeting the challenge of disability or chronic illness — A family guide.* Baltimore: Brookes Publishing.

Goldstein, M. J., Baker, B. L., & Jamison, K. R. (1986). *Abnormal Psychology: Experiences, origins, and interventions,* (2nd ed.). Boston: Little, Brown.

Goldstein, M. J., Judd, L., Rodnick, E. H., Alkire, A., & Gould, E. (1968). A method for studying social influence and coping patterns within families of disturbed adolescents. *Journal of Nervous and Mental Disease, 147*, 233–251.

Gourash, N. (1978). Help-seeking: A review of the literature. *American Journal of Community Psychology, 6*, 413–423.

Grailiker, B. V., Fischer, K., & Koch, R. (1962). Teenage reaction to a mentally retarded sibling. *American Journal of Mental Deficiency, 66*, 838–843.

Greenfeld, J. (1973). *A Child Called Noah.* New York: Warner Books.

Griest, D. L., & Forehand, R. (1982). How can I get any parent training done with all these other problems going on?: The role of family variables in child behavior therapy. *Child and Family Behavior Therapy, 4*, 73–80.

Gross, A. M., Eudy, C., & Drabman, R. S. (1982). Training parents to be physical therapists with their physically handicapped child. *Journal of Behavioral Medicine, 5*, 321–327.

Grossman, F. K. (1972). *Brothers and sisters of retarded children.* Syracuse: Syracuse University Press.

Grossman, H. J. (1983). *Classification in mental retardation.* Washington, DC: American Association on Mental Deficiency.

Gunn, P., & Berry, P. (1987). Some financial costs of caring for children with Down syndrome at home. *Australia and New Zealand Journal of Developmental Disabilities, 13,* 187–193.

Hall, M. C., & Nelson, D. J. (1981). Responsive parenting: One approach for teaching single parents parenting skills. *School Psychology Review, 19*, 45–53.

Hargis, K., & Blechman, E. A. (1979). Social class and training of parents as behavior change agents. *Child Behavior Therapy, 1*, 69–74.

Harris, S. L. (1982). A family systems approach to behavioral training with parents of autistic children. *Child and Family Behavior Therapy, 4*, 21–35.

Harris, S. L. (1983). *Families of the developmentally disabled: A guide to behavioral intervention.* New York: Pergamon Press.

Harris, S. L., Wolchik, S. A., & Weitz, S. (1981). The acquisition of language skills by autistic children: Can parents do the job? *Journal of Autism and Developmental Disorders, 11*, 373–384.

Hazzard, A. P. (1981). *Enhancing children's attitudes toward disabled peers using a multi-media curriculum.* Unpublished doctoral dissertation, University of California, Los Angeles.

Heifetz, L. J. (1974). *Beyond freedom and dignity.* Doctoral dissertation, Harvard University.

Heifetz, L. J. (1977). Behavioral training for parents of retarded children: Alternative formats based on instructional manuals. *American Journal of Mental Deficiency, 82,* 194–203.

Hetrick, E. W. (1979). Training parents of learning disabled children in facilitative communicative skills. *Journal of Learning Disabilities, 12,* 275–277.

Hinshaw, S. P. (1987). On the distinction between attentional deficits/hyperactivity and conduct problems/aggression in child psychopathology. *Psychological Bulletin, 101,* 443–463.

Hinshaw, S. P., & Erhardt, D. (in press). Behavioral treatment of attention deficit hyperactivity disorder. In V. B. Van Hasselt & M. Hersen (Eds.), *Handbook of behavior therapy and pharmacotherapy for children: A comparative analysis.* New York: Grune & Stratton.

Hinshaw, S. P., Henker, B. & Whalen, C. K. (1984). Self-control in hyperactive boys in anger-inducing situations: Effects of cognitive-behavioral training and of methylphenidate. *Journal of Abnormal Child Psychology, 12,* 55–77.

Hirsch, I., & Walder, L. (1969). Training mothers in groups as reinforcement therapists for their own children. *Proceedings of the 77th Annual Convention of the American Psychological Association,* 561–562.

Hollingshead, A. B. (1957). *Two-factor index of social position.* Unpublished manuscript, Yale University.

Holroyd, J. (1974). The Questionnaire on Resources and Stress: An instrument to measure family response to a handicapped family member. *Journal of Community Psychology, 2,* 92–94.

Horner, R., Dunlop, G., & Koegel, R. L. (Eds.) (1988). *Generalization and Maintenance: Lifestyle Changes in Applied Settings.* Baltimore: Brookes Publishing.

Hudson, A. M. (1982). Training parents of developmentally handicapped children: A component analysis. *Behavior Therapy, 13,* 325–333.

Intagliata, J., & Doyle, N. (1984). Enhancing social support for parents of developmentally disabled children: Training in interpersonal problem solving skills. *Mental Retardation, 22,* 4–11.

Jahn, D. & Lichstein, K. (1980). The resistive client: A neglected phenomenon in behavior therapy. *Behavior Modification, 4,* 303–320.

Karoly, P., & Rosenthal, M. (1977). Training parents in behavior modification: Effects on perceptions of family interaction and deviant child behavior. *Behavior Therapy, 8,* 406–410.

Kashima, K. J. (1983). *Improving maintenance of parent teaching: An intervention following participation in a behavioral training program for parents of mentally retarded children.* Unpublished Master's thesis, University of California, Los Angeles.

Kashima, K. J., Baker, B. L., & Landen, S. L. (1988). Media vs. live-directed training for parents of retarded children. *American Journal on Mental Retardation, 93,* 209–217.

Kaufman, S. (1988). *Retarded isn't stupid, Mom!* Baltimore: Brookes Publishing.

Kazdin, A. E. (1977). Assessing the clinical or applied importance of behavior change through social validation. *Behavior Modification, 1,* 427–452.

Kimberly, J. (1976). Organizational size and the structuralist perspective: A review, critique, and proposal. *Administrative Science Quarterly, 21,* 571–597.

Kiresuk, T. J., & Sherman, R. E. (1968). Goal Attainment Scaling: A general method for evaluating comprehensive community mental health programs. *Community Mental Health Journal, 4,* 443–453.

Kleinbaum, D. G., & Kupper, L. L. (1978). *Applied Regression Analysis and Other Multivariate Methods.* North Scituate, MA: Duxbury Press.

Koegel, R. L., Glahn, T. J., & Nieminen, G. S. (1978). Generalization of parent training results. *Journal of Applied Behavior Analysis, 10,* 197–205.

Koegel, R. L., Rincover, A., & Egel, A. L. (1982). *Educating and understanding autistic children.* San Diego: College Hill Press.

Koegel, R. L., Russo, D. C., & Rincover, A. (1977). Assessing and training teachers in the generalized use of behavior modification with autistic children. *Journal of Applied Behavior Analysis, 10,* 197–205.

Kogan, K. L., & Tyler, N. B. (1978). *Comparing ways of altering parent-child interaction. (ERIC Document Reproduction Service No. ED 161 558).*

Kovitz, K. E. (1976). Comparing group and individual methods for training parents in child management techniques. In E. J. Mash, L. D. Hamerlynk, & L. C. Handy (Eds.), *Behavior modification approaches to parenting.* New York: Brunner/Mazel, 1976.

Kozloff, M. A. (1973). *Reaching the autistic child: A parent training program.* Champaign: Research Press.

Lachenbruch, P. A. (1975). *Discriminant analysis.* New York: Hafner Press.

Landen, S. L. (1984). *A behavioral training program for Spanish-speaking siblings of retarded children.* Unpublished manuscript, University of California, Los Angeles.

Landen, S. L., & Baker, B. L. (1986). *Intervention models for training Hispanic families.* American Association on Mental Deficiency Symposium: Denver, CO.

Laviguer, H. (1976). The use of siblings as an adjunct to the behavioral treatment of children in the home with parents as therapists. *Behavior Therapy, 7,* 602–613.

Lobato, D. (1983). Siblings of handicapped children: A review. *Journal of Autism and Developmental Disorders, 13,* 347–364.

Locke, H. J., & Wallace, K. M. (1959). Short marital-adjustment and prediction tests: Their reliability and validity. *Journal of Marriage and Family Living, 21,* 251–255.

Loney, J., & Milich, R. S. (1981). Hyperactivity, inattention, and aggression in clinical practice. *Advances in Developmental and Behavioral Pediatrics, 2,* 113–147.

Lovaas, O. I. (1981). *Teaching developmentally disabled children: The ME book.* Baltimore: University Park Press.

Lovaas, O. I. (1987). Behavioral treatment and normal educational and intellectual functioning in young autistic children. *Journal of Clinical and Consulting Psychology, 55,* 3-9.

Lovaas, O. I., Berberich, J. P., Perloff, B. F., & Schaeffer, B. (1966). Acquisition of imitative speech by schizophrenic children. *Science, 151,* 705–707.

Lovaas, O. I., Koegel, R. L., Simmons, J. Q., & Long, J. S. (1973). Some generalization and follow-up measures on autistic children in behavior therapy. *Journal of Applied Behavior Analysis, 3,* 131–166.

Lovaas, O. I., Smith, T., & McEachin, J. (1989). Clarifying comments on the Young Autism Study: Reply to Schopler, Short, and Mesibov. *Journal of Consulting and Clinical Psychology, 57,* 165–167.

Lyon, S., & Preis, A. (1983). Working with families of severely handicapped persons. In M. Seligman (Ed.), *The family with a handicapped child: Understanding and treatment* (pp. 203–232). New York: Grune & Stratton.

Magana, A. B., Goldstein, M. J., Karno, M., Miklowitz, D. J., Jenkins, J., & Falloon, I. R. H. (1986). A brief method for assessing expressed emotion in relatives of psychiatric patients. *Psychiatry Research, 17,* 203–212.

Marshall, V. (1986). *Family factors, aggressive symptomatology and treatment outcome in boys with attention deficit disorders.* Unpublished doctoral dissertation, University of California, Los Angeles.

Martin, B. (1977). Brief family intervention: Effectiveness and the importance of including the father. *Journal of Consulting and Clinical Psychology, 45,* 1002–1010.

Martin, J. P. (1980). Working with parents of abused and neglected children. In R. Abidin (Ed.), *Parent education and intervention handbook.* Springfield, IL: Charles C Thomas.

Mash, E. J., & Johnston, C. (1983). Parental perceptions of child behavior problems, parenting self-esteem and mothers' reported stress in younger and older hyperactive and normal children. *Journal of Consulting and Clinical Psychology, 51,* 86–99.

McAdoo, G. W., & DeMyer, M. K. (1978). Personality characteristics of parents. In M. Rutter and E. Schopler (Eds.), *Autism: A reappraisal of concepts and treatment.* New York: Plenum Press.

McAllister, R. J., Butler, E. W., & Lei, T. (1973). Patterns of social interaction among families of behaviorally retarded children. *Journal of Marriage and the Family, 35.*

McClannahan, L. E., Krantz, P. J., & McGee, G. G. (1982). Parents as therapists for autistic children: A model for effective parent training. *Analysis and Intervention in Developmental Disabilities, 2,* 223–252.

McClelland, D. C. (1978). Managing motivation to expand human freedom. *American Psychologist, 33,* 201–210.

McConachie, H. (1986). *Parents and young mentally handicapped children: A review of research issues.* London: Croom Helm.

McConkey, R., & McEvoy, J. (1984). Parental involvement courses: Contrasts between mothers who enroll and those who don't. In J. M. Berg (Ed.), *Perspectives and Progress in Mental Retardation, Vol. 1: Social, Psychological and Educational Aspects.* Baltimore: University Park Press.

McEachin, J. J. (1987). *Outcome of autistic children receiving intensive behavioral treatment: Psychological status 3 to 12 years later.* Unpublished doctoral dissertation, University of California, Los Angeles.

McMahon, R. J., Forehand, R., & Griest, D. L. (1981). Effects of knowledge of social learning principles on enhancing treatment outcome and generalization in a parent training program. *Journal of Consulting and Clinical Psychology, 49,* 526–532.

McMahon, R. J., Forehand, R., Griest, D. L., & Wells, K. C. (1981). Who drops out of treatment during parent behavior training? *Behavioral Counseling Quarterly, 1,* 79–85.

Miklowitz, D. J. (1985). *Family interaction and illness outcome in bipolar and schizophrenic patients.* Unpublished doctoral dissertation, University of California, Los Angeles.

Miklowitz, D. J., Goldstein, M. J., Faloon, I. R., & Doane, J. A. (1984). Interactional correlates of expressed emotion in the families of schizophrenics. *British Journal of Psychiatry, 144,* 482–487.

Miller, J. H. (1980). Structured training with parents of exceptional children. *Dissertation Abstracts International, 40(08),* 3908B.

Mira, M. (1970). Results of a behavior modification training program for parents and teachers. *Behaviour Research and Therapy, 8,* 309–311.

Mira, M., & Hoffman, S. (1974). Educational programming for multihandicapped deaf-blind children. *Exceptional Children, 40,* 513–514.

Morris, R. J. (1973). *Issues in teaching behavior modification to parents of retarded children.* American Psychological Association, 81st Annual Meeting, Montreal, Quebec, Canada.

Nay, W. R. (1975). A systematic comparison of instructional techniques for parents. *Behavior Therapy, 6,* 14–21.

Nomellini, S., & Katz, R. (1983). Effects of anger control training on abusive parents. *Cognitive Therapy and Research, 1,* 57–68.

O'Dell, S., Flynn, J., & Benlolo, L. (1977). A comparison of parent training techniques in child behavior modification. *Journal of Behavior Therapy and Experimental Psychiatry, 8,* 261–268.

O'Dell, S. L., Krug, W. W., Patterson, J. N., & Faustman, W. O. (1980). An assessment of methods for training parents in the use of time-out. *Journal of Behavior Therapy and Experimental Psychiatry, 11,* 21–25.

O'Dell, S. L., Mahoney, N. D., Horton, W. G., & Turner, P. E. (1979). Media assisted parent training: Alternative methods. *Behavior Therapy, 10,* 103–110.

O'Dell, S. L., Tarler-Benlolo, L., & Flynn, J. M. (1979). An instrument to measure knowledge of behavioral principles as applied to children. *Journal of Behavior Therapy and Experimental Psychiatry, 10,* 29–34.

O'Leary, K. D. (1980). Pills or skills for hyperactive children. *Journal of Applied Behavior Analysis, 13,* 191–204.

Olshansky, S. (1962). Chronic sorrow: A response to having a mentally defective child. *Social Casework, 43,* 191–194.

Olson, D. H., McCubbin, H. I., Barnes, H., Larsen, A., Muxen, M., & Wilson, M. (1982). *Family Inventories.* St. Paul, MN: University of Minnesota.

Olson, D. H., Russell, C. S., & Sprenkle, D. H. (1983). Circumplex model VI: Theoretical update. *Family Process, 22,* 69–83.

Olson, D. H., Sprenkle, D. H., & Russell, C. S. (1979). Circumplex model of marital and family systems I: Cohesion and adaptability dimensions, family types and clinical application. *Family Process, 18,* 69–83.

Oltmanns, T. F., Broderick, J. E., & O'Leary, K. D. (1977). Marital adjustment and the efficacy of behavior therapy with children. *Journal of Consulting and Clinical Psychology*, 45, 724–729.

Omizo, M. M., Williams, R. E., & Omizo, S. A. (1986). The effects of participation in parent group sessions on child-rearing attitudes among parents of learning disabled children. *The Exceptional Child, 33*, 134–139.

Ornitz, E. M. (1985). Neurophysiology of infantile autism. *Journal of the American Academy of Child Psychiatry, 24*, 251- 262.

Oster, A. (1984). Keynote address. In *Equals in this partnership: Parents of disabled and at-risk infants and toddlers speak to professionals* (pp. 26–32). Washington, DC: National Center for Clinical Infant Programs.

Padilla, A. M., Ruiz, R. A., & Alvarez, R. (1975). Community mental health services for the Spanish-speaking/surnamed population. *American Psychologist, 30*, 892–905.

Pasick, R. S. (1975). *Inclusion of siblings of the retarded in a training program in behavioral modification*. Unpublished doctoral dissertation, Harvard University.

Patterson, G. R. (1974). Interventions for boys with conduct problems: Multiple settings, treatments, and criteria. *Journal of Consulting and Clinical Psychology, 42*, 471–481.

Patterson, G. R. (1977). *Families: Applications of social learning to family life* (rev. ed.). Champaign, IL: Research Press.

Patterson, G. R., Cobb, J. A., & Ray, R. S. (1973). A social engineering technology for retraining the families of aggressive boys. In H. E. Adams & I. Umhel (Eds.), *Issues and Trends in Behavior Therapy*. Springfield, IL: Charles C Thomas.

Patterson, G. R., & Gullion, M. E. (1976). *Living with children: New methods for parents and teachers* (rev. ed.). Champaign, IL: Research Press.

Patterson, G. R., Reid, J. G., Jones, R. R., & Conger, R. E. (1975). *A social learning approach to family intervention*. Eugene, OR: Castalia Press.

Pickering, D., & Morgan, S. B. (1985). Parental ratings of treatments of self-injurious behavior. *Journal of Autism and Developmental Disorders, 15*, 303–313.

Pinkston, E. M. (1984). Individualized behavioral intervention for home and school. In R. A. Dangel and R. F. Polster (Eds.), *Parent training: Foundations of research and practice*, (pp. 202–238). New York: Guilford Press.

Pisterman, S., McGrath, P., Firestone, P., Goodman, J. T., Webster, I., & Mallory, R. (1989). Outcome of parent-mediated treatment of preschoolers with attention deficit disorder with hyperactivity. *Journal of Consulting and Clinical Psychology, 57*, 628–635.

Powell, R. H., & Ogle, P. A., (1985). *Brothers & Sisters: A special part of exceptional families*. Baltimore: Brookes Publishing.

Powers, M. D. (1988). Behavioral assessment of autism. In E. Schopler and G. B. Mesibov (Eds.), *Diagnosis and assessment in autism*. New York: Plenum Press.

Prieto-Bayard, M. (1987). *Coping with a retarded child: A psychosocial study of Spanish speaking mothers*. Unpublished doctoral dissertation, University of California, Los Angeles.

Prieto-Bayard, M., & Baker, B. L. (1986). Parent training for Spanish speaking families with a retarded child. *Journal of Community Psychology, 14*, 134–143.

Prieto-Bayard, M., Huff, R., & Baker, B. L. (1981). *Parent training for Spanish speaking families with developmentally disabled children: A formative evaluation*. Los Angeles: Western Psychological Association.

Reisinger, J. J. (1982). Unprogrammed learning of differential attention by fathers of oppositional children. *Journal of Behavior Therapy and Experimental Psychiatry, 13*, 203–208.

Rickel, A. U., Dudley, G., & Bermon, S. (1980). An evaluation of parent training. *Evaluation Review, 4*, 389–403.

Rimland, B. (1964). *Infantile autism: The syndrome and its implications for a neural theory of behavior*. New York: Appleton-Century-Crofts.

Rinn, R. C., Vernon, J. C., & Wise, M. J. (1975). Training parents of behaviorally-disordered children in groups: A three years' program evaluation. *Behavior Therapy, 6*, 378–387.

Ritvo, E. R., & Freeman, B. J. (1978). National Society for Autistic Children definition of the syndrome of autism. *Journal of Autism and Childhood Schizophrenia, 8*, 162–167.

Rodger, S. (1985). Siblings of handicapped children: A population at risk? *The Exceptional Child, 32*, 47–57.

Rodick, J. D., Henggeler, S. W., & Hanson, C. L., (1986). An evaluation of the family adaptability and cohesion evaluation scales and the circumplex model. *Journal of Abnormal Child Psychology, 14,* 77–87.

Rogers, T. R., Forehand, R., Griest, D. L., Wells, K. C., & McMahon, R. J. (1981). Socioeconomic status: Effects on parent and child behaviors and treatment outcome of parent training. *Journal of Clinical Child Psychology, 10,* 98–101.

Rogers, S. J., & Puchalski, C. B. (1984). Development of symbolic play in visually impaired infants. *Topics in Early Childhood Special Education, 3,* 57–64.

Rose, S. (1974a). Group training of parents as behavior modifiers. *Social Work, 19,* 156–163.

Rose, S. (1974b). Training parents in groups as behavior modifiers of their mentally retarded children. *Journal of Behavior Therapy and Experimental Psychiatry, 5,* 135–140.

Rosen, G. M. (1987). Self-help treatment books and the commercialization of psychotherapy. *American Psychologist, 42,* 46–51.

Ross, D. M., & Ross, S. A. (1982). *Hyperactivity: Current Issues, Research, and Theory, Second Edition.* New York: John Wiley and Sons.

Rutter, M. (1970). Autistic children: Infancy to adulthood. *Seminars in Psychiatry, 2,* 435–450.

Rutter, M. (1978). Diagnosis and definition of childhood autism. *Journal of Autism and Childhood Schizophrenia, 8,* 139–161.

Sadler, O. W., Seyden, T., Howe, B., & Kaminsky, T. (1976). An evaluation of "Groups for Parents": A standardized format encompassing both behavior modification and humanistic methods. *Journal of Community Psychology, 4,* 157–163.

Salzinger, K., Feldman, R.S., & Portnoy, S. (1970). Training parents of brain injured children in the use of operant conditioning procedures. *Behavior Therapy, 1,* 4–32.

Sandler, A., & Coren, A. (1981). Integrated instruction at home and school: Parents' perspective. *Education and Training of the Mentally Retarded, 16,* 183–187.

Sandler, A., Coren, A., & Thurman, S. K. (1983). A training program for parents of handicapped preschool children: Effects upon mother, father, and child. *Exceptional Children, 49,* 355- 358.

San Martino, M., & Newman, M. B. (1974). Siblings of retarded children: A population at risk. *Child Psychiatry and Human Development, 4,* 168–177.

Sarason, S. B. (1972). *The creations of settings and the future societies.* San Francisco: Jossey-Bass.

Schild, S. (1964). Counseling with parents of retarded children living at home. *Social Work, 9,* 86.

Schild, S. (1971). The family of the retarded child. In R. Koch & J. Dobson (Eds.), *The mentally retarded child and his family.* New York: Brunner/Mazel.

Schleifer, M., Weiss, G., Cohen, N., Elman, M., Cvejic, H., & Kruger, E. (1975). Hyperactivity in preschoolers and the effect of methylphenidate. *American Journal of Orthopsychiatry, 45,* 38–50.

Schneiman, R. S. (1972). *An evaluation of structured learning and didactic learning as methods of training behavior modification skills to low and middle socio-economic level teacher-aides.* Unpublished doctoral dissertation, Syracuse University.

Schopler, E., & Reichler, R. J. (1971). Parents as co-therapists in the treatment of psychotic children. *Journal of Autism and Childhood Schizophrenia, 1,* 87–102.

Schreiber, M., & Feeley, M. (1965). Siblings of the retarded: A guided group experience. *Children, 12,* 221–225.

Schreibman, L., & Britten, K. R. (1984). Training parents as therapists for autistic children: Rationale, techniques, and results. In W. P. Christian; G. T. Hannah, and T. J. Glahn (Eds.), *Programming effective human services.* New York: Plenum Press.

Schreibman, L., O'Neill, R. E., & Koegel, R. L. (1983). Behavioral training for siblings of autistic children. *Journal of Applied Behavior Analysis, 16,* 129–138.

Schwenn, M. (1971). *The effects of parent training on generalization of therapeutic behavior change in retarded children from an educational camp to home.* Unpublished senior honors thesis, Harvard University.

Search Institute. (1978). *Effecting utilization: Experimental use of consultants.* Phase one report, National Institute of Mental Health Grant No 5R01 MH 28498–02. Minneapolis, MN.

Sebba, J. (1981). Intervention for profoundly retarded mentally handicapped children through parent training in a preschool setting and at home. In P. Mittler (Ed.), *Frontiers of knowledge in mental retardation: Vol. 1, Social, educational and behavioral aspects.* Baltimore: University Park Press.

Shearer, D. E., & Shearer, M. S. (1976). The Portage Project: A model for early childhood education. In T. D. Tjossem (Ed.), *Intervention strategies for high risk infants and young children.* Baltimore: University Park Press.

Shenk, J. L. (1984). *Predictors of joining a parent training program for Spanish-speaking families with a mentally retarded child.* Unpublished master's thesis, University of California, Los Angeles.

Sherman, B. R. (1988). Predictors of the decision to place developmentally disabled family members in residential care. *American Journal of Mental Retardation, 92,* 344–351.

Shrybman, J. A. (1982). *Due process in special education.* Rockville, MD: Aspen.

Simeonsson, R. J., & McHale, S. M. (1981). Review: Research on handicapped children: Sibling relationships. *Child Care, Health and Developmen, 7,* 153–171.

Singh, N. N., Watson, J. E., & Winton, A. S. W. (1987). Parents' acceptability ratings of alternative treatments for use with mentally retarded children. *Behavior Modification, 11,* 17–26.

Solnit, A. J., & Stark, M. H. (1961). Mourning and the birth of a defective child. *Psychoanalytic Study of the Child, 16,* 523–537.

Steinbeck, J. (1986). *Sweet Thursday.* New York: Penguin Books.

Stokes, T. F., & Baer, D. M. (1977). An implicit technology of generalization. *Journal of Applied Behavior Analysis, 10,* 349- 368.

Strain, P. S., Steele, P., Ellis, T, & Timm, M. A. (1982). Long- term effects of oppositional child treatment with mothers as therapists and therapist trainers. *Journal of Applied Behavior Analysis, 15,* 163–169.

Strom, R., Ress, R., Slaughter, H., & Wurster, S. (1980). Role expectations of parents of intellectually handicapped children. *Exceptional Children, 47,* 144–147.

Sturmey, P., & Crisp, A. B. (1986). Portage Guide to Early Education: A review of research. *Educational Psychology, 6,* 139–157.

Tavormina, J. B. (1974). Basic models of parent counseling: A critical review. *Psychological Bulletin, 81,* 827–835.

Tavormina, J. B. (1975). Relative effectiveness of behavioral and reflective group counseling with parents of mentally retarded children. *Journal of Consulting and Clinical Psychology, 43,* 22–31.

Thomas, C. A. (1977). The effectiveness of two child management training procedures for high and low educational level parents of emotionally disturbed children. *Dissertation Abstracts International, 37,* A12.

Tornatzky, L. G., & Solomon, R. (1982). Contributions of social science to innovation and productivity. *American Psychologist, 37,* 737–746.

Turnbull, A. P., & Behr, S. K. (1986, May). *Positive contributions that persons with mental retardation make to their families.* Paper presented at the annual meeting of the American Association on Mental Deficiency, Denver.

Turnbull, A. P., Summers, J. A., & Brotherson, M. J. (1986). Family life cycle: Theoretical and empirical implications and future directions for families with mentally retarded members. In J. J. Gallagher & P. M. Vietze (Eds.), *Families of Handicapped Persons.* Baltimore: Brookes Publishing.

Turnbull, A. P., & Turnbull, H. R. (1982). Parent involvement in the education of handicapped children: A critique. *Mental Retardation, 20,* 115–122.

Turnbull, H. R., III, & Turnbull, A. P. (1985). *Parents speak out: Then and now.* Columbus, OH: Charles E. Merrill.

Valone, K., Goldstein, M. J., & Norton, J. P. (1984). Parental expressed emotion and psychophysiological reactivity in an adolescent sample at risk for schizophrenia spectrum disorders. *Journal of Abnormal Psychology, 93,* 448–457.

Valone, K., Norton, J. P., Goldstein, M. J., & Doane, J. A. (1983). Parental expressed emotion and affective style in an adolescent sample at risk for schizophrenia spectrum disorder. *Journal of Abnormal Psychology, 92,* 399–407.

Vaughn, C. E., & Leff, J. P. (1976). The measurement of expressed emotion in the families of psychiatric patients. *British Journal of Social and Clinical Psychology, 15,* 157–165.

Vaughn, C. E., Snyder, K., Jones, S., Freeman, W. B., & Falloon, I. R. H. (1984). Family factors in schizophrenic relapse: A replication. *Schizophrenia Bulletin, 8,* 425–426.

Wahler, R. G. (1980). The insular mother: Her problems in parent-child treatment. *Journal of Applied Behavior Analysis, 13,* 207–219.

Waisbren, S. E. (1980). Parents' reactions after the birth of a developmentally disabled child. *American Journal of Mental Deficiency, 84,* 345–351.

Watson, L. S., & Bassinger, J. F. (1974). Parent training technology: A potential service delivery system. *Mental Retardation, 12,* 3–10.

Webster-Stratton, C. (1985a). The effects of father involvement in parent training for conduct-problem children. *Journal of Child Psychology and Psychiatry, 26,* 801–810.

Webster-Stratton, C. (1985b). Predictors of treatment outcome in parent training for conduct disordered children. *Behavior Therapy, 16,* 223–243.

Webster-Stratton, C., Kolpacoff, M., & Hollinsworth, T. (1988). Self-administered videotape therapy for families with conduct-problem children: comparison with two cost-effective treatments and a control group. *Journal of Consulting and Clinical Psychology, 56,* 558–566.

Weinrott, M. R. (1974). A training program in behavior modification for siblings of the retarded. *American Journal of Orthopsychiatry, 44,* 362–375.

Weiss, G., & Hechtman, L. T. (1986). *Hyperactive children grown up.* New York: Guilford Press.

Weiss, G., Hechtman, R., & Perlman, T. (1978). Hyperactives as young adults: School, employer, and self-rating scales obtained during ten-year follow-up evaluation. *American Journal of Orthopsychiatry, 48,* 438–445.

Weiss, G., & Minde, K. K. (1974). Follow-up studies of children who present with symptoms of hyperactivity. In C. K. Conners (Ed.), *Clinical use of stimulant drugs in children.* Amsterdam: Excerpta Medica.

Weitz, S. E. (1981). A code for assessing teaching skills of parents of developmentally disabled children. *Journal of Autism and Developmental Disorders, 12,* 13–24.

Whalen, C. K. (1989). Attention deficit and hyperactivity disorders. In T. H. Ollendick & M. Hersen (Eds.), *Handbook of child psychopathology* (2nd ed.), pp. 131–169. New York: Plenum Press.

Whalen, C. K., & Henker, B. (1980). The social ecology of psychostimulant treatment: A model for conceptual and empirical analysis. In C. K. Whalen and B. Henker (Eds.), *Hyperactive children: The social ecology of identification and treatment* (pp. 3–51). New York: Academic Press.

White, O., Edgar, E., Haring, N. G., Afflick, J., & Hayden, A. (1978). *Uniform performance assessment system: Birth - 6 years level.* Seattle, WA: College of Education, University of Washington.

Wikler, L. (1981). Chronic stresses of families of mentally retarded children. *Family Relations, 30,* 281–288.

Wilson, J., Blacher, J., & Baker, B. L. (1989). Siblings of severely handicapped children. *Mental Retardation, 27,* 167–173.

Winton, P., & Turnbull, A. P. (1981). Parent involvement as viewed by parents of preschool handicapped children. *Topics in Early Childhood Education, 1,* 11–19.

Wolf, M. M. (1978). Social validity: The case for subjective measurement or how applied behavior analysis is finding its heart. *Journal of Applied Behavior Analysis, 11,* 203–214.

Wolfe, D. A., Aragona, J., Kaufman, J., & Sandler, J. (1980). The importance of adjudication in the treatment of child abuse: Some preliminary findings. *Child Abuse and Neglect, 4,* 127- 136.

Wolfe, D. A., St. Lawrence, J., Graves, K., Brehony, K., Bradlyn, D., & Kelly, J. A. (1982). Intensive behavioral parent training for a child abusive mother. *Behavior Therapy, 13,* 438–451.

Wolfensberger, W. (1969). The origin and nature of our institutional models. In R. B. Kugel & W. Wolfensberger (Eds.), *Changing patterns in residential services for the mentally retarded.* Washington, DC: President's Committee on Mental Retardation.

Wolfensberger, W., & Kurtz, R. A. (Eds.) (1969). *Management of the family of the mentally retarded.* Chicago: Follett.

Worland, J., Carney, R., Milich, R., & Grame, C. (1980). Does in-home training add to the effectiveness of operant group parent training? A two-year evaluation. *Child Behavior Therapy, 2,* 11–24.

Worland, J., Carney, R. M., Weinberg, H., & Milich, R. (1982). Dropping out of group behavioral training. *Behavioral Counseling Quarterly, 2,* 37–41.

Yasuda, P. (1986). *Family variables as predictors of successful parent training outcome with families of hyperactive children.* Unpublished doctoral dissertation, University of California, Los Angeles.

Yates, C. E. (1981). *Mother-son and father-son interactions in hyperactivity and the effects of Methylphenidate.* Unpublished manuscript, University of California, Los Angeles.

Young, L. (1964). *A study of child neglect and abuse.* Princeton: McGraw-Hill.

Zarfas, D. E., Lovering, B. I., & Robbins, H. J. (1975). Personnel training. In J. Wortis (Ed.), *Mental retardation and developmental disabilities: An annual review.* Vol. 7. (pp 299–312). New York: Brunner/Mazel.

Zebiob, L. E., Forehand, R., & Resnick, P. A. (1979). Parent-child interactions: Habituation and resensitization effects. *Journal of Clinical Child Psychology, 8,* 69–71.

ABOUT THE AUTHOR

Bruce L. Baker is Professor of Psychology and Director of the Clinical Psychology training program at the University of California, Los Angeles. He received his Ph.D. in clinical psychology from Yale University in 1966 and taught at Harvard University for nine years before moving to UCLA. He has directed the Children's Unit at Fernald State School for the Mentally Retarded and was the founder and director of Camp Freedom, a residential camp school for children with special needs. Dr. Baker's UCLA Project for Developmental Disabilities has studied the training of parents as teachers of their retarded children. He has more than 60 publications, among them his co-authored books *Abnormal Psychology; Experiences, Origins, and Interventions*, and *Steps to Independence: A Skills Training Guide for Parents and Teachers of Children with Special Needs*. Dr. Baker lives in Los Angeles and has three children, Kristen (19), Jason (15), and Alex (2), who have conducted their own ongoing parent training for him and his wife Jan.